Pulling out of the Nosedive:
A Contemporary Picture of
Churchgoing

What the 2005 English
Church Census reveals

D1146675

This Census was sponsored by:

The Ansvar Insurance Society
The Baptist Union of Great Britain
The Bible Society
Christian Aid
Church Mission Society
Church Pastoral Aid Society
Churches' Child Protection Advisory Service
The Economic and Social Research Council
(via the University of Manchester)
The Evangelical Alliance
Holy Trinity Church, Brompton
The Methodist Church
Moorlands College
Operation Mobilisation
The Salvation Army
Tearfund
World Vision

All royalties from this book will go towards
funding further research for the church

Pulling out of the Nosedive: A Contemporary Picture of Churchgoing

What the 2005 English Church Census reveals

Dr Peter Brierley

Christian Research, 2006

First British edition 2006

Christian Research ISBN: 978 1 85321 168 3

Published by Christian Research,
Vision Building, 4 Footscray Road,
Eltham, London SE9 2TZ September 2006
Phone: 020 8294 1989   Fax: 020 8294 0014
Email: admin@christian-research.org.uk
Web: www.christian-research.org.uk
and: www.ukchristianhandbook.org.uk

British Library Cataloguing Data
A catalogue record for this book is available
from the British Library.

Typeset by PencilSharp Ltd, Unit F8, Rake Industries,
Rake, Nr Petersfield, Hants GU31 5DU
Printed by Goodman Baylis, The Trinity Press,
London Road, Worcester WR5 2JH
Cover design by Paul Jones Associates, 98 Eden Way,
Beckenham BR3 3DH

Pulling out of the Nosedive: A contemporary picture of churchgoing

The Biggin Hill Air Fair is a popular annual event. It is always a thrill to watch planes old and new, large and small, executing their breath-taking aerobatics. The wing-walkers never fail to entertain as they perform on top of bi-planes that roll and dive before righting themselves again, and the Red Arrows are hugely impressive with their tight, impeccable formations, demonstrating a unique mastery of the skies.

The thunderous Tornado has always been a fascinating favourite, with its huge glowing after-burners and ability to sweep its wings back. It is invariably, however, the few remaining Spitfires that steal the show, as well as the hearts of the on-lookers, as they climb and weave their way up and up, only to fall dramatically, spiralling apparently out of control, before pulling out of their nosedive at the last second to claim the skies once more.

It is this ability to pull out of a nosedive which is a visual representation of the church in England today. During the 1990s it went into what seemed a disastrous nosedive. Of the million people who stopped attending church during that period, half a million were young people under the age of 15. In 1989 1.2 million under-15s attended church on a Sunday; by 1998 the number was down to 0.7 million. That was a catastrophe in the making, a gaping hole which continues while the remaining folk in that cohort grow older. Quite literally, it was a nosedive towards terminal tragedy.

Could the church ever pull out of such a nosedive? That was the essential reason for the 2005 English Church Census: to find out. This book gives the story of church life over the seven years 1998 to 2005. The church *is* pulling out of the nosedive, but is still going down. No levelling out is in sight yet, but astonishing things are happening.

Some leaders are taking the mega-decision to make the local expression of the Body of Christ relevant and accessible to those in the 21st century, often with huge implications of doing things differently. The church must continue to adapt if it is not to keep on losing attenders. It is always possible to nosedive a second time. The future is not the past revisited or re-branded.

Growth is occurring in many places, and a third, 34%, of all the churches in the country have grown over these 7 years. So *something* is definitely happening, by God's grace, and the church is not inexorably destined to die. But it still has to pull out of the nosedive fully if it is to become airborne again in the years to come. This book gives the results of the Census and suggests practical ways in which power can be restored so that we can fly on, *as we must!*

We are enormously grateful
for the cartoons. All, except that
in Chapter 7, are by Noel Ford.

That which appears in Chapter 1
also previously appeared in
the *Church Times* in May 2005.

The cartoon in Chapter 7 is
by Terri Dauncey and previously
appeared in *Quadrant* in May 1998.

The small illustrative line drawings
are by Alec Hitchins.

"There is no credit to be drawn from the virtue of one's past.
Look for the risk. Make it your watchword.
If you seek to save your life, corporate or individual,
I promise you – *Jesus promises you* – you will lose it.
Don't play it safe."

(Stan Mooneyham, President, World Vision, 1991)

If you only look at what is,
you might never attain what could be.

(Anon)

"Mind must be stronger,
heart must be bolder,
courage must be greater,
as our power grows less."

[The soldier Byrthwold, about to die in a battle in Maldon, Essex in
August, 991, recorded in the Old English poem, *Beowulf*]

"... leads you to believe a lie,
when you see with, not through the eye."

[William Blake, *The Everlasting Gospel,* lines 104,105]

"May the Lord Jesus put His hands on our eyes also,
for then we too shall begin to look at
not what is seen but at what is not seen."

[Prayer of Origen, one of the early church Fathers, who died c254]

CONTENTS

Foreword
by the Most Rev & Rt Hon Dr Rowan Williams, Archbishop of Canterbury

I am delighted to commend this book to you. As the Christian scene in England becomes ever more richly diverse it is really helpful to have a comprehensive picture of what is going on. This book fulfills that need.

One of the most striking findings concerns the number of thriving churches which have been started by immigrant communities. This is having a big impact in our major cities, where black majority churches are growing fast. People from ethnic minorities are also bringing new life and energy into churches from established denominations such as the Church of England. This is one of the reasons why the Anglican Diocese of London, for example, is now growing steadily.

The success of black majority churches reminds us that hope for the Church as a whole rests on growth and change in each local church, and it is at this local level that this book rightly focusses. One of the most encouraging results of the Census is the evidence that churches of all types and sizes can grow and develop. This includes churches whose history has been one of decline. There is a positive message here for every leader of every local church.

This book also gives us a reading on the success of new churches which are quite different from our traditional ideas about what a church should be like. Anglicans and Methodists call these "Fresh Expressions of Church". There is interesting evidence in these pages about their growth to date, and we must work and hope to see them having lasting and substantial impact.

The last English Church Census, carried out in 1998, showed an alarming decline in the number of children and young people in church. These latest results suggest that we have yet to reverse this, but at least the rate of change has slowed. It has often been said that children are not just the future of the church, they are the church. Based on the findings of this Census, we still have some way to go to give effect to this maxim.

I am very thankful that God enabled Peter Brierley and his team – supported and encouraged by their sponsors – to undertake the huge job of carrying out this Census. It is my prayer that He will use the results to challenge, equip and energise us as we seek to build Christ's kingdom in this country.

✝ Rowan, Cantuar

Introduction

It was one of those totally unexpected repercussions. Detailed preparations for the 2005 English Church Census had been going on for months. Letters advising it was coming in several weeks' time had been sent to all the 24,000 clergy in England, as well as all the senior leaders so that they knew what would happen. Details of hundreds of new churches, and church closures, were sent to Christian Research in response to this mailing, for which we were very grateful.

Now, Sunday 8th May had arrived! I was at a Conference that weekend, and had to get a taxi for my interview on the *Sunday* programme on BBC Radio 4. When I returned the others all said, "It was on television!"

"What was?" I asked.

"The Church Census," they all replied excitedly. "On BBC main news at 7.00 am, with pictures of different churches." Well! We later learned it was also on BBC News 24, Ceefax, Radio 2 and in three successive news bulletins on Radio 4. It had also been carried by Reuters.

During my *Sunday* interview I had been allowed to quote my colleague's phone number as our office was closed. She was listening to the programme and was astonished to hear her own number being given on the air. Within minutes, her phone was ringing, and of the 19 calls that day 5 were from churches who had not received their form, 4 of whom downloaded it from the internet in time for their morning service!

The following day our 3 telephone lines were swamped the entire day, and we had a tidal wave of emails! Such was the enthusiasm for the 2005 English Church Census. "Must have spent a lot of money on advertising," some said, but while we had put small advertisments in the church press "Will you count? 8th May English Church Census" we were amazed at the huge interest, which was far beyond our own capacity to generate.

WILL YOU COUNT?

8th May
**English Church
Census**
www.ecc05.org.uk

The consequence was that thousands of forms were completed and returned to us. It was not all good news, however. We learned that the Royal Mail had not dealt with several of the 80 sacks of Census mail we had entrusted to them three weeks earlier, so that several hundred, maybe thousands, of forms actually never arrived. It meant we had to send an extra large number of reminder letters five weeks after Census Sunday.

A team effort
There are 37,500 churches or congregations in England, so contacting them all for a special event like a Church Census requires much co-ordinated activity.

Crucial to the whole process is funding. I am grateful to Bill Lattimer, Christian Research's Business Development Manager, for writing an excellent proposal, which helped to generate support for the Census both from various denominations and from Christian organisations.

We had financial support from Ansvar Insurance Company, the Baptist Union of Great Britain, the Bible Society, Christian Aid, the Church Mission Society, the Church Pastoral Aid Society, the Churches' Child Protection Advisory Service, the Economic and Social Research Council, the Evangelical Alliance, Holy Trinity Brompton, the Methodist Church, Moorlands College, Operation Mobilisation, the Salvation Army, Tearfund and World Vision.

We are especially grateful to David Voas, University of Manchester, who wrote a detailed proposal for the Economic and Social Research Council, which was successful and provided our first academic grant (Christian Research not having sufficient full-time researchers to apply in its own name). Collectively all these bodies provided the £100,000 this entire exercise has cost.

We are also grateful to many senior leaders who supported this Census by being willing to serve as its Council of Reference. These were: Bishop Dr Joe Aldred (Churches Together in Britain and Ireland), Viscountess Gill Brentford (then the Third Estates Commissioner, Church of England), Rt Rev Pete Broadbent (Bishop of Willesden, Church of England), Gerald Coates (Team Leader, Pioneer), Rev David Coffey (Moderator, Free Churches Group), Rt Rev Kieran Conry (Bishop of Arundel and Brighton, Roman Catholic Church), Rev Dr David Cornick (General Secretary, United Reformed Church), Rev Joel Edwards (General Director, Evangelical Alliance), Rev John Glass (General Superintendent, Elim Pentecostal Church), Rev Katei Kirby (Director, African and Caribbean Evangelical Alliance), General John Larsson (at that time the International Leader, Salvation Army), His Eminence Cormac Murphy-O'Connor (Cardinal Archbishop of Westminster, Roman Catholic Church), Pastor Cecil Perry (President, Seventh-day Adventist Church), His Grace Abba Seraphim (Metropolitan of Glastonbury, British Orthodox Church), Dr Neil Summerton (Executive Chairman, Partnership, Christian Brethren), Rev Michael Townsend (Chairman of Leeds District, Methodist Church) and Rev Dr Nigel Wright (Principal, Spurgeon's Baptist College). To all these we are most indebted.

The Census Steering Committee consisted of Rev Derek Allan (Baptist Union of Great Britain), Ian Farthing (Tearfund), Rev Kenneth Howcroft (Methodist Church), Alistair Metcalfe (World Vision), Major David Pickard (Salvation Army), Philip

Poole (Bible Society), Russell Price (Church Mission Society), and David Voas (Manchester University), sometimes represented by Alasdair Crockett (University of Essex). They helped us in many ways, not least in working through the many suggested questions, the results of the pilot exercise (we sent an initial draft to 100 churches of different denominations), and in trying to get the wording as intelligible as possible. They proved tremendously helpful too when it came to publicity about the Census results and checking the draft of this book.

The staff of Christian Research have all been involved: Heather Wraight (Deputy Director) who organised the initial mailing, reminder, data entry and much more, Bill Lattimer with much advice on numerous occasions, Gwen Gowers (Personnel Assistant) who kept us all sane and organised, dealt with many email or phone questions about the form and sorted out address list queries by the hundred, Kim Miles (Research Officer) who provided the large majority of the analyses and gave valuable help with the design of the questionnaire, and Vicky Wharton (Administration Officer) who kept a tally of forms received and provided background support in a hundred different ways. So much from so few? Well, we work hard, and enjoy it!

Then there were a large number of people who helped us part-time, whether in getting the mailings ready, phoning (especially black church leaders to get data), or basic data entry. These were: Carrol Barham, Ronnika Barham, Vicky Bayliss, Clara Bickford, Tolulalo Bolaji, Joan Cheesman, Richard Cooper, Jonathan Eades, Charlene Fernandez, Josh Gowers, Joan Haffner, Peggy Hale, Sarah Harding, Victoria Hunt, Andrew Junaid, Ben Keating, James Lumgair, Ratidzo Maboreke, Naomi Maxim, Ernel McIntosh, Rachel Paris, Stephanie Pathimagaraj, Katie Radcliffe, Sarah Radcliffe, Maureen Ross, Lindsay Rowden and Hannah Wright. Rev Onye Obika, General Secretary of the International Ministerial Council of Great Britain, kindly offered that he and some of his staff would phone their member churches. The work would never have been done without this army of helpers, so to all of them huge thanks. You will appreciate that this whole exercise was a real team effort.

Questionnaire design

There is no such thing as a perfect questionnaire. We had the competing demands of asking questions to give us the basic data which would compare with previous studies, the need to ask much more about midweek activity, the questions that the larger sponsors wished us to included, and all within the overall demands of a maximum size of two sides of one page in a type size large enough to read!

Altogether information was received from 18,720 churches or congregations by the time we stopped entering data on our computers, and details from a further 39 were received subsequently. Several dozen other churches returned details more than six months after the Census, for which we are also grateful. Three-quarters of those supplying information returned one of our forms. We were also able, however, to input data of total attendance, sometimes with additional information, which was very kindly supplied by 10 Church of England and 8 Roman Catholic Dioceses, the Baptist Union of Great Britain, the Fellowship of Independent Evangelical Churches, the Salvation Army and 91 Methodist Circuits for the remainder.

This gives a total overall response rate of 50.02%, a very much higher response to a postal survey than most research companies expect to achieve today. We are grateful to the army of people who completed the forms or helped us get so much information. That the response rate was so high again shows something of the interest in this Census. The rate at which the forms came back for the first six months is illustrated in the graph in Figure 0.1, showing the considerable improvement after the reminder was sent out after 2 months:

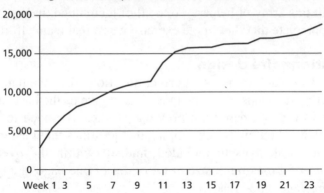

Figure 0.1: The speed at which forms were returned

Was the response reasonable?

There are two facets to this. In terms of the overall percentage, the 50% achieved in 2005 compares to a 33% response in 1998, and to 70% in 1989. In the 2002 Scottish Church Census we had 52%. So this suggests a very strong commitment to the process and an earnest desire to learn what is happening.

In statistical terms a response rate of 50% is certainly robust enough for reasonable reliability. The statistical accuracy of any survey is dependent on three things: the actual level of accuracy desired (usually taken on what is technically called a 95% confidence interval, though other percentages are perfectly possible); the percentage value emerging from the results (percentages closer to 50% are slightly less accurately measured than smaller percentages), and the number on which the percentage is based. Of these three the last is the most important. To illustrate these variations, take the overall 2005 finding that 6.3% of the population attend church on Sunday. As it was based on a response rate of 50% of the churches this figure is subject to a variation of ± 0.3%[1], that is, the true figure is between 6.0% and 6.6%; by convention we take the midpoint value of 6.3%.

The other facet to the question, "Are the overall results reasonable?", is whether or not they compare reasonably with existing figures collected quite independently from the different denominations. Not every denomination collects attendance information, and some, like the Baptist Union of Great Britain, collect it, but do not publish it. The Church of England, the Roman Catholic Church and the United Reformed Church however all collect and publish such information.

The Church of England publishes a variety of attendance data; here, and throughout this book, we take their "Usual Sunday Attendance" (USA) data as this is comparable to the information collected by other denominations, and to previous Censuses. This is the lowest of the figures produced by the Church of England's Research and Statistics Department: "Average Sunday Attendance" (ASA) for example is at least 10% higher, and furthermore increased between 2002 and 2003 while the USA decreased. The ASA is measured over a month, and will therefore include special services such as Harvest services, Parade, other All Age services and Baptism services. Such data is clearly useful, but it isn't directly comparable to the data that we collected in the Census or to other denominations' data. When in 1979 we tried to collect figures averaged over a month, the response rate was lower, and subsequently we were advised that, statistically, measuring on a "typical" Sunday was as accurate[2].

Figures published for the years immediately prior to the 2005 Census year are given in Table 0.2[3].

Table 0.2: Attendance information published

Year	Church of England USA	Roman Catholic Church[4]	United Reformed Church
2001	938,000	954,132	81,228
2002	917,000	934,200	79,473
2003	902,000	n/a	75,980
2004	n/a	n/a	72,166
Straight line 2005 projection	865,000	874,400	69,500
English Church Census 2005	**867,400**	**875,600**	**68,700**

The "straight line projection" is based on the 2, 3 or 4 figures given above and projected to 2005 for ease of comparison. The closeness of the Census figures with these projections suggests that the overall results at least for these three major denominations are reasonable, and on that basis, it is assumed that the other figures likewise will probably be of the right order of magnitude, and that the conclusions drawn are likely to be correct.

Jurisdictions

In common with previous studies, the fourth English Church Census included both the Channel Islands and the Isle of Man. It is of course recognised that these two territories are separate jurisdictions legally, but most of the major denominations include supervision of their churches within an appropriate Diocese or Region which is based in England. These two territories are therefore analysed along with the 47 counties in England and included in the commentary where appropriate. This note is to assure those who live on these islands that their special legal status is understood and recognised!

How was the Census carried out?

A number of church leaders were asked in 2003 whether a further Census should be undertaken in 2005, and they unanimously were positive. The Board of Christian Research concurred. So a proposal was written and requests for sponsorship made. When sufficient support was forthcoming, action began! That included forming the Census Steering Committee which first met in September 2004; they agreed the final questionnaire at their meeting in March 2005. (For questionnaire see associated results volume *Religious Trends* No 6, 2006/2007).

An initial mailing to all the 38,000 churches on our database took place in February to let churches know the Census would take place on 8th May 2005, and asked them to let Christian Research know of any new churches which had been started in their locality or any which had closed. A huge and very helpful response to this letter was received. At the same time every senior leader (Bishop, Archdeacon, Vicar-General, Regional Minister, Chairman, Superintendent, Moderator, District Commander, etc.) was informed that the Census was taking place.

The Census covered all Christian denominations, which included all Free, Protestant, Anglican, Roman Catholic and Orthodox Churches, that is, all those accepting the Trinitarian formula of belief in God the Father, God the Son and God the Holy Spirit in one Essence. This excludes the Jehovah's Witnesses, Mormons, Christian Scientists, Christadelphians, Jews, Muslims, Hindus and members of other non-Trinitarian or non-Christian groups. Collectively the active religious people thus excluded represented 4% of the UK population in 2005[5].

The crucial mailing took place in April 2005, with a covering letter indicating that the information provided would be treated as confidential. No information on any individual church would be released without its approval. Likewise churches were able to tick appropriate boxes to indicate whether or not they wished to receive future mailings, according to the Data Protection Act.

The thousands of returned forms were then individually checked, and entered on to the Christian Research computers, an exercise which was finally completed in October 2005. Then the analysis began!

Why choose May 8th?

May 8th was chosen as it was a day outside holidays and half-terms, away from Bank Holidays and Festivals, and the week before Pentecost Sunday, when some churches hold special services. It was not a cold winter's day, but one where we were kindly given mild weather. No Sunday is ever "average" but there is no real reason to think that the church attendance that Sunday was overall above or below the usual number.

1 The overall findings

During a summer holiday in north eastern Scotland I took the new funicular railway to the top of the Cairngorms. It happened to be a glorious sunny day, and the view from the new restaurant was absolutely spectacular. You could see for miles, and, with no clouds or mist, could take in a whole panorama. Being able to see the whole picture allowed the particular mountain I was standing on to be put into perspective. You could observe peaks elsewhere, and look at curious rocky outcrops, different in colour from the rest, all of which helped to make up the entire scene.

A church Census fulfils a similar function – it enables the "big picture" to be seen, and the irregularities which are part of it. The view gives the framework for the detail. Some of those differences are important as they help pinpoint changes and can enable leaders to consider alternative strategic actions. Big surveys give the overview and paint the broad picture into which the ups and downs of individual churches fit.

Why, therefore, another Census? To evaluate current activity, to understand better the macro picture and the contrasting trends which compose it, and especially to provide data resources to enable action by church leaders.

Was another Census strictly necessary? After all, if 12% of the English population went to church in 1979, and 10% in 1989 and 7.5% in 1998, it is obvious that the percentage is decreasing. Yes, that is obvious, but is the decline continuing as rapidly as expected? Have the many mission activities of the last five years helped to reduce the drop? Only a major study such as another Census can really answer such questions.

The changing context

Church life is always lived in a national and local context. Such wider factors are also part of the "big picture", and it is worth briefly looking at some of these before we focus specifically on church life.

Societal factors

Continued immigration. One of the features of British life over the last decade has been the continued influx of many who want to live in this country. Asylum seekers and refugees frequently make the news headlines, sometimes in their desperate attempts to get here somehow. The basic facts are that over the years 1995 to 2005 some two million additional people are living in England, because of the 1.2 million immigrants, mainly from the EU, in addition to natural population increase of 0.8 million. The English population thus increased from 48.4 million in 1995 to 50.4 million in 2005. Some of these people are Christian and will attend a local church – and in some cases, have started one!

Continued rise in cohabitation and single parent families. Focussing only on families, in 1995 70% of families were married couples (with or without children), 10% were cohabiting couples (with or without children) and 20% were single parents (the overwhelming majority being single mothers). By 2005 these percentages had become, respectively, 56%, 15% and 29%[1] – an enormous change in just 10 years. If these changes continue at the same rate in the future, then by 2015 they will have become 42%, 20% and 38% respectively, as illustrated in Figure 1.1. The marital status of churchgoers nationally is not definitively known (though see Figure 6.8), but, again focussing only on families and leaving aside the many widowed and single people in church, then an estimate for 2001 would suggest that of the families attending churches, 92% are married couples, 2% cohabiting couples, and 6% single parents[2] – percentages which are massively different from the general population. These trends may inhibit church attendance by some.

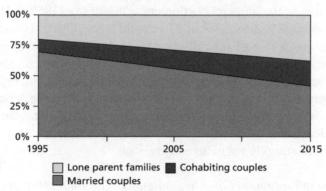

Figure 1.1: Proportions of different types of family

Sunday Shopping. Legislation was passed in 1994 allowing shops to open for 6 hours on a Sunday, and in 2006 the larger stores had hoped, unsuccessfully, for this to be increased to 9 hours, from 9.00am to 6.00pm. The 2002 Scottish Church Census showed that fewer women in the 30-44 age-group were attending church[3], and Focus Groups which explored why showed that this was the impact of employment in retail trading and care, which, while open to both genders, tend to be taken more by women than men. As will be seen, this is a real concern in England also, even without extra legislation extending shopping hours.

Competition. Sunday shopping is not the only competitor. Many schools and sports clubs now have fixtures on a Sunday morning, thereby making it more difficult for some children to get to Sunday School. In addition, many churches are finding it harder to get Sunday School teachers willing and able to teach every week, moving to a rota system instead. Children find it harder to

relate to different teachers on successive weeks, especially if
they are irregular themselves.

Impact on children. There are many pressures on children and
young people today. One is the fact that a third are growing up
without having their two natural parents in the same home[4].
Another is the huge proportion engaging in sex (18% of 16 year
old boys, 38% girls; 33% of 17 year old boys, 43% girls[5]), and the
consequent rise of sexually transmitted diseases and abortions
among those under 20. Some churchgoing young people, tempted
by such practices, drop out of church attendance, feeling that their
life-style is inappropriate – and Christians do not always practice
forgiveness. Many children are unable to attend Sunday morning
services because they then visit "absent" parents, are involved in
sport, or struggle to get up early enough.

Growth and impact of other religions. The increasing presence
of other religions may be highlighted in terrorist or other high
profile activity, but the basic numbers bear it out also, due in
part to the continuing number of immigrants. The number of
active Muslims (attending mosque once a year) has increased
from 630,000 in 1995 to 890,000 by 2005, and is likely to reach
1.24 million by 2015[6]; other religions are growing less quickly[7].
This growth is unlikely to affect church attendance as such, but
is a constant challenge to it, and a comparison to which the
media draw much attention.

Positive Church factors
Church planting. When the Archbishop of Canterbury, Dr
Rowan Williams, was appointed in 2003, he brought an emphasis
on what is termed "fresh expressions" of church. A movement of
that name has been formed under his aegis which is promoting
different ways of church life. An important report, *Mission-
shaped Church*[8], was presented to the General Synod in January
2004 by the Committee's chairman, Graham Cray, Bishop
of Maidstone[9]. It emphasised the re-thinking necessary for

assessing what kinds of church might currently be acceptable. "Emerging church" is another expression indicating vitality, alternatives, and perhaps a new beginning for relevant evangelism. A major Church Planting Conference in Sheffield in March 2006 drew 450 people.

Alpha Courses. The Alpha Course, originated by Holy Trinity, Brompton Road, London (HTB), is well known, and has been a powerful force in Britain, and indeed around the world, in the last 10 years. Eight million people have now attended such a course worldwide (to end 2005)[10] and in 2005 more people attended an Alpha course in England than in 2004, just as more attended in 2004 than 2003[11]. When HTB commissioned MORI to undertake a national awareness poll, they found that 22% of the population knew Alpha was a Christian instruction course. Other, less publicised courses, such as Emmaus and Christianity Explored, have also had a significant impact.

Information Technology (IT). The 1990s saw a dizzying display of ever more dazzling machines, particularly electronic gadgetry, with technology becoming increasingly smarter, faster and smaller. This rise has gathered momentum in the 21st century, with use of blackberry devices, iPods, MP3s, Satnav, digital/ interactive TV, broadband in more than 50% of British households in 2005, etc. Into this age of technology, the church has to make its mark, and although some feel that it was initially slow in taking advantage of it, this is much less the case now. The use of IT is a major attraction for some young people in going to church! It challenges our habitual ways of thinking in old linear patterns. In opening the November 2005 General Synod of the Church of England, the Queen said, "When so much is in flux, when limitless amounts of information, much of it ephemeral, are instantly accessible, there is renewed hunger for that which endures and gives meaning. The Christian Church can uniquely speak to that need"[12].

Culture still Christian. Much has been written about the changed and changing culture of our times, including the move from modernism to post-modernism. In an excellent book looking at the impact culture has on a person's spirituality, and their usage of the Occasional Offices for Christian baptism, marriage and funerals, Alan Billings, an Anglican parish priest in Kendal and Director of the Centre for Ethics and Religion at Lancaster University, writes, "The culture of this country is without question more secular than it was, though it is a secular culture that puts a high premium on emotion rather than reason . . . a turn to the self, a turn inward. Nevertheless, the culture is still deeply influenced by the Christian religion, and most people think of themselves as Christian. . . . People may lead more secular lives, but they retain sacred hearts."[13] However, Manchester University researcher, David Voas, has shown that "the proportion of people who believe in God is declining faster than church attendance."[14]

Negative church factors

Few major campaigns. In the 1980s Billy Graham and Luis Palau held major missions in England. In the 1990s the Pentecostals had special missions with Morris Cerullo in London and the JIM Campaign [=Jesus in Me] in the northwest, and the German evangelist, Reinhard Bonké, posted a gospel to every household in Britain for Easter 1994. But since then there have been few similar campaigns other than the J John campaigns, although Morris Cerullo held another Mission to London in 2006. Such impact they bring to the Christian scene, even if only temporary, has been lost.

Post-Christendom. Numerous books have been written in the 1995-2005 decade describing the implications of current church changes. *The Death of Christian Britain*, by the Scot Callum Brown[15] has perhaps been the most well-known, but there are many others[16]. Some feel we are in the closing stages of church as it has been known for past centuries, and are trying to think "what next" for British, European and western Christianity. The uncertainty of what the future holds can lead to a loss of confidence and reduced commitment for some churchgoers.

Time pressure. It can always be said that people are too busy, but European-wide statistics show that British people work longer hours than in any other European country. One British study showed that 40% of managers work more than 50 hours a week, 2% more than 80 hours; 60% often or always worked in the evenings; 66% said they felt under constant time pressure[17]. If you are under pressure, is your priority as a committed Christian always to go to church on a Sunday? A 2003 survey of Archdeacons found 11% of them worked over 80 hours a week[18].

The sexuality debate. The ordination of a practising homosexual, Gene Robinson, as the Bishop of New Hampshire in the United States, created a huge furore throughout the Anglican Communion. A report commissioned to look at the implications of this action, the Windsor Report, chaired by the Archbishop of Ireland, Robin Eames, did not satisfy everyone. The potential appointment of a non-practising homosexual as Bishop of Reading, Jeffery John, created a similar uproar in England, especially in the Diocese of Oxford, where the Bishop's chaplain was kept busy answering thousands of letters! Jeffery John's name was eventually withdrawn although he subsequently became the Dean of St Albans Cathedral. The Anglican Mainstream organisation has declared the topic of sexuality of major first order priority[19]. This type of concern, while originating in the Anglican Communion, is not confined to the Church of England.

Women bishops? Whether the natural fulfilment of the ordination of women as priests is to ordain some of them as bishops is being debated within the Church of England. If agreed, it could cause major disruption in church life, and some would leave or join (or start) a separate "continuing" congregation.

All these factors do not just add up to massive change in the last 10 years, but in their own way impact church people, and with that their church attendance to a greater or lesser extent.

Something must be happening – churches are opening!

Between 1998 and 2005 some 1,100 churches were newly opened in England – congregations not there 7 years previously! That's an average of 3 new churches opening every week. However, this is fewer than opened between 1989 and 1998 when it was 4 per week. There are two particular groups of these new congregations, described below. Both can claim at least 300 such churches started in the last few years, and they show a vigour and urgency for evangelism which is far-reaching and important. Whether this trickle of life and energy (and very different forms of worship) will turn into a stream, and that stream turn into a river, is far too early to say, but the initial and expanding phenomenon is remarkable.

- There is what is called the "fresh expression" church, an emerging church, a mission-shaped church: new names and titles for what might have been called "church planting" a few years ago, but with an enthusiastic emphasis on mission and non-traditional styles of worship not always associated with previous church plants[20]. Fresh Expressions is an Anglican organisation headed by Steven Croft to help research, encourage and enable such churches. It is supported by the Archbishop of Canterbury who said, "Fresh Expressions is to enable more and more people to engage with Jesus Christ."[21] Such churches are probably mostly Anglican, but for Census purposes they were separately designated[22].

- A large number of churches started by ethnic minority groups, across a whole variety of languages, particularly in the years since 1998. Some of these are just single congregations started by immigrants keen to spread the gospel, especially among their own language and culture. Others by those sent as missionaries from Africa or the Caribbean or Asia to help evangelise the "mother country which gave them the gospel a century or so ago". The Black majority churches are mostly Pentecostal, so are included under that heading, while other ethnic minority churches, often non-charismatic, are included within the "Smaller Denominations" group.

The 1990s was a church planting decade, encouraged by the Challenge 2000 Conferences in 1992 and 1995 in which the target of collectively starting 20,000 new congregations by 2000 was adopted. Although this target was unrealistic, many denominations did encourage the starting of new congregations, explaining the relatively large numbers of newly opened churches in the early 1990s. Different factors were at work:

- *Anglican*. With the introduction of women priests into the Church of England, a number of ministers left and formed various "Continuing" congregations[23], the largest of which was the Anglican Catholic Church which started with 27 congregations in 1992.

- *New Churches*. The New Churches (House Churches) had expanded very rapidly in the 1980s and much the same energy was put into fresh congregations in the 1990s. Far fewer New Churches have opened since, suggesting they recognised the need to consolidate their growth, especially those streams associated with the vision of the Challenge 2000 Conferences. Newfrontiers and Vineyard Churches, however, have been church planting very strongly in the last decade.

- *Orthodox*. The Orthodox Church began expanding in England in the 1990s, and has continued into the new century through the policy of ordaining many part-time non-stipendiary priests[24], who begin a congregation where they live. The Orthodox do not call this church planting or mission activity, but many others would!

- *Pentecostal*. Kensington Temple, a major Elim Pentecostal Church, sought to begin 2,000 new churches in the 1990s. "They managed 126 churches with many hundreds of additional cells but the initial goal was not reached."[25]

- *Smaller Denominations*. A number of ethnic minority churches also began in the 1990s, something which has continued since, especially since the beginning of the new century.

Some of these trends have passed with the start of a new century, apart from the continuing enthusiasm of the immigrant churches. Table 1.2 shows that churches have been both opened and closed in *all* denominational groups in the last 7 years. In this fourth Census, for the first time, Hospital services have been included where appropriate; these are part of the "All Others" in the Smaller Denominations category and are recorded as newly opened, although some will have been meeting long before 1998.

It is still true that 3 congregations have started on average every week since 1998! Is *something* really happening?

Table 1.2: Number of churches 1979-2005, by denomination[26]

Year	Ang-lican	Baptist	Roman Cath'c	Indep-endent	Meth-odist	New	Orth-odox	Pente-costal	United Ref'ed	All others	TOTAL
1979	16,960	2,211	3,673	3,011	7,636	419	97	1,772	1,829	1,456	39,064
1989	16,373	2,339	3,824	3,097	6,740	1,026	114	1,951	1,681	1,462	38,607
Opened	+120	+105	+65	+53	+70	+490	+144	+355	+28	+437	+1,867
Closed	-212	-31	-118	-907	-570	-127	0	-201	-145	-446	-2,757
1998	16,281	2,413	3,771	2,243	6,240	1,389	258	2,105	1,564	1,453	37,717
Opened	+89	+58	+11	+247	+23	+89	+65	+207	+18	+276	+1,083
Closed	-123	-85	-126	-209	-264	-171	-6	-85	-112	-118	-1,299
2005	16,247	2,386	3,656	2,281	5,999	1,307	317	2,227	1,470	1,611	37,501

Church closures

However against these exciting numbers of new openings of congregations must be set a slightly higher number of closures. Over 1,300 churches have ceased since 1998, making the net number of churches in England in 2005 just over 200 less than in 1998. However, it should be noticed that far fewer churches have closed in the past 7 years than the previous 9 (1,300 compared with 2,750).

The changes since 1989 are shown in Table 1.2, which gives the net effect of openings and closures, where "opened" and "closed" each refer to the periods 1989-1998 and 1998-2005.

Some of the factors behind these closures are:

- *Independent*. Many smaller churches, especially the lone individual independent churches[27], closed in the 1990s, as well as some in the "Smaller Denominations" category, but the number of Independent churches is increasing again partly because of the "Fresh Expression" congregations.

- *Methodists*. The Methodists went through a severe time of re-organisation and re-appraisal in the 1990s leading to many closures of churches in particular areas, a policy which has continued since although at a slower rate.

- *Pentecostal*. Some of the new churches started by the Elim Pentecostal Church in the 1990s had to close after a year or so.

- *Rationalisation* in the larger, more institutional denominations, continues and inevitably this means making some churches redundant.

This is a list more of *which* churches have closed, rather than *why* churches close. An article in *Christianity* suggested that lack of vision for the future and a culture of preference more than purpose were the key reasons[28], but arguments for and against closure, especially of rural churches, have been detailed elsewhere[29].

The overall finding

The overall result of the Fourth English Church Census was that on 8th May 2005, or an equivalent Sunday, there were 3,166,200 people, adults and children, in church in England. This is 6.3% of the population.

There are two elements to look for in statistics – the overall strength (what is the number?) and how is it moving (where is it going?). The second is as important as the first. Trend information gives us this second vital arm of understanding what is happening in the world, and in English church life in particular. The previous studies showed that:

• In 1979 there were 5.4 million in church, 11.7% of the population.

• In 1989 there were 4.7 million in church, 9.9% of the population.

• In 1998 there were 3.7 million in church, 7.5% of the population.

This Census shows:

• In 2005 there were 3.2 million in church, 6.3% of the population.

It may be seen that over the 9 year period 1989 to 1998, 1 million fewer people went to church, but in the seven years 1998 to 2005 only half a million have stopped attending, fewer than might have been expected. That has to be good news, but of course it raises the question "why?" A million loss over 9 years (or a 1.7 million loss over 19 years) would be about a 800,000 loss in 7 years, so as the church has "only" lost 500,000, it "gained", as it were, about 300,000 people.

Where have they come from? As will be shown in the following chapters essentially three broad sources – the Black majority and other ethnically diverse churches have been expanding rapidly, the white churches also have seen people come to faith through Alpha and other like courses or related evangelistic events, and from the stimulus of the "Fresh Expressions" movement. Why then have we declined? Because while we have gained a large number we have lost twice as many through death or people simply giving up going to church so often. (The number dropping out from loss of faith is fairly small). It had been hoped that the impact of some of the new experimentation would make a real difference on numbers; this result suggests it has not yet had that effect. The many Willow Creek Conferences, Purpose-Driven Church emphasis, the charismatic renewal, the cell church programme may all have been important but their cumulative impact has not been sufficient to offset the decline in other areas. This is disappointing; it also shows that a vibrant future will not be the past reviewed or re-branded[30].

The number found in 2005 *includes* some of the early results of the many "fresh expression" churches, and the results of the explosion of ethnic churches. If these were removed from the overall numbers, there would be at least 125,000 fewer people in church, giving a total of 3.04 million or just 6.0% of the population. In other words, the decline in most churches is accelerating. The results are therefore very serious.

These basic overall numbers are illustrated in Figure 1.3; the nose-dive out of which we need to come. It should be noted that the number of years between each vertical bar is different:

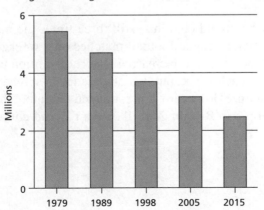

Figure 1.3: English church attendance 1979-2015

Some may say that the 6.3% of the population in church on 8th May is a far cry from the 72% who claimed to be Christian in the 2001 Census. This is certainly true, and reasons for the gap and whether the 72% really measures *religious* affiliation have been debated by academics and others in the years since the Census[31]. However, as Reginald Bibby points out[32], the line in the 1970s Bonnie Tyler song *It's a Heartache* "Love songs last longer than lovers ever do" can be translated "Religious identification lasts longer than involvement ever does", which does not necessarily contradict the finding of rapid decline in belief already mentioned if people identify with religion more because of heritage reasons than faith reasons.

It could be argued that this result confirms some of the trends in Europe where what Grace Davie calls "vicarious religion" is taking place. Vicarious religion is "the notion of religion formed by an absent minority on behalf of a much larger number who not only understand but clearly approve of what the minority is doing."[33] This means that people are seen to believe on behalf of others and invoke moral codes on behalf of others[34]. Research undertaken in the immediate aftermath of the first Scottish Church Census in 1982 among men who had stopped going to church found that they reckoned "their wives went on their behalf". This attitude, however, is not immutable, but is changing.

The 6.3% who attend church is still three times the number of those who attend League football matches on a weekend, even though their numbers are increasing. Nearly 3 million people go to the cinema each week, but that attendance is spread across 7 days not just one. However, "it is estimated that more than twice as many people in Britain go to Ikea than attend church every Sunday."[35]

Some questions

We need to ask some questions to ensure that we are interpreting these numbers correctly.

What do we mean by "church"? "Church" was defined for the purpose of this Census as *a body of people meeting on a Sunday in the same premises primarily for public worship at regular intervals.* The congregations approached thus included normal church buildings, and also those meeting for worship in school chapels, Armed Forces chaplaincies[36], and those in hospital chapels. Congregations which meet on Saturdays (like the Seventh-day Adventists, or Catholics taking Vigil Mass) were counted in. Churches whose services are held fortnightly or monthly were also counted in, but not those used less frequently. Congregations who do not own a building but hire a local school or civic hall for their meetings were included. Some people meet for worship during the week, and these numbers were also counted, but not included in the Sunday total.

Was it an average Sunday? May 8th was the 60th anniversary of VE Day, and a number of churches held special commemoration services. Some indicated to us that they included all the non-regulars who attended that day, others omitted them, and yet others took the Census on another day in order to get a more normal Sunday. Some drew attention to the Census in their weekly news-sheet[37]. We have not included, for example, the estimated 2,000 people who attended the Cenotaph Service that day, nor those who may have visited the Church of Fools or other like web-based churches (whose numbers are not known). No Sunday is ever "average" but there is no reason to think that the church attendance that Sunday was abnormal.

Was the response rate adequate? The response rate of 50% is very high by normal statistical standards. In terms of denominational response, the overall figure breaks down as follows:

	%
Baptist	67
Smaller denominations	57
Anglican	55
Catholic	54
Independents	50
New Churches	49
United Reformed	44
Methodists	37
Pentecostal	30
Orthodox	7

The two largest individual denominations, Anglican and Catholic, both responded better than average[38]. As the figures in Table 0.2 indicate, the grossed up figures suggest the Census findings are very reasonable. Likewise for the United Reformed Church. While it is disappointing that only a third of Pentecostal churches responded, this is in large part due to the difficulty of tracking down black church leaders, many of whom have full-time jobs in addition to their church responsibilities.

It is obviously of concern that there was such a low response from the Orthodox Churches, but 8th May happened to be "low" Sunday[39], or the Sunday after their Easter, when many of their churches were closed. However, even if the grossed up figures are say 100% wrong (which is unlikely), the resulting extra 25,000 worshippers will not change the overall figure very much, and the total numbers would still be 6.3% of the population.

Estimates have been made for those who did not respond, partly on the basis that their figures would on average be similar to those who did respond, but also by comparing the resulting totals to see if the trend in their figures was reasonable compared with the pre-vious study or with published denominational or other figures.

Were the right questions asked? The basic questions on total attendance, numbers attending twice, and children, with an age/gender breakdown have been the same since 1989 and have been used identically in three Scottish Church Censuses. The age-groups were extended in this Census from the six used previously. to nine, but this will not affect the total numbers recorded. Furthermore the draft ques-

Are we supposed to count how many are in at the start of your service or how many there are left at the end?

tions were freshly piloted for this Census, so that while it is always easy to blame the wording of the question, it seems that the questions this time were probably as correct as they could be. We didn't foresee the one in Noel Ford's cartoon[40] though!

Some churches didn't have a service that day! Almost 3% of English churches did not hold a service on 8th May, some 973 churches in total. This figure is likely to be understated since many churches not holding a service that day will not have replied. These were mostly churches in Remoter Rural areas whose practice is to hold a service every fortnight or month[41], some members of whose congregations will perhaps have attended a service in a neighbouring hamlet or village.

These churches which had a zero congregation on Census Sunday were not assumed to have closed, but rather were amalgamated with the other linked churches in recording the results. Thus if there were three linked rural churches, two of which had no service on 8th May, and the third church had 75 people who were a mixture from all three congregations, the church where the service was actually held was recorded as having 75 present and the other two as zero, but not closed. This means that the correct number is included in the overall total, and the size of that congregation is also correctly recorded, and not put as, for example, three congregations of 25 each.

Rates of decline
The 2005 figure of 3,166,200 people in church is a drop of 15% from the 1998 figure of 3,714,700. This works out at a decline of -2.3% per year. Between 1989 and 1998 the numbers attending church dropped at the rate of -2.7% per year, and between 1979 and 1989 the numbers dropped at the rate of -1.4% per year. So the *rate of decline* is not quite as great as it was in the 1990s but is still considerably more than it was in the 1980s. We are coming out of the nosedive, but no U-turn is yet in sight – we are still dropping.

If the figure of 2.47 million by 2015 turns out to be correct, then numbers will have dropped by then at the rate -2.5% per year, implying that the existing rate of decline is set to continue and probably to worsen slightly[42].

Had the impact of the growing ethnic minority and independent churches not happened, and the total church attendance in 2005 was 3.04 million instead of 3.17 million, the drop between 1998 and 2005 would have been at the rate of 95,000 people per year. If the 2015 estimate of 2.47 million still held, then this would mean that between 2005 and 2015 numbers would decrease at 60,000 a year, a massive difference from the 95,000 for 1998 to 2005. This suggests that the growing ethnic and independent churches are critical for the wellbeing of the future church life in England, and hold the balance between a reducing rate of decline and an increasing rate of decline.

Further analyses
The questionnaire asked for a wide variety of further information. The following chapters analyse the basic data essentially

one factor at a time, though two or more are used where the subsequent analysis gives important information. All the data are also broken down by county and some by Local or Unitary Authority. These Tables are too extensive to be included here, so are given at length in the companion volume, *Religious Trends* No 6, 2006/2007, published simultaneously with this book. A copy of the questionnaire used in the Census is also included in *Religious Trends*.

Additional analyses are also included in this edition of *Religious Trends*, as are coloured maps to show the variations of church-going across England. For those interested in such data, *Religious Trends* can be purchased through Christian Research's website www.christian-research.org.uk.

Assessing change, understanding trends, evaluating the future, looking at the national picture, all build up into the importance of taking strategic action. This is especially considered in the last chapter; for those not wanting the detail, feel free to jump straight to Chapter 12!

So what does all this say?

This introductory chapter has shown:

- There have been many societal and ecclesial changes in the last few years, making a further Census very timely.

- An excellent response was received, especially by the largest denominations, meaning that the results can be read with confidence.

- While many new churches have been started between 1998 and 2005, slightly more have closed, bringing the total number of churches or congregations of all denominations to 37,501 in May 2005.

- The number of churches closing in the 7 years 1998-2005 was at a much slower rate than closures in the previous nine years.

- The overall finding was that on 8th May 2005, 3.2 million people attended church in England, 6.3% of the population.

- Unfortunately it is not as many as might have been expected from the energy seen in the many new churches which have been started, but on the other hand, the average decrease in numbers is less than occurred during the 1990s.

2 Going down Lewisham High Street
[Denominational analysis]

Every so often I travel down Lewisham High Street in south east London. No visitor would fail to recognise yet another new black church has opened, often above a shop, with a name fascinating to white Anglo-Saxon ears, such as the Kingsvine Church, or the Global Revival Christian Centre, or Anointed Word Ministries or the Shiloh Church of God. This is just a microcosm of the plethora of new black churches starting and growing in all their diversity, and it is a wonderful sight.

So before we look in detail at the 10 groups into which the 227 different denominations in England 2005 are divided, let us begin with where church life is exciting, growing and changing rapidly.

Ethnic churches

Many of these 227 denominations relate to ethnically diverse groups[1], which may be divided into four main categories:

1) The Catholic churches which naturally are included within the Roman Catholic group, such as the Croatian or Hungarian churches;

2) The (largely) charismatic Black churches which are included within the Pentecostal group;

3) The (largely) non-charismatic churches of non-Afro-Caribbean origin which are included as "Protestant Overseas National Churches" within the "Smaller Denominations" group such as the Chinese, Korean, Tamil churches or those springing from an explicitly European origin like the Italian, Portuguese or Spanish; and

4) The 22 separate Orthodox denominations most of which are based around their own ethnic, racial or cultural peoples and may thus also be referred to as "ethnic" churches.

Collectively these ethnically diverse churches are important as the number of their congregations is increasing as are the numbers attending them. Table 2.1 shows the breakdown of these four denominational groups, and lists as (5) the other non-white churchgoers who intermingle with many white and other ethnicities in various congregations. It ignores "white" churchgoers, who are decreasing, even though of course white is one ethnicity, as ethnicity as a whole is looked at in more detail in Chapter 5.

Table 2.1: Attendance in ethnic churches, 1998 and 2005

	1998	Change	2005
1) Catholic Overseas National Churches	12,300	+42%	17,500
2a) New Testament Church of God	14,700	+37%	20,100
2b) Church of God of Prophecy	5,600	+21%	6,800
2c) Other Afro-Caribbean churches	84,000	+49%	125,000
3) Protestant Overseas National Churches	9,200	+110%	19,300
4) All Orthodox denominations	25,200	+ 2%	25,600
Total attendance at ethnic churches	**151,000**	**+42%**	**214,300**
5) Non-white churchgoers attending other churches	289,100	+8%	311,300
All white churchgoers	3,274,600	−19%	2,640,600
Total church attendance	**3,714,700**	**−15%**	**3,166,200**

Table 2.1 shows that these various ethnically diverse groups are *all growing*, whether they are Catholic, Charismatic, Non-charismatic or Orthodox. Why this growth? For various reasons:

• Some can be attributed to immigration, which at current rates is bringing an extra million people into England every 7 years. These are those looking for employment, relatives of those already here, asylum seekers and others. For example, 7 new Croatian Catholic churches started between 1998 and 2005, almost certainly to meet the needs of Croatian immigrants.

- Some are "missionary" stations of an overseas denomination[2], say in Nigeria, which is establishing one or more congregations in England often "to help evangelise the British people" but sometimes (as with the Koreans) to minister to those of their own culture or race. Some of these denominations consist as yet of just one congregation.

- Some of the Charismatic and Orthodox groups especially are strong in planting new churches for those already living in Britain, or, as with the Orthodox, ordaining many new non-stipendiary (unpaid) ministers who begin a new congregation where they already live.

- Some are churches which come about from Christians eager to evangelise, especially among those not yet fluent in another language who would prefer to worship in their own language if at all possible.

This growth suggests that if "something has been done right" between 1998 and 2005, this must be part of it, even if their existence could imply that some immigrants do not always feel welcome in existing congregations. Table 2.1 shows that the Black churches are the most numerous (and impact areas like Greater London especially), but all the various ethnically diverse groups are important.

While all growth is exciting and significant, the growth reflected in Table 2.1 represents but 7% of the total churchgoers in England in 2005, so it is to the others that we now turn, starting with the Institutional churches.

Institutional v non-institutional

For simplicity of analysis, the 227 English denominations are divided into 10 broad categories, of which a third are in the "Pentecostal" group and another quarter are collected together and simply called "Smaller denominations". In addition, 4 categories are additionally termed "institutional" (Roman Catholic,

Anglican, Orthodox and United Reformed Church or URC) because in at least one country of the world the dominant denomination in that group is the State or Established Church (Presbyterian acting in this capacity for the URC). The other six groups thus are "non-institutional" churches or, more simply, "Free Churches". The basic figures for these two larger divisions are shown in Table 2.2, and are illustrated in Figure 2.3[3].

The Institutional churches between them account for 3.7% of the English population, of which the Roman Catholics are 1.8%, the Anglicans 1.7%, and the Orthodox and URC 0.2%. The non-institutional are collectively 2.6% of the population.

Table 2.2: Attendance in institutional and non-institutional churches, 1979–2015

	1979	Change	1989	Change	1998
4 Institutional categories	3,862,000	−19%	3,143,800	−25%	2,357,600
6 Non-institutional groups	1,579,000	+1%	1,599,000	−15%	1,357,100
Total church attendance	**5,441,000**	**−13%**	**4,742,800**	**−22%**	**3,714,700**
	1998	Change	**2005**	Change	2015E
4 Institutional categories	2,357,600	−21%	**1,859,200**	−26%	1,327,200
6 Non-institutional groups	1,357,100	−4%	**1,307,000**	−8%	1,147,000
Total church attendance	**3,714,700**	**−15%**	**3,166,200**	**−19%**	**2,474,200**

E = Estimate

Figure 2.3: Total English church attendance, 1979–2015

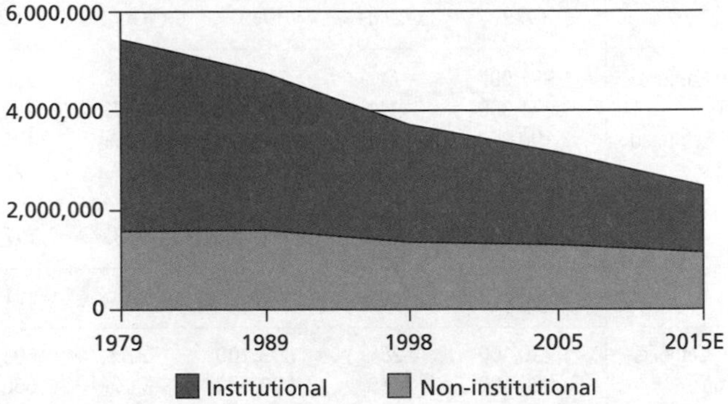

Figure 2.3 shows that it is the Institutional churches which are declining more rapidly, although it also shows that the Free churches are declining. If these rates of decline continue to 2015 then the collective attendance of the Institutional churches will by then be only slightly greater than that of the Free churches. Part of the reason for the smaller Free church decline between 1998 and 2005 is that all the ethnic minority churches except the Catholics (which are relatively small) are in the Free church grouping and are growing.

The Institutional churches

Table 2.4 gives the numbers and Figure 2.5 graphs the four Institutional churches and projects their figures to 2015[4]. It shows that while the Roman Catholic Church has seen greater decline before 1998 than the Anglican Church, both are likely to decline between 2005 and 2015 more slowly than the URC.

The overall figure in 2005 is close to what might have been expected had we only had the earlier figures to go by. However, the 2005 attendance figures are higher than expected for the Anglicans[6], but are all *lower* than might have been expected[7] for the Catholics, United Reformed and Orthodox.

Table 2.4: Institutional church attendance, 1979–2005

	1979	Change	1989	Change	1998
Roman Catholic	1,991,000	−14%	1,715,900	−28%	1,230,100
Anglican	1,671,000	−24%	1,266,300	−23%	980,600
United Reformed	190,000	−21%	149,300	−18%	121,700
Orthodox	10,000	+23%	12,300	+105%	25,200
Total	**3,862,000**	**−19%**	**3,143,800**	**−25%**	**2,357,600**
	1998	Change	2005	Change	2015E
Roman Catholic	1,230,100	−28%	**893,100**	−32%	608,000
Anglican	980,600	−11%	**870,600**	−24%	660,000[5]
United Reformed	121,700	−43%	**69,900**	−53%	33,100
Orthodox	25,200	+2%	**25,600**	+2%	26,100
Total	**2,357,600**	**−21%**	**1,859,200**	**−29%**	**1,327,200**

E = Estimate

Figure 2.5: Institutional church attendance, 1979–2015

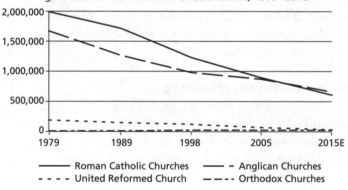

Roman Catholic churches

The "Roman Catholic" category includes a few smaller denominations which do not recognise papal authority, but the Roman Catholic Church in England accounts for 98% of attendance in this group. These churches collectively are, however, declining more than twice as rapidly as the Anglicans, but because they were larger than the Anglicans in 1998 they are still larger in 2005. Details are in Table 2.6:

Table 2.6: Roman Catholic church attendance

	1979	Change	1989	Change	1998	Change	2005
RC Church in England	1,978,300	−14%	1,703,800	−29%	1,217,800	−29%	875,600
Overseas and other Catholics	12,700	−5%	12,100	+2%	12,300	+42%	17,500
Total Catholic	1,991,000	−14%	1,715,900	−28%	1,230,100	−28%	893,100

The Roman Catholic churches have seen much decline across England, but this decline is not evenly spread. It is slightly less in the south east than elsewhere, and in each of the four Catholic Provinces there is at least one county where Mass attendance has bucked the overall trend. Mass attendance grew between 1998 and 2005 in four counties: Northumberland, Somerset and in West Sussex, all by 2% each, and in Hertfordshire by 1%, while it only reduced slightly in Kent (−1%) and Buckinghamshire (−9%)[8].

Anglican churches

The main part of the Anglican group, 99.6%, is of course the Church of England. Apart from the Free Church of England which is the largest and which began in 1863, most of the various other denominations are very small and were formed during the latter half of the 1990s in protest at the ordination of women. These have sometimes subsequently split further or re-grouped, and some of their priests have been re-admitted into the Church of England[9]. Table 2.7 on the next page gives the Usual Sunday Attendance which is measured by the different Censuses.

While the Anglican churches are in overall decline, that is not universal across the whole of England. Anglican attendance grew in two counties between 1998 and 2005 – in Herefordshire

Table 2.7: Anglican church attendance

	1979	*Change*	1989	*Change*	1998	*Change*	**2005**
Church of England	1,666,100	*−24%*	1,260,800	*−23%*	975,900	*−11%*	**867,400**
Other Anglicans	4,900	*+12%*	5,500	*−15%*	4,700	*−32%*	**3,200**
Total Anglican	**1,671,000**	*−24%*	**1,266,300**	*−23%*	**980,600**	*−11%*	**870,600**

by 4% and in Kent by 1%, and declined by less than 10% in 16 others (a third of the country)[10].

Between 1979 and 1989 Anglican numbers dropped at about 40,000 a year, and while this was a little less in the period 1989 to 1998 (30,000 a year), an age-adjusted "straight line" estimate of the future Anglican numbers from these years would suggest continued declines of about 40,000 a year. Actually between 1998 and 2005, and between 2005 and the estimated Anglican attendance in 2015 the decline is about 20,000 a year. This is illustrated in Figure 2.8.

Figure 2.8: Anglican attendance – expected and actual

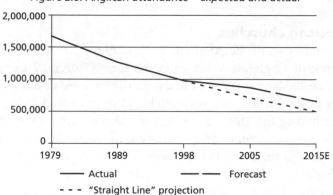

So the Church of England is not declining as rapidly as it has been. It is perhaps some 100,000 people stronger than might have been expected given the declines of the past, and this optimism is built into the 2015 forecast also, as part of the Anglican component given in Table 2.4. The Church of England is, however, still declining, even if the rate of attrition is not as great as it has been[11]. It is far too early to say whether this will eventually become a U-turn[12]. Large ships have to go a very long way before they can turn round.

The impact of this not-so-fast-as-expected decline is that in most counties the number of Anglican churchgoers is a higher proportion of all churchgoers in 2005 than in 1998. This may readily be seen in looking through *Religious Trends*, where the percentage strength of each denomination in each county is given[13].

United Reformed Church

The Presbyterians are one of the Institutional churches (as the Church of Scotland is the legally recognised church in Scotland), but are represented in England by the United Reformed Church (URC) whose origins in 1972 included the merging of the Presbyterian Church of England with others[14]. The URC figures include a small percentage (1.7%) of the attendance which comes from the few Church of Scotland, Free Church of Scotland or other Presbyterian churches in England. Although the URC has declined the most of all the Institutional churches, it has also seen growth in church attendance between 1998 and 2005 in Cleveland, Cornwall and Oxfordshire, albeit from small base numbers in each county[15].

Orthodox churches

The Orthodox figures include all 22 denominations, but five-sixths, 85%, are Greek Orthodox churches. These have spread further throughout England since 1998 when they had no presence at all in 17 counties, but in 2005 were only absent in three: Cleveland, Cumbria and Northumberland. This has been achieved by the ordination of many more clergy in this period, some 23 priests in the Greek Orthodox Church alone, as well as other priests coming as immigrants.

The policy has been deliberate – all Greek Orthodox priests are non-stipendiary (except 2 in their London Diocese) and part-time. Suitable people are ordained and start new churches in their home or locality. Other denominations would call this church planting or mission, but these words are not usually used in an Orthodox context[16]. The consequence is that Orthodox attendance has increased by over 10% in 8 counties, albeit often from a small base. They are the only Institutional church to have grown throughout the period 1979–2005, even though the most recent estimate is based on a very small response.

Non-institutional Free church attendance
Table 2.9 gives the basic total figures for each denominational group, and Figure 2.10 graphs these, again with a projection to 2015.

The Pentecostals are on the verge of replacing the Methodists as the third largest denomination in the country, although they are only a third of the size of either the Catholics or Anglicans. Figure 2.9 also suggests that they are the only group among these six which is likely to grow further in the next decade, something which is consistent with earlier forecasts.

Methodists
The Methodists are the third fastest declining denomination, behind the United Reformed Church and the Catholics. The Methodist Church of Great Britain (MCGB) accounts for 98% of the Methodists in England, the residual churches being largely the Independent Methodist Church and the Wesleyan Reform Union (which are both declining) and the Free Methodist Church (which is small but growing). In 2003 the MCGB entered into a Covenant with the Church of England, and more sharing of ministry is consequently taking place; a full merger may occur in the future.

Table 2.9: Free church attendance, 1979–2005

	1979	*Change*	1989	*Change*	1998
Methodists	621,000	*−18%*	512,300	*−26%*	379,700
Pentecostals	228,000	*+4%*	236,700	*−9%*	214,600
Baptists	290,000	*−7%*	270,900	*+2%*	277,600
Independent Churches	235,000	*−27%*	298,500	*−36%*	191,600[1]
New Churches	64,000	*+161%*	167,000	*+20%*	200,500[1]
Smaller denominations	141,000	*−19%*	113,600	*−18%*	93,100
Total	**1,579,000**	*+1%*	**1,599,000**	*−15%*	**1,357,100**

	1998	*Change*	**2005**	*Change*	2015E
Methodists	379,700	*−24%*	**289,400**	*−31%*	200,000
Pentecostals	214,600	*+34%*	**287,600**	*+3%*	298,000
Baptists	277,600	*−8%*	**254,800**	*−11%*	226,000
Independent Churches	191,600[1]	*−1%*	**190,500**	*−11%*	170,000
New Churches	200,500[1]	*−8%*	**183,600**	*−10%*	166,000
Smaller denominations	93,100	*+9%*	**101,100**	*−14%*	87,000
Total	**1,357,100**	*−4%*	**1,307,000**	*−12%*	**1,147,000**

[1] Revised figure E = Estimate

Figure 2.10: Free church attendance, 1979–2015

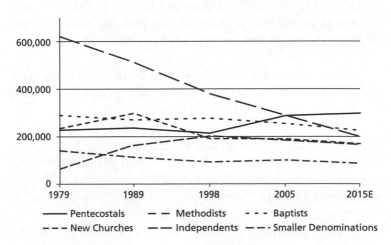

The Methodists closed 264 churches between 1998 and 2005, more than any other denomination (see Table 1.1). They also restructured their central organisation in the 1990s, but this has not reversed the decline. Their big problem, as with the URC, is the age of those who attend their churches – a large proportion are elderly, and hence may lack the energy necessary for rejuvenation. It is also off-putting for young newcomers.

The Methodists declined everywhere in England with only 2 counties declining by less than 10% of their 1998 attendance, Surrey (–8%) and Leicestershire (–9%)[17].

Pentecostal churches

The Pentecostal group contains a mixture of the mainly white denominations Elim, Assemblies of God and the Apostolic Church and the many Afro-Caribbean churches, which are largely black. These latter include the larger and longer established denominations like the New Testament Church of God and the Church of God of Prophecy.

The "white" group are 49% of the total (against 51% in 1998) and growing, except for the Apostolic Church, with the two largest having reversed declines in the 1990s. This is largely because they have both resumed church planting in earnest; each has started some 30 new congregations in the last 5 years.

The "black" group are 51% of the total Pentecostal attendance, five-sixths of which are the many newer groups which have begun mainly in the last 10 or 15 years.

The Pentecostal decline in attendance in the 1990s was probably due to the smaller number of church plants which they undertook in the latter half of the 1990s, something which has been reversed in the 21st century.

Their overall experience of growth between 1998 and 2005 has not

Table 2.11: Pentecostal church attendance, 1979–2005

	1979	Change	1989	Change	1998	Change	2005
Assemblies of God	86,500	−12%	75,700	−21%	59,900	+13%	67,600
Elim Pentecostal	44,500	+13%	59,000	−25%	44,300	+41%	62,500
New Testament Church of God	9,400[1]	+11%	10,400[1]	+41%	14,700	+37%	20,100
Church of God of Prophecy	9,100[1]	−13%	7,900[1]	−29%	5,600	+21%	6,800
The Apostolic Church	5,900	+25%	7,400	−18%	6,100	−8%	5,600
All other denominations	72,600	+5%	76,300	+10%	84,000	+49%	125,000
Total	**228,000**	**+4%**	**236,700**	**−9%**	**214,600**	**+34%**	**287,600**

[1] Estimated, based on membership

been uniform across the country: they have declined in the north west[18] and south west of London[19], but grown especially where the black population now live, in the urban and many suburban areas[20]. The Pentecostals have also grown throughout the rural areas of England, apart from a couple of rural counties[21].

Baptist churches

After holding their own for 20 years, the Baptist churches have declined since 1998, something the Research Department of the Baptist Union of Great Britain (BUGB) has reported[22]. The BUGB encompassed five-sixths, 83%, of all attendance in 2005, but while attendance has been decreasing, member-ship has increased[23]. Table 2.12 shows the main constituent denominations of the Baptist group, the 14 English churches of the Old Baptist Union now being absorbed into the main Baptist Union.

The Baptist decline has affected the Union most, but the Grace Baptists, strong in the south east of England, have seen a modest growth. The Independent Baptists have seen their previous growth

Table 2.12: Baptist church attendance, 1979–2005

	1979	Change	1989	Change	1998	Change	2005
Baptist Union of GB	249,400	–9%	226,700	+2%	232,200	–9%	212,200
Old Baptist Union	1,400	–21%	1,100	–18%	900		
Independent Baptists	13,400	+43%	19,200	+27%	24,400	–9%	22,100
Grace Baptist	17,200	–1%	17,100	–7%	15,900	+4%	16,600
Gospel Standard	8,600	–21%	6,800	–38%	4,200	–7%	3,900
Total	**290,000**	**–7%**	**270,900**	**+2%**	**277,600**	**–8%**	**254,800**

drop, despite more such churches being started or incorporating churches which have left the Baptist Union. The latter are easy to classify as "Baptist"; some of the other "Independent Baptists" are not so easily identified. It maybe that the decline here but reflects an incorrect designation of "independence" and thus some churches being consequently included within the "other churches" of the Independent group. Perhaps some of the growth seen there should be more properly allocated here.

The Baptist churches grew more than 10% in East and South Yorkshire, between 1% and 9% in six other counties[24], and remained fairly stable across the majority of the south of England and parts of the Midlands.

Independent churches

There are many different groups of independent churches. The Christian Brethren are the largest single group, followed by the Fellowship of Independent Evangelical Churches (FIEC), not to be confused with the much smaller Union of Evangelical Churches (UEC) which mostly operates in Essex and Suffolk.

Congregational churches have traditionally been independent, and after the formation of the United Reformed Church in 1972 (when the Congregational Union of England and Wales joined with the Presbyterian Church of England), the Congregational churches which continued formed the Congregational Federation and the Evangelical Fellowship of Congregational Churches (EFCC).

Boarding schools ("residential schools" in Table 2.13) appear to have fewer boarders partly due to the high cost of fees, or make church attendance optional rather than compulsory. There are still some, however, which have public services on a Sunday. Whether these are strictly "independent churches" is open to discussion, but they have been consistently classified to this group.

Table 2.13: Independent churches attendance, 1979–2005

	1979	Change	1989	Change	1998	Change	2005
Christian Brethren (Open)	64,000	+10%	70,500	−21%	49,900	−8%	46,000
FIEC	63,100	+63%	102,700	−57%	43,800	+4%	45,400
Residential Schools	47,000	+7%	50,200	−37%	31,600[1]	−43%	18,000
Christian Brethren (Closed)	10,200	+21%	12,300	+17%	14,400	−15%	12,300
Congregational Federation	12,700	+20%	15,200	−28%	11,000	−11%	9,800
EFCC	9,300	+18%	11,000	−33%	7,400	−7%	6,900
Churches of Christ	5,700	−7%	5,300	−43%	3,000	0	3,000
UEC	2,000	−20%	1,600	−37%	1,000	0	1,000
All others	21,000	+41%	29,700	−1%	29,500[1]	+2%	30,100
Emerging churches	~	n/a	~	n/a	~	n/a	17,600
Total	**235,000**	**−27%**	**298,500**	**−36%**	**191,600**	**−1%**	**190,500**

[1] Revised figure

Independent churches generally saw decline apart from a small increase in the FIEC, and an increase in the "others", which might otherwise be termed independent Independent churches. There are several thousand such churches[25], which are scattered across different denominational groupings. For convenience they are gathered together in Table 2.14.

Table 2.14: Totally independent church attendance, 1979–2005

	1979	Change	1989	Change	1998	Change	2005
Other Pentecostals	72,600	+5%	76,300	+10%	84,000	+49%	125,000
Independent New Churches	32,800[1]	+75%	57,400[1]	+25%	71,200	−14%	60,900
Independent Independent	21,000	+41%	29,700	−1%	29,500[1]	+2%	30,100
Independent Baptists	13,400	+43%	19,200	+27%	24,400	−9%	22,100
Overseas Nationals	3,100	+13%	3,500	+163%	9,200	+110%	19,300
Emerging churches	~	n/a	~	n/a	~	n/a	17,600
Total	142,900	+30%	186,100	+17%	218,300	+26%	275,000

[1] Estimated pro rata from 1989 and 2005 proportions

Collectively these churches have attracted an increasing number of people since 1979, and in 2005 were some 9% of total churchgoers. One of the features emerging from this Census therefore is this continuing *increase in independency* shown in Table 2.14. While this may be seen from the numbers attending independent churches, the same movement can be detected in the mainstream denominations where a number of churches act independently while remaining in their denomination.

Emerging churches

The same acting of independence while remaining within their mainstream denomination might also be said about the "emerging churches"[26], a group coded deliberately separately for this Census so that "Fresh Expression" and such like churches might be identified, although not a separate denominational group. "Fresh Expression" churches, at least as Anglicans and Methodists see them, have been defined as follows:

"A fresh expression is a form of church for our changing culture established primarily for the benefit of people who are not yet members of any church. It will come into being through principles of listening, service, incarnational mission and making disciples. It will have the potential to become a mature expression of church shaped by the gospel and the enduring marks of the church and for its cultural context."[27]

At the time of the Census, Fresh Expressions had some 200 such congregations listed on their website, and by various means we were able to track others. Altogether 40 such churches replied, with an average congregation of 59 people each. Assuming there might have been some 300 such congregations mid-2005, this gives the 17,600 attenders noted in Table 2.14, and thus have been included in the figures of independency. By March 2006, the number had grown to 420 congregations with 25,000 people, including 8,000 children.

Such a substantial number attending "Fresh Expression" churches is both important and encouraging. However, given that the English churches collectively lost 80,000 people per year between 1998 and 2005, it is going to need 1,400 such churches *started every year* just to stem the tide, assuming their size continues at nearly 60 people per congregation (which is high for most church plants). As only this number of congregations have been started in the *7 years* 1998 to 2005, this kind of momentum would appear very unlikely. This is not to negate the experimentation and risk-taking that Fresh Expressions engenders, but simply to indicate that such congregations, important though they are, are unlikely by themselves to be able to stem the tide of declining numbers. Other innovations, strategies and changes will be needed as well under the leading of the Holy Spirit. Perhaps that will bring Fresh Expressions "in every parish" as Steven Croft, Archbishops' Missioner and Team Leader of Fresh Expressions would wish[28].

Some of the Fresh Expression churches are part of an existing denomination, but have been separated so that this new movement can be looked at as an entity. Nor is it necessarily true that all Fresh Expression attenders are new people; it is most unlikely that they are. One survey in the 1990s, unfortunately not repeated since, found that about 70% of people joining the New Churches were transfers from other congregations, and perhaps the same kind of proportion is true of these Fresh Expression churches also. There will, however, probably be an increasing number of people *returning* to church, such as has been found in the *Back to Church* Sundays started in 2004 by the Diocese of Manchester[29]. The actual number of genuine converts may well be very small[30].

"Fresh Expressions" is one of the names commonly given to new types of churches. Such new forms of churches may be, for instance, café style services where people sit at a table with food and drink while participating in a service, or a service where dance takes a significant part of the proceedings, or new styles of music are explored, or where acting out of plays or playlets is key, or having the sermon in, say, four 5-minute slots, or other radical ways of worship[31]. They may just be a website[32]. These "churches" are called by different names, and include Mission-shaped Churches[33], Diaconal Church[34], Mixed-economy church[35], Emerging church, and so on. An introductory Reading Guide has been published[36]. In an article, the Bishop of London wrote "the truth is that the Church is being re-imagined and recalled to its primary task."[37]

Stuart Murray Williams has analysed the many new forms of church and classifies them into three broad groups: Mission-led, Community-led and Worship-led, which he describes as respectively refocusing, reconfiguring and re-imagining[38]. He would further sub-divide them as follows:

- Mission-led: (a) Restructuring churches for mission, (b) Importing church into new places, and (c) Incarnating church into different cultures.

- Community-led: (a) Churches shaped by community engagement, and (b) Churches shaped by community dynamics.

- Worship-led: (a) Alternative worship, (b) Culture-specific worship, (c) Customised worship, and (d) New monasticism.

George Barna, the American researcher, has found that "evangelical Christians are those most likely to get involved in an alternative form of the Christian church – and also the group most likely to participate in both a traditional church and alternative church form."[39] Could this be true in England?

New churches

The New Churches, or House Churches, began in the 1970s and rapidly expanded during the 1980s by planting many fresh congregations. They also formed various "streams" or mini-denominations. They continued to grow in the 1990s though at a smaller rate. They have declined between 1998 and 2005 partly because some streams have closed down (like Cornerstone) or because they have split into different groups (like Covenant and Ichthus) or found the transition to new senior leadership difficult.

In addition to those in known streams there are many other churches, often with names like the "Pentbury Community Church" signifying the locality in which it is situated, which broadly follow most but not all of the New Church theological and charismatic principles[40]. These are, nevertheless, quite independent of any stream, so estimating their number is difficult, and, again, it may be that some of these should have been classified as "other Independent" or vice versa. The overall number is quite large, amounting to about a third of all New Church churchgoers, as may be seen in Table 2.15.

Some of the groups existing in 2005 either did not exist in 1989 or were not constituted in the same way, so comparative figures for years prior to 1998 are not given. The major two New Church streams which have grown strongly since 1998 are Newfrontiers and Vineyard Churches, mostly because they continue to plant new churches. Newfrontiers do this very vigorously, starting 65 fresh fellowships between 2000 and 2003 for example[41].

Table 2.15: New Church stream attendance, 1998–2005

	1998	Change	2005
Newfrontiers	20,300	+70%	34,600
Association of Vineyard Churches	6,500	+78%	11,600
Salt and Light	9,600	+11%	10,700
Ground Level	6,700	+21%	8,100
Pioneer	9,200	−24%	7,000
Ichthus Christian Fellowship	27,300	−75%	6,800
Jesus Fellowship/ Multiply	3,300	+36%	4,500
Covenant/ Ministries without Borders[42]	17,000	−77%	3,900
Smaller New Church streams	29,400	+21%	35,500
Independent New Churches	71,200[1]	−14%	60,900
Total	**200,500**	**−8%**	**183,600**

[1] Revised figure

New Churches have seen overall attendance increases of at least 10% in 10 counties, urban and rural, and smaller increases in six others[43].

Smaller denominations

There remain a number of Smaller denominations, the largest of which are listed in Table 2.16.

The "all others" category includes the British Conference of Mennonites, the Countess of Huntingdon's Connexion churches (which collectively are growing slowly), the various Holiness churches (of which the Church of the Nazarene is the largest and whose Northern Province has experienced 12% growth between 1998 and 2005), the Worldwide Church of God and various small Liberal Catholic Churches.

The growth in these Smaller denominations comes primarily from the Overseas Nationals churches, already noted, and small growth among the Religious Society of Friends, or Quakers[44], and the Seventh-day Adventists. The last of these has both white and black congregations; the black Adventist congregations in the main are growing and the white ones tend to be declining.

Table 2.16: Smaller denomination church attendance, 1979–2005

	1979	Change	1989	Change	1998	Change	2005
Salvation Army	107,500	−27%	78,400	−35%	51,100	−7%	47,600
Overseas Nationals	3,100[1]	+13%	3,500[1]	+163%	9,200	+110%	19,300
Seventh-day Adventists	14,100	+19%	16,800	−10%	15,100	+11%	16,800
Religious Society of Friends	3,300	+9%	4,100	+110%	8,600	+2%	8,800
Lutheran Churches	8,300	−23%	6,400	−39%	4,400	−5%	4,200
Moravian Church	2,900	−14%	2,500	−36%	1,600	−25%	1,200
All others	1,800	+6%	1,900	+63%	3,100	+3%	3,200
Total	141,000	−19%	113,600	−18%	93,100	+9%	101,100

[1] Estimate

The three largest Overseas Nationals churches are all Asian: the many Chinese Churches, the Asian Christian Fellowship Churches and the Korean Churches, all of which are growing. The next largest groups are the Tamil Churches and Portuguese Churches (also both growing), showing growth is not confined to people from any one continent. There are, however, many smaller churches for groups who have come from a particular country, such as the Dutch, French, Greek, Hungarian, Iranian, Italian, Japanese, Spanish, Swahili, Swiss or Turkish churches.

While the Smaller denominations are growing in most parts of England, decline of at least 10% from the 1998 attendance was seen in several rural counties[45] and two urban ones (Cleveland and Merseyside).

A couple working in Stepney sometimes use the chapel of Queen Mary University as a venue for a prayer meeting. One day when they were using it in 2005, Jason, a student from China, wandered in, "intrigued by what he might find there. He was not planning to go to church that day but he tells us he just felt a desire to go in that day. We invited him to join us for church the following week at our house. . . . A few months after we first met him he asked if he could become a Christian. Sitting in our lounge drinking mugs of tea . . . we prayed for him before he made his own prayer in Mandarin."[46]

LEPs

Local Ecumenical Partnerships (LEPs) involve two or more denominations (sometimes up to six!) working together in the context usually of a single church building and/or single congregation. There are various types of LEPs – a united congregation, a shared building, a shared ministry, a shared congregation, a local covenant, a sponsored body, or a mixed group in some other way[47].

In 1989 there were 1,138 LEPs in England, 738 of which were united congregations. Although some new LEPs are still being formed, the number had decreased to 910 in 2005. About 600, or two-thirds, of these involve the Anglican church[48] as one partner, a reduction from the 729 in 1989.

In 2005 the average LEP congregation was 69 people, making the total LEP attendance 62,800, or 2.0% of the total. They were not measured separately in 1998 but in 1989 their congregations totalled 101,100 people, 2.1% of all churchgoers. They thus declined 38% in these 16 years, a little faster than the 32% for church attendance generally between 1989 and 2005.

The average age of LEPs churchgoers is 40, younger than the overall average of 45, because they tend to have a smaller proportion of older people.

Size of churches

With a known attendance of a particular denominational group and the number of churches in that group, a simple division gives the average size of a church. These numbers are given in Table 2.17.

The average congregation in 2005 was 84 people including the many relatively large Catholic congregations; if these are excluded the average Protestant congregation was 67 people, a decline of a third, 32%, since 1979. How these sizes are distributed is considered in a later chapter. Four denominations had an average below the overall Protestant number – the Anglicans, the Smaller denominations, the United Reformed Church and the Methodists.

Table 2.17: Average attendance by denomination, 1979–2005

	1979	1989	1998	2005
Catholic	505	449	326	244
New Churches	153	163	180	140
Pentecostals	129	121	102	129
Baptist Churches	131	116	123	107
Independent Churches	91	108	85	84
Orthodox	91	108	113	81
Smaller denominations	84	63	52	63
Anglican	99	77	60	54
United Reformed	107	89	78	48
Methodists	81	76	61	48
Overall average	**139**	**123**	**98**	**84**
Average excluding Catholics	98	87	73	**67**

Geographical variations

Across the English counties the numbers attending church have mostly declined. The average decline between 1998 and 2005 is 15%, but this varies:

- It is –25% or more in 5 counties: the Isle of Wight (–31%), Merseyside (–30%), Cornwall (–26%), Wiltshire and Lancashire (both –25%).

- It is between –10% and –24% in the 35 counties not specified above or below.

- The decline is in single digits in 5 counties: Somerset (–9%), Buckinghamshire, Northamptonshire and Gloucestershire (all –8%) and Kent (–6%).

- Numbers attending have grown in just 2 counties: Greater London and Herefordshire (both +1%).

The growth in Herefordshire is from 9,700 people in 1998 to 9,900 in 2005, well within the margin of error for estimating the figures. In Greater London, however, the increase is from 618,000 in 1998 to 623,000 in 2005, which is statistically significant.

Greater London

Greater London emerges as the one county with both the largest attendance (representing a fifth, 20%, of all English church-goers), and where the trends have been reversed, and church attendance has *increased*. The number of churches has also increased in Greater London: from 3,827 in 1998 to 4,059 in 2005. While 8 other counties[49] have also seen the number of their churches increase, none have done so in substantial quantities, except the West Midlands (up from 1,231 to 1,281) and for the same reason as in Greater London: a large increase in the number of Pentecostal churches. In London's case these churches went from 875 in 1998 to 1,005 in 2005, and virtually all the new churches were black churches, Caribbean or African.

Greater London's Pentecostal attendance increased by +68% in the seven years to 2005, up from 94,000 to 153,000, with a consequential average increase in congregation from 107 to 152. This 153,000 people represents 53% of all Pentecostal attenders, that is, over half the country's Pentecostals are in London!

However, such figures do not tell the whole story. One of the key reasons for the increase has been the continued growth of the Kingsway International Christian Centre, a Nigerian congregation based in Hackney under the leadership of Pastor Matthew Ashimolowo, which in 2005 had an estimated regular Sunday congregation of over 10,000 people. Kensington Temple, a much longer established main line Elim Pentecostal congregation but with large numbers of ethnic minority participants[50], also has significant numbers, well into five figures, although spread over a number of associated congregations.

The other very large London church, included with the Independent group, is Hillsong, originally from Sydney, Australia, which used to meet in the Mermaid Theatre near Blackfriars, but had to move to the Dominion, one of the West End's biggest theatres, because of capacity crowds. It attracts upwards of 5,000 young people in their twenties across 7 Sunday and one Saturday night services[51], and saw some 1,500 come to faith through its work in 2004 alone[52]. (It should be noted in passing that this is not the only thriving Australian-initiated church in England: the Hope City Church in Sheffield attracts 1,000 people, and its founder, Dave Gilpin, has seen it spread to Leeds, Liverpool and Manchester[53]).

Greater London also has an above average number of people attending church in their 20s compared with other parts of the country. Many are students, but others are beginning their professional careers often in the City. Many of these attend Anglican churches like All Souls, Langham Place or Holy Trinity, Brompton with regular Sunday congregations in excess of 2,000 people. Such "mega-churches" are very rare elsewhere in England (excluding Catholic churches). Other Anglican churches, like St Helen's, Bishopsgate have regular congregations in four figures.

However, it should be noted that all of the above comments on Greater London churches actually refer to churches in *Inner*

London, and it is the Inner London church attendance which has increased, not that of Outer London. Inner London attendance increased by 11%, while that of Outer London fell by 6%. This is discussed further in Chapter 5 on ethnic attendance.

London therefore is different in its church attendance. However, in the years 1998 to 2005, the Baptists, Independents, New Churches, Orthodox and Pentecostals all grew (as did the Anglicans in the north of London, location of the Diocese of London), whereas in the nine years 1989 to 1998, the Anglicans as a whole, as well as the United Reformed and the Smaller Denominations all saw growth.

Summary of main findings

This chapter, focussing on denominational attendance, has shown:

- There are three growing denominational groups: The Pentecostals (+34%), the Smaller Denominations (+9%), and the Orthodox churches (+2%). Of these, only the Orthodox also grew between 1989 and 1998.

- All the various independent churches taken together as a separate group also grew.

- The main reason for this growth is the large number of new ethnic diversity churches being started, partly as a result of the influx of new people into England. This includes many black people whose charismatic/Pentecostal churches are particularly based in Greater London, but also in other urban areas. Those from Indian or other Asian countries which in the main are not charismatic are included among the "Smaller Denominations".

- Institutional church attendance has continued to decline at a far greater pace than non-institutional, but the pace of decline of Anglican churches has slowed markedly, and has not been as fast as had been expected.

- Greater London is the only county where church attendance has increased by several thousand people in the first few years of the 21st century. It is untypical, however, because of the proliferation of black churches and relatively large numbers of churched young people in their 20s. Inner London's church attendance grew, but Outer London's declined.

- The average size of a Protestant congregation in 2005 was 67 people, a quarter of the average Catholic Mass attendance.

Looking beyond the detail

Four elements stand out from this analysis of denominational church attendance which are important for church leaders:

A) The fact that the Church of England has not decreased as much as might have been expected (which is explored further in later chapters);

B) The increasing amount of independency (and the implications of what this might mean for the major denominations);

C) The importance of the many burgeoning ethnic diversity churches, the reasons for that growth and spontaneity, and whether other churches could follow their example; and

D) The uniqueness of church life in the capital – growing overall, with several mega-churches (of different denominations), and with much youthful attendance and exuberance (which is also explored later in more detail).

3 Halfway up the candle
[Churchmanship analysis]

The Census questions are divided into groups, and the title of each of these is printed vertically alongside the question to save taking up precious horizontal room on the form where space is scarce. One subject had only one question, and its title "churchmanship" was too long when turned sideways for the actual question, so the word "ethos" was substituted. This meant that in the "other" box, provided for those who did not fit into one of the categories of churchmanship on the form, there were many interesting descriptions of churchmanship. One was "halfway up the candle", used as the heading for this chapter with permission of the vicar of that particular Anglican church[1]. It seems to summarise where many people found themselves!

The options given in the question have been extensively pilot tested, and were the same as used in the 1989 and 1998 studies, thus allowing continuity. Each minister is asked to tick up to three of the nine options listed to express the churchmanship of his/her *congregation*, that is, not his/her own churchmanship which may be different. For purposes of analysis all the members of his/her congregation are assumed to have that particular churchmanship, and while in practice this will rarely be the case, studies of individual congregations[2] have shown that usually about two-thirds of a congregation would agree with its minister's description.

The combination of ticks given on the form is then translated into one of seven churchmanships, one of which, "evangelical", is further broken down into three components. Full details of this process are given in *Religious Trends*[3] which also lists all the various combinations used both in this Census and that of 1989. Just under half, 44%, ticked one box only, a third, 34%, ticked two, and most of the rest ticked three, although inevitably a few ticked four or more! A brief summary of this process for ease of reference is given in the box.

Churchmanship allocations

The **Catholic** category was nearly all those who ticked "Catholic", independent of how many other boxes were ticked, unless they also ticked "Anglo-Catholic".

Anglo-Catholics were those who ticked "Anglo-Catholic" together with any other boxes or none.

Liberals were all those who ticked "Liberal".

Low Church were those who ticked "Low Church" unless they also said that they were "Broad" or "Charismatic".

Broad were those who ticked "Broad" unless it was in combination with "Evangelical" or "Liberal".

Broad Evangelical were those who ticked "Broad" and "Evangelical" unless they also said they were "Charismatic".

Charismatic Evangelical were those who ticked "Charismatic" on its own or with any other combination. The great majority of these also ticked "Evangelical" although a few also ticked "Catholic".

Nearly all of the **Mainstream Evangelical** category were those who just ticked "Evangelical". It also includes any evangelicals who did not tick "Broad or "Charismatic".

The few minor variations to these allocations are listed in *Religious Trends.*

The terms used were not defined on the form – no space – so inevitably the answers will reflect slightly different theological understandings. Some definitions have been published, however[4].

One form in every 22 had something written in the "other" box, and the full list of these, apart from when the church's denomination was confused with its churchmanship, is given in *Religious Trends*[5]. The most popular word, used across several denominations but not on the Census form, was "Traditional", which a number further defined on individual forms by their ticks as Broad or Low Church (the most popular two) followed by Liberal, Orthodox or Evangelical – or perhaps, had they thought of it, "halfway up the candle"?

Churchmanship of churchgoers

The purpose of looking at the answers to this question is to ascertain the churchmanship of those attending church in May 2005. Two-fifths, 40%, were Evangelical, followed by a quarter, 27%, who were Catholic. This latter term is not to be confused with "Roman Catholic", a denominational label, although a very large proportion of Roman Catholics, 87%, would define themselves as of "Catholic" churchmanship. The description "Catholic" is also used by 72,000 Anglicans[6], 3,000 Methodists and 1,000 Independent churchgoers.

"Evangelical" is further broken down into three sub-categories – Broad, Mainstream and Charismatic. These were defined as indicated in the box on the previous page[7].

Table 3.1 shows the proportions of each churchmanship in 2005, and compares these with the previous studies[8]:

Table 3.1: Churchmanship of churchgoers, 1989–2005

Churchmanship	1989 %	1998 %	2005 %
Anglo-Catholic	4	5	5
Broad	9	9	9
Catholic	39	27	27
Evangelical	30	37	40
Liberal	10	11	9
Low Church	6	8	7
Others	2	3	3
Base (=100%)	4.7mn	3.7mn	3.2mn

There have been two main changes since 1989 – a decrease in the number who are Catholic (which took place mostly during the 1990s), and an increase in the proportion who are Evangelical. The percentage of Liberals has declined slightly since 1998, but otherwise the proportions have changed little since 1989.

The 2005 percentages mean that each week 2.5% of the English population are Evangelical churchgoers, 1.7% Catholic, and 2.1% all the other categories combined.

All groups have declined

Unlike the 1990s when two churchmanship groups grew in absolute numbers (the Mainstream Evangelicals and the Others), between 1998 and 2005 every group declined, although some much more than others, as Figure 3.2 on the next page indicates[9].

It can be seen from Figure 3.2 that it is the Liberals and those who are Low Church who have seen the greatest decline and the Mainstream and Charismatic Evangelicals who have seen the least.

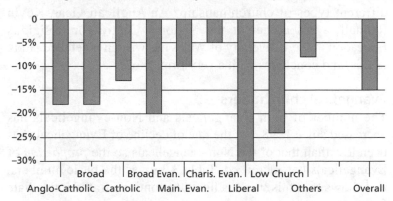

Figure 3.2: Rate of decline by churchmanship, 1998–2005

These results match the findings of Professor Paul Heelas in his book *The Spiritual Revolution* in which he researches some of the reasons why, according to the sub-title, "religion is giving way to spirituality"[10]. While he charts the decline of the "congregational domain", he reports a research project based in Kendal where he looked for specific evidence for alternative spiritualities in what he calls the "holistic milieu". He found the latter are growing, and concludes that of the four different spiritualities in Britain today:

- Holistic milieu, subject-life spirituality, is faring best;

- Religions of experiential humanity and experiential difference (which we would call mainstream and charismatic evangelicalism respectively), placing spirituality within a life-as frame of reference, tend to be faring relatively well;

- Religions of difference (broadly equivalent to Catholicity), which emphasise life-as "oughts", tend to be faring relative badly; and

- Religions of humanity (which we would call Broad and Liberal), paying least attention to unique subjectivities, tend to be faring worst[11].

Could this suggest that different types of people are drawn to different types of churchmanship? An Anglican vicar, Kevin Randall, a researcher at the National Centre for Religious Education at the University of Wales has written a detailed study of this, and concludes with a very firm "No"[12].

Evangelical churchgoers

The number of both Evangelicals and Non-evangelicals has decreased since 1998, but the rate of decline of Evangelicals has been less than that of the Non-evangelicals so the *proportion* of Evangelicals has increased. Table 3.3 gives the basic numbers, and shows that this trend is likely to continue in the immediate future.

Table 3.3: Attendance in Evangelical and Non-evangelical churches, 1989–2015

	1989	Change	1998	Change	**2005**	Change	2015E
Evangelical	1,430,400	−3%	1,391,300	−9%	**1,264,800**	−12%	1,111,900
Non-evangelical	3,312,400	−30%	2,323,400	−18%	**1,901,400**	−23%	1,462,300
Total	**4,742,800**	**−22%**	**3,714,700**	**−15%**	**3,166,200**	**−19%**	**2,574,200**
Evangelical %	*30%*		*37%*		***40%***		*43%*

E = Estimate

However in this Evangelical trend, it is important to note the dominant role of Evangelicals in Greater London. Table 3.4 breaks down the Evangelical attendance between those going to church in Greater London and those going elsewhere.

Evangelicals are consistently growing in Greater London because of their black component, while Evangelicals in the rest of England are declining, although Evangelicals outside London have not declined quite as fast as Non-evangelicals.

Table 3.4: Evangelical attendance in Greater London and
elsewhere, 1989–2015

	1989	Change	1998	Change	**2005**	Change	2015E
Greater London	216,800	+23%	265,800	+9%	**289,300**	+10%	317,400
Rest of England	1,213,600	−7%	1,125,500	−13%	**975,500**	−19%	794,500
Total Evangelicals	**1,430,400**	**−3%**	**1,391,300**	**−9%**	**1,264,800**	**−12%**	**1,111,900**
Greater London %	15%		19%		23%		29%

E = Estimate

Evangelicals only grew between 1998 and 2005 in the counties of
Buckinghamshire, East Yorkshire, Gloucestershire, Herefordshire
and the Channel Islands. The combined growth of these 5 areas
was from 48,800 to 52,200, just 3,400 people or +7%, whereas the
Greater London growth was from 265,800 to 289,300, 23,500
people or +9%. The main engine of Evangelical growth is the
change taking place in Greater London, not outside it.

What is happening in Greater London is therefore particularly
important for the growing influence of Evangelicals generally.
The proportion of all English Evangelicals located in Greater
London is rapidly growing, likely to increase from 15% of
the total in 1989 to double that (29%) by 2015 if present trends
continue[13]. In order to understand why, we need to break down
the Evangelical total into its constituent parts.

Types of evangelicals
Table 3.5 on the next page breaks down the Evangelical total
into the three groups which form the total.

The proportion of Broad Evangelicals has decreased since 1989,
mostly during the 1990s, but the proportions of both Mainstream
and Charismatic Evangelicals have increased. The term

Table 3.5: Churchmanship of Evangelical churchgoers, 1989–2005

Evangelical churchmanship	1989 %	1998 %	2005 %
Broad Evangelical	9	6	6
Mainstream Evangelical	8	17	18
Charismatic Evangelical	13	14	16
TOTAL Evangelical	30	37	40

"Mainstream" was not used on the Census form[14] and has simply been used to distinguish this group from Broad and Charismatic. The major increase in the proportions of Mainstream Evangelicals also occurred in the 1990s, but the increase in the Charismatic Evangelical percentage has occurred both in the 1990s and since.

Table 3.6 gives the actual numbers behind these proportions and shows how they have changed over the years 1989 to 2005 and might change if projected to 2015.

Table 3.6: Type of Evangelical churchmanship, 1989–2015

	1989	Change	1998	Change	**2005**	Change	2015E
Broad	414,600	–47%	217,900	–20%	**175,500**	–38%	109,000
Mainstream	384,600	+68%	645,500	–10%	**584,700**	–11%	519,200
Charismatic	631,200	–16%	527,900	–5%	**504,600**	–4%	483,700
Total Evangelicals	**1,430,400**	**–3%**	**1,391,300**	**–9%**	**1,264,800**	**–12%**	**1,111,900**
Broad %	29%		16%		**14%**		10%
Mainstream %	27%		46%		**46%**		47%
Charismatic %	44%		38%		**40%**		43%

E = Estimate

The story in Table 3.6, which is illustrated in Figure 3.7, is that the proportion of Broad Evangelicals will continue to decline both in numerical terms and as a proportion of the whole, for reasons which we will look at shortly. There is however a slowly changing balance between the Mainstream Evangelicals, which became the majority in the 1990s, growing at the expense of the Broad Evangelicals, and the Charismatic Evangelicals which are a substantial and growing minority, reflecting the growth of the many Black churches nearly all of whom are Charismatic Evangelical.

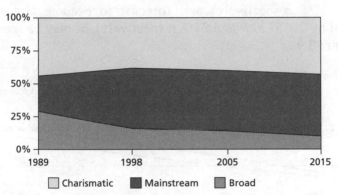

Figure 3.7: Proportions of Evangelicals, 1989–2015

Table 3.8 repeats Table 3.6 but gives the figures only for Greater London, with the first percentage underneath the total line the same as in Table 3.6, that is, the proportion that each group is of the whole, but the second percentage is the proportion of Greater London evangelicals of all evangelicals in England.

Table 3.8: Type of Evangelical churchmanship in Greater London, 1989–2015

	1989	Change	1998	Change	2005	Change	2015E
Broad	37,100	−52%	17,900	−9%	16,300	−15%	13,900
Mainstream	67,300	+88%	126,700	+9%	137,700	+10%	151,300
Charismatic	112,400	+8%	121,200	+12%	135,300	+12%	152,200
Total Evangelicals	**216,800**	**+23%**	**265,800**	**+ 9%**	**289,300**	**+10%**	**317,400**
Broad %	17% / 9%		7% / 8%		6% / 9%		4% / 13%
Mainstream %	31% / 17%		48% / 20%		47% / 24%		48% / 29%
Charismatic %	52% / 18%		45% / 23%		47% / 27%		48% / 31%

E = Estimate

Evangelical growth in Greater London is among both the
Mainstream and Charismatic Evangelicals, with the latter marginally outstripping the former by 2015. Both groups are
growing strongly, however, and are equally important. They
are also both becoming an increasingly large proportion of
Mainstream and Charismatic Evangelicals in the whole of
England, being about a quarter of the total in 2005 (24%
and 27% respectively) and forecast to become almost a
third by 2015 (29% and 31% respectively), as may be seen in
Figure 3.9.

Figure 3.9: The growing influence of Evangelicals in Greater London as a

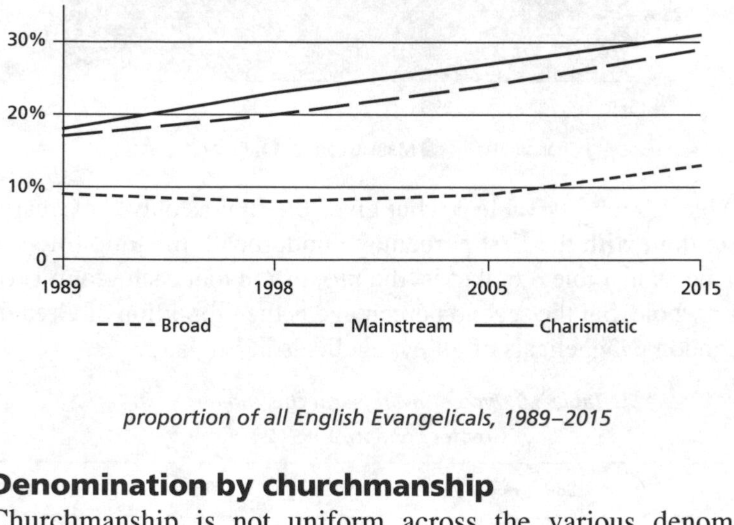

proportion of all English Evangelicals, 1989–2015

Denomination by churchmanship
Churchmanship is not uniform across the various denominational groupings. Some churchmanships are very much
associated with particular denominations, as Figure 3.10
indicates, the basic underlying figures being given in *Religious
Trends*[15].

The main allegiances are:

• Evangelicals are the substantial majority of churchgoing

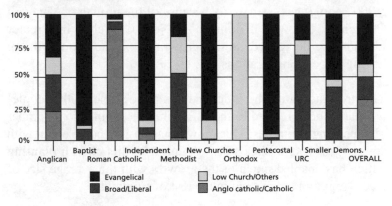

Figure 3.10: Churchmanship of churchgoers by denomination, 2005

Baptists, Independents, New Churches and Pentecostals, and just a majority among the Smaller denominations.

- The Orthodox and Roman Catholics essentially have their own, almost unique, brand of churchmanship, the Anglicans being the only other group to have a noticeable Catholic element.

- The Methodists and United Reformed Church are strongly Broad or Liberal, with a significant proportion in the Smaller denominations also in those churchmanships. The Methodists have a substantial proportion who are Low Church.

- The Anglicans are the only denomination where all four types illustrated in Figure 3.9 are reasonably strongly represented.

These become important when the denominational growth in Greater London is ascertained. The only groups showing growth between 1998 and 2005 were the Baptists (+1%), New Churches (+15%), Independents (+21%) and Pentecostals (+63%), all essentially Evangelical denominations. The Smaller denominations declined (–7%) between 1998 and 2005.

The growth in the New Churches in Greater London (some 5,000 people) has been partly because of the growth of Vineyard Churches. The actual number of New Churches in Greater London has decreased, so this growth has come about through having larger congregations.

The growth among the Independents (also some 5,000 people) has partly been related to the FIEC churches, but also a number of Emerging Churches. This growth has largely come about with some 43 new churches starting, and it is this church planting which has enabled much of the growth, with the average size of a congregation larger than in the rest of England[16].

The growth among the Pentecostals (some 59,000 people) is the huge growth of the Afro-Caribbean churches, with some 130 new Pentecostal congregations, offsetting closures in other parts of the country. The growth in Greater London represents four-fifths, 81%, of the entire Pentecostal growth in England between 1998 and 2005.

Thus the Evangelical growth seen in Greater London is largely due to the enthusiasm of the black diversity churches in both church planting and seeing individual congregations increase in size. Non-black Evangelicals play a part but they are, at best, but a seventh of the growth that is taking place.

It would seem vital that this phenomenon be recognised by the senior church leadership in Greater London – whatever their denomination. This emphasis on London being different is help-fully explored in an Anglican context by Bob Jackson in his book *The Road to Growth*[17]. He explains that when David Hope was Bishop of London (broadly the Boroughs in the north and north-west of the capital) in 1993 he introduced Mission Action Plans (MAPs) for every parish, something which his successor, Richard Chartres, has continued. "Every church was asked to look at its parish in a mission-oriented way under three headings: recruiting new believers; renewing the household of faith; and rebuilding a broken world." The consequence of this Diocesan activity was overall growth in his Diocese in church attendance in the 1990s which has continued since.

Figure 3.10 is also useful in suggesting why the Broad Evangelicals have declined faster than other types of Evangelical. The Methodists as a denomination have declined sharply since 1998, itself a considerable decline from 1989. Some Methodists describe themselves as "Broad Evangelicals" so that the decline in the latter is partly because of the decline in the denomination.

Churchmanship by denomination

The other way of looking at churchmanships and denominations is to ascertain what proportion of a particular churchmanship is in a particular denomination. Table 3.11 gives this for 2005 (where "0" means under 0.5% and "~" means none at all); figures for 1989 and 1998 may be worked out from *Religious Trends*[18]. The percentages add to 100% at the foot of each column.

The Table shows that:

• Anglo-Catholics are most likely to be Anglican, and Catholics most likely to be Roman Catholic.

• Broad churchgoers if not Anglican are likely to be Methodist or Roman Catholic.

• There are some Evangelicals in every denomination except the Orthodox, and 3% of the total are Roman Catholic. A quarter of Evangelicals are Anglican and another quarter Pentecostal.

• Two-fifths of Liberals are Anglican and a quarter are Methodist.

• Half of those who are Low Church are Anglican and a third are Methodist.

Table 3.11: Denomination of churchgoers by Churchmanship, 2005

Denomination	Anglo-Catholic %	Broad %	Catholic %	Evangelical %	Liberal %
Anglican	90	46	9	23	40
Baptist	~	2	~	18	6
R Catholic	4	16	91	3	4
Independent	5	2	0	13	1
Methodist	1	26	0	4	24
New Churches	~	0	~	12	1
Orthodox	0	0	0	~	~
Pentecostal	~	1	~	22	1
URC	~	4	0	1	12
Smaller Dens.	~	3	~	4	11
BASE (=100%)	146,500	288,600	854,500	1,264,800	298,100

Denomination	Low Church %	Others %	Evan: Broad %	Evan: Main. %	Evan: Charis %	**Overall %**
Anglican	52	8	60	13	23	**28**
Baptist	3		7	25	13	**8**
R Catholic	1	14	~	5	2	**28**
Independent	4	4	5	23	4	**6**
Methodist	33	3	12	3	3	**9**
New Churches	0	26	0	8	21	**6**
Orthodox	~	25	~	~	~	**1**
Pentecostal	0	9	13	14	33	**9**
URC	4	0	2	1	1	**2**
Smaller Dens.	3	0	1	8	0	**3**
BASE (=100%)	210,100	103,600	175,500	584,700	504,600	**3,166,200**

- Those of other churchmanships are spread across virtually every denomination, and are growing in many counties outside Greater London.

- Three-fifths of Broad Evangelicals are Anglican.

- A quarter of Mainstream Evangelicals are Baptist and another quarter are in the Independent group.

- A third of Charismatic Evangelicals are Pentecostal, a quarter Anglican and a fifth New Churches, but there are a few in every denomination except the Orthodox, and 2% are Roman Catholic.

Size of churches by churchmanship

The churchmanship of congregations is not necessarily in the same proportion as church attendance. The actual numbers for churches are in *Religious Trends*[19], but given the number of churches and the number of churchgoers, the average attendance may be worked out. It is important to see both how this varies over time and how it compares with other denominational groups. Table 3.12 is a complicated looking Table but shows the average congregation for three different groups of churchmanship in Anglican and other denominations in which they are strong, as well as the overall total, since 1989[20]. The two churchmanships not given in this Table, Low Church and Other, account for 15% of churches in each year, and about 10% of churchgoers.

Table 3.12 shows two things: the average attendance has decreased whatever the churchmanship or denomination, and the Anglo-Catholics/Catholics have the largest average congregations, followed by the Evangelicals and then the Broad/Liberals. In general terms congregations are getting smaller whatever their background or affiliation.

Change of churchmanship

Has churchmanship changed since 1998? In two-thirds, 67%, of churches it has remained the same. Of the remaining 33%, 7% are between different types of Evangelicals, 4% by Anglo-Catholics or Catholics changing, and the majority of the rest being change by those who are Broad or Liberal. 5% of those now Broad were previously something else, as opposed to 6% of those formerly Broad now being different, and 7% of those who were Liberal now being something else. Details are in *Religious Trends*[21].

Table 3.12: Proportions of Churches and Churchgoers by selected church-manships and denominations, with average congregational size, 1989–2005

Anglo-Catholic/ Catholic	Anglicans			Roman Catholic		
	1989	1998	2005	1989	1998	2005
Churches	52%	55%	56%	45%	43%	43%
Churchgoers	15%	17%	20%	82%	81%	78%
Average congregation	73	45	48	454	277	238

Broad/Liberal	Anglicans			Methodists		
	1989	1998	2005	1989	1998	2005
Churches	25%	22%	22%	23%	22%	24%
Churchgoers	25%	19%	20%	25%	19%	25%
Average congregation	95	77	71	86	67	65

Evangelicals	Anglicans			New Churches		
	1989	1998	2005	1989	1998	2005
Churches	41%	35%	33%	7%	9%	8%
Churchgoers	38%	35%	29%	12%	13%	12%
Average congregation	71	60	48	164	137	126

Anglo-Catholic/ Catholic	Methodists			**All Denominations**		
	1989	1998	2005	**1989**	**1998**	**2005**
Churches	1%	1%	1%	*21%*	*21%*	*20%*
Churchgoers	0%	0%	0%	*43%*	*31%*	*32%*
Average congregation	97	56	90	*248*	*147*	*131*

Broad/Liberal	United Reformed			**All Denominations**		
	1989	1998	2005	**1989**	**1998**	**2005**
Churches	8%	9%	8%	*29%*	*26%*	*25%*
Churchgoers	11%	10%	8%	*19%*	*20%*	*18%*
Average congregation	106	92	60	*81*	*78*	*63*

Evangelicals	Pentecostals			**All Denominations**		
	1989	1998	2005	**1989**	**1998**	**2005**
Churches	14%	13%	14%	*35%*	*38%*	*40%*
Churchgoers	15%	15%	22%	*30%*	*37%*	*40%*
Average congregation	122	105	132	*105*	*96*	*85*

Summary of main findings

So what has this Chapter shown? We have found:

- While the terminology of "churchmanship" may be confusing for some, requiring extra explanation, the most popular designation, Evangelical, was used by two-fifths, 40%, of all English congregations, a slight increase on the 37% in 1998.

- This was followed by a quarter, 27%, who were Catholic, the same percentage as in 1998. Those who were Broad/Liberal were next, with 18%, down from 20% in 1998.

- Evangelicals are declining less quickly than non-Evangelicals, so the proportion of Evangelicals among all churchgoers is increasing, and is likely to continue to do so for the immediate decade ahead.

- However, much of this Evangelical growth is because of the rapid increase in the number of Pentecostals especially in Greater London. This is driven in turn by the growth of the Afro-Caribbean churches in the capital.

- About a quarter, 23%, of all Evangelicals in England are to be found in Greater London, up from 19% in 1998, and which could become 29% by 2015.

- While all types of Evangelicalism are declining, Charismatic Evangelicals are declining less rapidly than Mainstream, and both much less rapidly than Broad Evangelicals. Consequently the proportion of Charismatics among Evangelicals is increasing.

- The Charismatic Evangelicals in Greater London are already more than a quarter, 27%, of those in the whole of England, a percentage which is also set to increase.

- Churchmanship is largely predicated by one's denomination, with the Anglicans the only denominational group with a significant spread across all churchmanships.

- The average size of a congregation has been decreasing, from 248 in 1989 for Anglo-Catholic/Catholics to 131 in 2005; from 81 to 63 for Broad/Liberals, and from 105 to 85 for Evangelicals.

Looking beyond the detail

Elements which stand out from this analysis which are important for church leaders include:

A) The growth being seen in London is not being replicated elsewhere. Two factors are highlighted here – the explosion of black Afro-Caribbean church growth largely through planting new congregations, and, at least among the Anglicans in London north of the Thames, a concentration on specific mission activity. Both of these actions could be copied by other churches in other areas.

B) This begs another interesting question for broader application: is the growth seen in London primarily because churches are *black* or because they are eminently involved in *church planting* or because that combination is especially important in *London*?

C) The average size of congregations is decreasing whatever their churchmanship. Bob Jackson highlights the importance of size – smaller churches and larger churches often grow more than middle-sized churches[22]. While other factors are also important, different sizes of congregations require varying leadership gifts. It is important to match leadership gifting with size of congregation.

D) Evangelicals are not declining as fast as other churchmanships. What are the components of evangelical theology or practice which contribute to their relative success, and could others from different backgrounds so identify with these that their experience matches that of the Evangelicals?

E) One key component of evangelicalism is the Charismatic Evangelicals who are declining slightly less quickly than the Mainstream. Is this due solely to their emphasis on the Holy Spirit or could there be other factors? For example, many charismatic churches have joined the New Wine network. Could their fellowship together be a mechanism for encouraging mission and growth?

F) If an increasing proportion of Evangelicals are located in Greater London, then obviously a smaller proportion are located outside London. How can London church leaders best help those in other parts of England?

4 Oh, to be in England!
[Environmental analysis]

There is something especially appealing about the English countryside, and Browning's poem is but one of many extolling its wonders:

Oh, to be in England
    Now that April's here,
And whoever wakes in England
    Sees, some morning, unaware,
That the lowest boughs and the brushwood sheaf
    Round the elm-tree bole are in tiny leaf,
While the chaffinch sings on the orchard bough
    In England – now![1]

Part of that idyll in many cases is a delightful village church nestling among the trees with its over-arching sense of being untouched by time. There are many such English churches – over 15,000 in a rural setting in 2005, two-fifths, 41%, of the total. More than 9,000 of these are in remoter rural areas, those parts of England where 4% of the population lives and, according to Government figures, where the population grew fastest during the 1990s[2]. However, some 8% of church-  goers (twice the population percentage) lived in such areas in 2005, against 11% in 1989, suggesting perhaps that those who move to the country do not always embrace the local church[3]. The issues of the number of such churches, their declining attendance, and their long-term viability are a critical part of the future of the church in England.

Bruce Cameron, the previous Primus of the Scottish Episcopal Church, tells of a rural parish he knew which had shrunk to just three elderly ladies. When it was suggested that their church should be closed, they were determined not to let that happen, and invited their friends and neighbours to join them on Sunday. Within two years, the congregation had increased to 15 people, an impressive growth in statistical terms, although still probably an unviable number to keep their building open. "But," said the Primus, "it made me give them a further five year extension."

Measuring churchgoing by environment

In the 1989 English Church Census, respondents were asked to indicate in which one of eight types of environment classification their church was located. A very high percentage answered that question[4], the answers to which were used to analyse the results both in 1989 and in this present 2005 survey. Both the number of churches and number of churchgoers are broken down by county in *Religious Trends*[5] for 1989 and 2005, but only the national total is available for 1998. The percentage of churches and churchgoers in each environmental type in 2005 is shown in Table 4.1:

Table 4.1: Percentage of churches and churchgoers by Environment, 2005

2005	City Centre %	Inner City %	Council Estate %	Suburban/ Urban fringe %	Separate Town %	Other built-up area %	Commuter Rural[6] %	Remoter Rural[7] %	BASE (=100%)
Churches	4	8	7	23	13	4	16	25	37,501
Churchgoers	5	12	7	36	17	4	11	8	3,166,200

This Table immediately shows three differences in the relative percentages:

- There are proportionately more **Inner City** churchgoers than churches. This is because there are many Roman Catholic churches in Inner City areas, with a very high average attendance in comparison with other churches.

- There are many more churchgoers in **Suburban Areas** and **Separate Towns** pro rata to the number of churches. But it is in such areas that the bulk of the population lives[8] (56%) so it shouldn't be surprising that more than half (53%) of churchgoers live in such places also. That the churchgoers are a lower percentage than the population shows that church attendance proportionately in other areas is higher even if the actual numbers are much smaller.

- **Rural churches** are smaller than average. Proportionately there are twice as many rural churches as churchgoers (41% to 19%), taking both Rural categories together.

Changes over time

Figure 4.2 shows the changing proportions of churchgoers in each environmental type since 1989[9]:

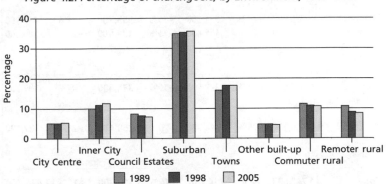

Figure 4.2: Percentage of churchgoers, by Environment, 1989–2005

The relative proportions of churchgoers living in Council Estates and in Commuter and Remoter Rural areas has declined between 1989 and 2005. In City Centres and Other built-up areas it has remained stable, but in the Inner City, Suburban areas and Towns the percentage has grown. Part of the reason for the Inner City growth is that this is where many of the black majority churches are located. The growth in the Towns is partly because this is where church planting often takes place: in 1989 there were 4,600 churches in English towns, and 4,800 by 2005. The increase in the Suburban areas has probably more to do with the fact that other areas (Inner City apart) have declined faster, meaning that the Suburban areas, although also in decline, have maintained a slightly larger share of the whole. The basic numbers behind Figure 4.2 are given in Table 4.3, which also projects them to 2015:

Table 4.3: Church attendance by Environment, 1989–2015

Environment	1989	Change	1998	Change	2005	Change	2015E
City Centre	235,100	−21%	186,200	−12%	**163,500**	−18%	134,300
Inner City	467,300	−12%	409,200	−10%	**368,400**	−11%	326,400
Council Estate	385,300	−28%	277,300	−19%	**223,500**	−40%	134,400
Suburban/ Urban Fringe	1,639,500	−21%	1,300,500	−14%	**1,123,600**	−20%	900,400
Separate Towns	755,400	−14%	651,300	−15%	**553,300**	−13%	482,900
Other built-up areas	219,300	−24%	165,800	−16%	**139,000**	−21%	109,500
Rural Commuter areas	540,500	−26%	399,500	−16%	**335,500**	−41%	199,200
Remoter Rural areas	500,400	−35%	324,900	−20%	**259,400**	−28%	187,100
Total	**4,742,800**	**−22%**	**3,714,700**	**−15%**	**3,166,200**	**−19%**	**2,474,200**

The projections suggest:

- City Centre, Suburban areas and Other built-up areas will continue to decline in numbers at about the average for the country.

- Inner City and Separate Town attendance will buck the trend somewhat. The Inner City projection assumes the continuing vibrancy of ethnic diversity, and that the number of large Roman Catholic churches will continue, even though their Mass attendances dwindle. Town attendance assumes that new churches will continue to start there, perhaps becoming a particular focus for the Emerging Church movement.

- The areas of serious concern are the much larger-than-average declines in attendance in Council Estates and Commuter Rural areas.

Environment by denomination

The various denominations are not spread equally across the different environments. Their proportions are shown in Table 4.4 on the next page, the percentages adding to 100% in each row.

The Table shows that the Orthodox have a high percentage of their attendance in City Centres, although their numbers are extremely small (are only present in 22 cities); the Roman Catholics, Orthodox and Pentecostals are strong in the Inner City; the Roman Catholics and Pentecostals likewise on Council Estates; nearly half the United Reformed churchgoers are in Suburban areas; a third of New Churches are in Separate Towns; Anglicans, Baptists, Independent and New Churches have a high relative percentage in Commuter Rural areas; as do the Anglicans, Independents and Methodists in Remoter Rural areas.

Table 4.4 shows attendance, not where church buildings are located. Their percentages are not the same! Table 4.5 gives the average 2005 congregation, derived from the attendance given in Table 4.4 and the number of churches which are in *Religious Trends* for those who need them[10].

Table 4.4: Percentage of church attendance, Environment by Denomination, 2005

Denomination	City Centre %	Inner City %	Council Estate %	Sub-urban %	Separate Towns %	Other built-up %	Commuter Rural %	Remoter Rural %	Base (= 100%)
Anglican	7	7	6	35	13	4	15	13	870,600
Baptist	3	6	4	41	20	4	15	7	254,800
Roman Catholic	4	14	9	39	18	5	6	5	893,100
Independent	4	6	5	40	16	3	16	10	190,500
Methodist	3	5	6	38	24	6	8	10	289,400
New Churches	2	7	5	29	31	5	13	8	183,600
Orthodox	16	35	1	28	12	3	4	1	25,600
Pentecostal	8	40	10	19	13	3	6	1	287,600
United Reformed	5	4	5	45	23	4	7	7	69,900
Smaller denoms.	5	7	6	39	23	5	9	6	101,100
Overall	**5**	**12**	**7**	**36**	**17**	**4**	**11**	**8**	**3,166,200**

Table 4.5: Average size of congregation, Environment and Denomination, 2005

Denomination	City Centre	Inner City	Council Estate	Sub-urban	Separate Towns	Other built-up	Commuter Rural	Remoter Rural	**Overall**
Anglican	71	68	73	107	97	79	37	20	**54**
Baptist	99	98	66	123	118	57	132	69	**107**
R Catholic	239	360	176	348	239	336	121	106	**244**
Independent	73	51	54	112	81	50	90	70	**84**
Methodist	(65)	49	61	80	98	53	27	15	**48**
New Churches	(200)	128	83	146	177	136	148	89	**140**
Orthodox	182	107	17	89	48	53	29	(100)	**81**
Pentecostal	154	141	98	145	105	86	184	(76)	**129**
United Reformed	78	31	50	63	50	38	26	28	**48**
Smaller denoms.	(102)	44	43	76	53	91	59	72	**63**
Overall	**98**	**118**	**91**	**131**	**115**	**93**	**55**	**28**	**84**

Where the average congregation is based on very small numbers[11] the figure has been put in brackets in Table 4.5; these numbers are less reliable than the others. It is clear from the small average numbers in some environments, including the Remoter Rural areas, that the long-term viability of some of these churches is questionable, particularly when the cost of upkeep of their buildings (especially if they are listed) is included.

Some of the denominations in the Remoter Rural areas have seen their congregations shrink appreciably. The Methodists, for example, had an average Remoter Rural congregation of 35 people in 1989, which dropped to 25 by 1998, and which has now declined to 15. Anglicans had an average Remoter Rural congregation of 37 people in 1989, which dropped to 23 in 1998, but has decreased much more slowly to the 2005 figure of 20 – another example of the Anglicans not declining as fast as might have been expected given their 1990s experience.

The number of Independent churches in Remoter Rural areas increased from 240 in 1998 to 280 in 2005, and their average attendance hardly changed – moving from 73 in 1998 to 70 in 2005.

In Gorsley, Herefordshire, a Baptist church has built a huge youth block, with separate rooms for each age-group, in order to cater for the many young people who come each week.

"In rural communities . . . faithful worship, even by only a few people, can have significance beyond the church walls. . . . In some small communities, there can be an unspoken understanding that the prayer and worship life of the village sustains others in their lives and work"[12].

Listed church buildings

Two denominations, Anglicans and Methodists, have the highest numbers of listed churches, although the Church of England numbers are way in excess of the Methodists – more than 11,000 and 600 respectively in 2003[13]. For the Church of England, this represents nearly three-quarters of all its churches: over a quarter, 27%, of the

Church of England church buildings are Grade I listed, a further quarter, 26%, are Grade II*, and almost a quarter, 23%, are Grade II; only 24% are not listed. The map shows the counties where more than 80% of Church of England buildings were listed in 1989. Their annual repair bill for listed buildings was £130 million in 2004[14]. Closing such churches, even when deemed desirable to do so, is not a quick or easy process. Sometimes redundant

churches are sold to other faiths[15], transformed into residential dwellings, or sold as offices or commercial premises.

Some living churches, in their concern to remain open and valuable to their community, put their building to an imaginative use during the week such as Shipbourne Parish Church in Kent in which a weekly Farmer's Market is held, or Sheepy Magna Church in Leicestershire which provides a Post Office 2 days a week after the village one closed in 2003, or the village church in Thorndon, Suffolk, where a café church is held[16]. Anglican rural churches were encouraged to "do what was best for their communities" in a debate on rural affairs in the February 2006 Synod[17].

Churchmanship of churches by environment

The churchmanship of churches varies by the various environments as the next Table shows, where the columns add to 100%, and the figures in bold indicate areas significantly different from the average.

There are many Catholic churches in the city areas, and fewer in Other built-up and Remoter Rural areas. Mainstream Evangelicals

Table 4.6: Churchmanship of Churches by Environment, 2005

Churchmanship	City Centre %	Inner City %	Council Estate %	Sub-urban %	Sep Towns %	Other built-up %	Commuter Rural %	Remoter Rural %	OVER-ALL %
Anglo-Catholic	8	7	5	5	3	5	5	5	5
Broad	12	7	10	12	11	12	16	18	13
Catholic	21	20	23	16	18	10	12	11	15
Broad Evangelical	8	8	8	10	10	10	8	6	8
Mainstream Evangelical	23	24	21	18	23	23	14	13	18
Charismatic Evangelical	10	19	17	19	18	17	10	6	14
Liberal	11	7	8	10	8	9	16	15	12
Low Church	4	7	6	7	6	11	15	20	11
All others	3	1	2	3	3	3	4	6	4
BASE (= 100%)	1,662	3,110	2,463	8,550	4,797	1,498	6,142	9,279	37,501

are similar, although also strong in Towns and Other built-up areas. Charismatic churches are especially to be found in Inner City and Suburban areas, and least in Remoter Rural areas. Liberal churches are less to be found in the Inner City, and Low Churches are especially in the Commuter and Remoter Rural areas.

Changes in the environment

Many changes are taking place in the English landscape, and change in the rural areas are not the only ones. Nevertheless these are substantial. A useful list in the book *Changing Rural Life*[18] included changes in:

- The general outlook (costs of rural life may outweigh the benefits),

- Employment (rural incomes not as high),

- Housing (affordable accommodation often not available),

- Transport (life can be difficult without access to a car),

- Health services provision (hospital access can be difficult),

- Deprivation (few jobs for the young; loneliness for the elderly).

One of the most publicised churches in the autumn of 2005 was St Mary Magdalene in the (Commuter Rural) village of Lundwood, near Barnsley, South Yorkshire where 10 people attended. It was a run down church, with paint peeling from its front wall. An American Anglo-Catholic priest, Father James McCaskill, was inducted and challenged to see if he could swell the congregation within a year – under the full glare of Channel 4's extensive TV publicity in its 3 part programme *Priest Idol*. Father James visited his local pub, took advice from a neighbouring incumbent, went to the local school, appointed brand consultants and consulted with his Archdeacon, Jonathan Greener. He *did* succeed although was unable to draw in the young people. A caring congregation, a warm welcome, a determined leader, relevant speaking and a vision or expectation of change made the difference.

The Congregational Church in Cawsand, Cornwall, closed in 2000, but re-opened in 2005 with 30 members in the congregation for two services a month. The remaining members in 2000 were too few and too elderly to enable the church to continue, but Rev Jill Stephens, the Congregational Federation South West Area support worker was concerned to keep it going. After a community meeting, help was given to refurbish the hall, build a kitchen and put in heating. The church now has a regular Tuesday coffee shop, a monthly children's workshop on a Saturday, and, for the last two years, has performed mystery plays in the summer[19]. Friendship, warmth of welcome, a willingness to be involved, and a determination to keep the church alive provided a seaside miracle[20].

Growth by environment

Having conducted previous Censuses, information from churches responding in 1989 and 1998 can be compared with the information given in 2005, allowing an analysis of whether churches have been growing or not. Nearly 5,000 churches which answered both the 1998 and 2005 studies had answered the question on their environment in 1989, which was not asked subsequently. This is a more than sufficient number on which to estimate growth.

"Growth" and "Decline" were defined in the 1998 survey as churches which had grown or declined at least 10% between 1989 and 1998; the same proportionate rate of growth was used for the shorter period 1998 to 2005 so that growth over the two periods could be equally compared. This is looked at in more detail in Chapter 9. "Stable" churches were those whose Sunday attendance had changed less than 10% in either direction.

Figure 4.7 shows the percentage of churches which either grew, remained stable or declined broken down by environment[21], in the order of growth (37% of remoter Churches grew compared to 32% of Council Estate churches).

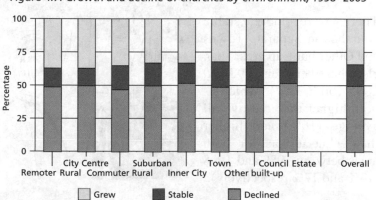

Figure 4.7: Growth and decline of churches by environment, 1998–2005

It is obvious from Figure 4.7 that there is no significant variation in proportions of churches growing by the different environments. Environmental location is not a factor in causing churches to grow, something which other research has found[22]; leadership and vision are the vital factors.

However, it is equally true that Figure 4.7 does show that there are a few minor variations, some of which are of particular interest. For example, 37% of both City Centre and Remoter Rural churches grew between 1998 and 2005, which is both higher than the overall average (34%) and two or three times higher than in the period 1989 to 1998 (14% and 13% respectively)[23]. This growth in Remoter Rural areas is both significant and important, and is consistent with a modelling exercise undertaken by the Future Foundation for Rural England and Wales, which found a steady growth in rural populations[24].

Over half, 52%, of both the Inner City and Council Estate churches declined between 1998 and 2005, which is slightly greater than the overall average (50%) but lower for both areas than in the period 1989 to 1998 (64% and 73% respectively).

Obviously, in the places the people aren't going out to the church, the Church should be going out to the people!

There were more stable churches in Separate Towns and Other built-up areas than elsewhere between 1998 and 2005 (both 19%), which is both higher than the overall average (16%) and higher than what it was for both areas between 1989 and 1998 (14% and 12% respectively).

Age by environment

Knowing the ages and church environment of nearly 600,000 attenders enabled further analyses. The details are given in Table 4.8[25]; similar analyses were not made in previous surveys:

Table 4.8: Proportions attending church by age-group and environment, 2005

Age-group	City Centre %	Inner City %	Council Estate %	Sub-urban %	Separate Towns %	Other built-up %	Commuter Rural %	Remoter Rural %	Overall %
Under 11	13	11	13	14	13	14	12	15	**13**
11–15	5	5	7	7	6	6	6	5	**6**
16–19	7	4	5	5	5	5	3	5	**5**
20–29	10	6	9	7	7	8	6	9	**7**
30–44	20	13	14	17	15	16	14	17	**16**
45–64	22	25	24	23	24	22	26	24	**24**
65–74	14	23	16	15	17	15	19	14	**17**
75–84	7	11	10	9	10	10	11	9	**10**
85 & over	2	2	2	3	3	4	3	2	**2**
Average age	**42**	**49**	**44**	**44**	**45**	**44**	**48**	**43**	**45**

There are two environments where the average age is much less than the overall average of 45, and two where it is much greater. The two which are less, those attending churches in City Centres and Remoter Rural churches are characterised by a higher percentage of people under 45 than across all churches: 55% in City Churches and 51% in Remoter Rural churches, against the average of 47%.

Having a greater proportion of churchgoers in their twenties might have been expected in City Centre churches where often there are many students, and large successful churches, but it is an unexpected finding that this is also true of Remoter Rural churches. Presumably this helps to explain the fact that in both environments, the proportion of growing churches is above the average.

When a friend of mine, the editor of a well-known woman's magazine, married a few years ago, she and her husband decided to buy a listed building in a very remote part of North Yorkshire – with internet facilities she was able to continue her researching and writing and earn a reasonable living in a very acceptable way.

Church attendance in the Local Authority of Ryedale which includes many acres of the North Yorkshire Moors has seen its church attendance *increase* not decrease. It is up by only +3%[26], not enough to keep up with the population increase since the percentage of the population in church has decreased from 7.4% in 1998 to 7.1% in 2005, but this illustrates the changes which are taking place.

The Archdeacon of Harlow, Peter Taylor, had to take a service in a very remote part of Essex in the autumn of 2005 for a church which at that time had no vicar. He was amazed that some 50 people were present, and even more surprised when he realised that at least half of them were under 40. It is perhaps not surprising that the Bishop of Exeter, Michael Langrish, wants the Government "to recognise the contribution that rural churches make to their communities by involving them more in decisions that affect their areas"[27].

An article in *Reader's Digest* indicated that a substantial number of people are "greenshifting"[28], migrating to the rural areas of England and towards a simpler lifestyle. It reported that the Countryside Agency had found that 352,000 people moved from urban to rural living in the four years to 2004[29]; "two-thirds of all houses are scooped up by people from the southeast"[30].

As already mentioned, the general population of Remoter Rural areas grew the fastest in the 1990s, and "greenshifting" younger people are perhaps as likely to move to such areas as older people who are retiring. The Remoter Rural areas have the *highest* percentage of children under 11 of all the various environments.

Researcher Charlotte Craig analysing some of Leslie Francis' data has suggested that churches in urban and rural areas may attract different types of churchgoers, urban churches attracting more "intuitive" people, rural more "sensing" people using the Myers-Briggs terminology for the different ways in which people perceive information[31]. At least with respect to age, which may not be a relevant variable, Table 4.8 would query this conclusion.

There is a difference between "Remoter Rural" and "Commuter Rural" in terms of church life with the former buoyant and the latter having a higher proportion of stable churches than the average.

The two areas which are less well placed with regard to age are the Inner City areas and the Commuter Rural locations. They have respectively 39% and 41% of their churchgoers under 45, against the average of 47%. The Inner City areas especially have many Roman Catholics attending; it is not always easy to move from such places, and employment elsewhere is not always forthcoming.

"Commuter Rural" was defined on the 1989 questionnaire as a "Dormitory area"; the government defines it as a "Rural Amenity area". Neither of these expansions of meaning are particularly helpful – perhaps "Commuter Rural" are those towns and villages which have a good variety of facilities, including road and rail links to larger towns and cities, as well as doctors and schools. Perhaps they are the places many people look to settle down in, as they near retirement. Both the Inner City and Commuter Rural areas had a higher percentage of those 65 or over than the overall average of 29% – 36% and 33% respectively; no other environment was over 30%.

Frequency of attendance by environment

Chapter 7 looks at the variations of frequency of church attendance in more detail, and here we will look only at those who
attend monthly or more frequently. Figure 4.9 shows the variations in proportions attending at various frequencies within the
different environments[32], with the most frequent on the left.

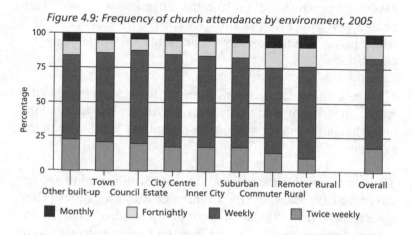

Figure 4.9: Frequency of church attendance by environment, 2005

There are some interesting variations reflected in this bar-chart.
There are three environments where the proportion attending
twice weekly is higher than the overall average of 18% (Other
built-up areas, Separate Towns and Council Estates).

Some years ago Christian Research had the privilege of undertaking Strategic Reviews of a number of Deaneries (groups of about
15 churches) in the Anglican Diocese of Rochester. One of these
Deaneries was in what used to be called a working-class area,
and it was immediately obvious that although the numbers
attending church were relatively small, those who did go were
fiercely loyal to their church and attended as often as they could.
This is precisely what is reflected in Figure 4.9 for Council Estate
churchgoers whose percentage of "only" going fortnightly or
monthly is much less at 12% than the overall figure of 17%, and

their proportion attending twice weekly is higher than average at 20%[33]. Also, the Roman Catholics have many churches on Council Estates and they emphasise weekly attendance.

The two environments where the proportions attending fortnightly or monthly are highest are the two rural environments, at 24% and 23% respectively against an average of 17%. This is almost certainly because many churches in these areas do not hold weekly services so that weekly attendance even if desired isn't possible!

Other notable features
So what has this Chapter shown?

- While church attendance may be summarised as 24% in city areas, 57% in suburban areas and 19% in rural areas, this is not where the churches are located! A fifth, 19%, of them are in city areas, two-fifths, 40%, in suburban areas and two-fifths, 41%, in rural areas.

- This has immediate and obvious problems of average size of churches in different environments and viability where churches are located in relatively small population centres, and for Anglicans (and to a much lesser extent the Methodists) problems with listed buildings.

- *City Centre*. 4% of all churches; 5% of churchgoers; 2% of ministers[34]. High proportion of total Orthodox attendance in City Centres. A quarter, 23%, of City Centre churches are Mainstream Evangelical. More churches are growing here than average; more younger congregations than average.

- *Inner City*. 8% of churches; 12% of churchgoers, an increasing proportion; 5% of ministers. A mix of ethnically diverse Pentecostal churches, large Roman Catholic centres, and some key Orthodox congregations. Low percentage of Broad churches. A quarter, 24%, of churches are Mainstream Evangelical. Although attendance is declining, it is not declining as much as it was. Older congregations on average.

- *Council Estates.* 7% of churches; 7% of churchgoers; 5% of ministers. Percentage of churchgoers declining and likely to drop further in years ahead. Strong Roman Catholic and Pentecostal presence. Loyal congregations who attend very regularly.

- *Suburban/Urban fringe.* 23% of churches; 36% of church-goers; 24% of ministers. Percentage of churchgoers increasing. Half of United Reformed churchgoing in suburban churches.

- *Separate Towns.* 13% of churches; 17% of churchgoers – the latter an increasing percentage; 13% of ministers. Towns have seen a number of new church plants started. A quarter, 23%, of churches are Mainstream Evangelical. One third of New Church attendance in towns. Churches are more stable than average, and more go twice weekly than average.

- *Other built-up areas.* 4% churches; 4% churchgoers; 5% of ministers. A quarter, 23%, of churches are Mainstream Evangelical. Churches are more stable than average, and more go twice weekly than average.

- *Commuter Rural areas.* 16% of churches; 11% of church-goers; 18% of ministers. Numbers attending church are a declining proportion and likely to drop further in years ahead. Anglicans, Baptists, Independent and New Churches strong here. Areas have seen many social changes, but are perhaps where people like to settle down. Older congregations, and less frequent attendance (services not every Sunday).

- *Remoter Rural areas.* 25% of churches; 8% of churchgoers; 28% of ministers. Proportion attending church has been decreasing and likely to decrease much further in days ahead. Anglicans, Independents and Methodists strong. One fifth, 20%, of churches are Low Church. Many very small congregations, but Anglicans did not decline as fast 1998–2005 as they did 1989–1998. Many social and struc-tural changes in these areas, where population growth has been greatest in the 1990s. Younger congregations than most, and more growing churches than average. Have highest percentage of children attending.

Looking behind the detail

There are some surprises here and things to watch:

A) The Remoter Rural areas may have fewer people going to church, with consequent problems of viability, but many of these churches are growing, with a good proportion of young people, and those in their 20s, in attendance. Some might see little future for these churches, but a fair number at least are not about to die. What can churches in other environments learn from those living in the most inaccessible parts of our country?

B) City Centre churches are untypical of the majority. They will include some of the very large London churches in the centre. How can their influence be shared with other churches in different locations?

C) Inner City areas are a cultural kaleidoscope. Older Catholic churches are alongside vibrant Afro-Caribbean fellowships whose worship styles could not be more different. The Orthodox present a third very different spirituality also. A mix of growing and declining congregations. Can one tradition even think of working with the others?

D) Suburban and Town churchgoing is the main engine of English Christianity. Solid, stable, strong commitment especially in the Towns. If the church is to be changed it is in these areas where the impact has to be made in terms of sheer volume of numbers.

E) Commuter Rural churches are seen not to be in the same league as Remoter Rural churches. One gets the impression these churchgoers are perhaps more comfortable, less positive in reaching out, least likely to embrace radical change.

If true, how can they be altered? If false, why are they continuing to decline?

Resources

The Commission for Rural Communities has the motto "tackling rural disadvantage" and seeks to advise the Government on their "Choice and Voice" agenda. Some opportunities of dialogue and involvement especially with respect to rural areas are available. Details are on their website[35].

5   Beating the drums
[Ethnicity analysis]

Given a chance, everywhere that Archbishop John Sentamu travels, he will take his drums. He plays them on every possible occasion, even during his enthronement service on 30th November 2005 as 97th Archbishop of York in York Minster! John Sentamu comes from Uganda, and the drums were part of his boyhood, and are part of his culture today. That culture, and the expression of Christianity which goes with it, is *very* different from the white Anglo-Saxon culture that has shaped Christianity in this country.

The ethnic expression of other Christian cultures is one classification that the English church must learn to appreciate if it is to be relevant in the UK today. The Archbishop's message was blunt: "The church in England must rediscover her self-confidence and self-esteem . . . why have we in England turned this glorious Gospel of life in the Spirit into a cumbersome organisation that repels, and whose people are dull, complacent, judgmental and moralising?"[1]

Classification
After much research, what is now called the Office for National Statistics[2] (ONS) found, in time for the 1991 Population Census, an acceptable question to ask people about their ethnic background, and it was included for the first time that year. The 1998 English Church Attendance Survey used a similar classification, which involves six broad categories:

• White, which will include those of non-British but European origin, as well as those from North America, Australia or New Zealand;

- Black Caribbean/African/Black Other, including the many African and West Indian people some of whom are immigrants, but many of whom are English being now in their third generation here, abbreviated for simplicity to "Black";

- Chinese/Korean/Japanese, abbreviated for simplicity to "Chinese"[3];

- Indian/Pakistani/Bangladeshi, abbreviated for simplicity to "Indian";

- Other Asian, which will include Filipinos, Malaysians, Singaporeans, Thai and Vietnamese;

- Other Non-White, which will include those from the South American continent.

Some of these categories were extended by the ONS for the 2001 Population Census, but the resulting categories took up too much space on the Church Census form, so we retained the 1998 formulation for the 2005 English Church Census which allows ready comparison. The one category which should, nevertheless, have been included was "mixed" to reflect the categorisation especially of children who have one white and one Afro-Caribbean or Asian parent[4].

Ethnic growth

However, whatever the classification, the 2005 English Church Census shows that there has been considerable growth in church attendance among those coming from a non-white ethnic background, as Table 5.1 makes clear, so much so that one person in six going to church in 2005, 17%, was non-white! This is double

It's all here in black & white – and, er... brown & yellow...

ETHNICITY ANALYSIS

the percentage of non-whites in the 2001 general population[5] and half as much again as the estimated proportion in 2005 (shown in Table 5.1)[6]. Black church attendance is at least three times their proportion in the population, and Chinese more than double. On the other hand, Indian church attendance as a percentage of Indians in England is only about a third of their numbers. Other groups (Other Asian and Other Non-White) are above the national proportions but closer to them.

Table 5.1: Church attendance by ethnicity, 1998 and 2005

	1998	Change	2005	Percentage of total		National percentage		
				1998 %	2005 %	1998 %	2001[7] %	2005E %
White	3,274,600	−19%	2,640,600	88.1	83.4	93.8	91.4	88.3
Black	268,600	+23%	331,400	7.2	10.4	1.9	2.6	3.8
Indian	54,300	+ 9%	59,400	1.5	1.9	3.0	4.1	6.0
Chinese	54,700	+ 3%	56,400	1.5	1.8	0.3	0.4	0.8
Other Asian	36,300	+24%	45,000	1.0	1.4	0.4	0.7	1.3
Other Non-White	26,200	+27%	33,400	0.7	1.1	0.6	0.8	1.0
Total	**3,714,700**	**−15%**	**3,166,200**	**100.0**	**100.0**	**47mn**	**49mn**	**50mn**
Total Non-White	**440,100**	**+19%**	**525,600**	**11.9**	**16.6**	**6.2**	**8.6**	**11.7**

Non-White church attendance has increased by a fifth, +19%, in the period 1998 to 2005, a total of over 85,000 people, or an increase of more than 12,000 per year. The White community meanwhile has dropped by almost a fifth, −19%, or a loss of over 630,000 people, equivalent to 90,000 people per year. This difference is huge and very important for the future of Christianity in this country. As the detailed denominational background given in Table 2.1 in Chapter 2 shows, two-fifths, 41%, of the Non-White attendance[8], has been seen in ethnic minority congregations, with the remainder being intermingled in White congregations, up from 34% in 1998.

The bulk of the Non-White attendance is the Black churchgoers, over three-fifths, 63%, of the total (marginally up from 61% in 1998). Black church attendance has increased by nearly 63,000 people in the seven years to 2005 to reach a total of 330,000, or just over 10% of total English church attendance. The other ethnic minority groups total nearly 200,000 people, or 7% of total attendance. Thus only five-sixths, 83%, of churchgoers in England are White (who are not of course necessarily English!).

The reasons for this growth come partly from immigration, although this applies rather less to the Black community from the West Indies who have been in England for longer. Immigration has been a significant factor however for those coming from Africa, among whom a number of deliberate missionary plants has occurred. A list of the major Black Majority Churches whose headquarters are outside the UK is given in a book by Mark Sturge[9], former General Director of the African and Caribbean Evangelical Alliance. This desire to be "reverse missionaries" does not apply only to Africans; there are Indian missionaries doing similar work, especially in the Roman Catholic church[10]. Nor should it be assumed that black ministers are always responsible for predominantly black churches; some look after essentially White congregations[11].

Mark Sturge also makes clear that the key reason why the Black churches have made such an impact is their natural evangelism and spiritual impact on the one hand and their intense community involvement in the other. The two have gone hand in hand. This reflects research in the United States where, when asked what was the top priority in their life, African-Americans were twice as likely as White people to say their faith (27% to 15%)[12].

Other research has shown that those in the professional and managerial classes who are Caribbeans, Indians, Pakistanis or white migrants predominantly come from working class backgrounds (while fewer than half of white non-migrants do so). This is because migrants entering Britain experience downward mobility, but have aspirations for their children (perhaps partly why they migrated). In addition the overall expansion of higher class jobs has provided opportunities from which their children have benefited. Migrant parents encourage their children to gain good qualifications, and this may help to explain why the churches attended by those who are Christian among them are growing so fast – perhaps they are using their faith and business experience in their evangelistic activities and are able to support their church's programme financially because they are in good jobs[13].

Although the Chinese and Korean Churches are strong in Britain, especially the former with so many Chinese spread across the UK[14], their evangelism has had less overall impact in terms of numbers these past few years. Much of the growth in the other ethnic communities has been strongly helped by continuing immigration often because of employment.

This issue of employment can be illustrated by the fact that while 10% of the staff on the register of the Nursing and Midwifery Council were trained outside the UK, this was true of 40% of the new entrants on the register in 1999, and over 90% of these are from outside Europe. In 2003 nearly a third, 29%, of all the doctors employed by the NHS were foreign-born, of whom the large majority were trained outside the European Economic Area. Over 40% of the dentists added to the General Dental Council's register in 2003 were overseas educated. As George Alagiah says in a forthcoming book, "The trend is clear: an ever-growing dependency on the skills of foreign workers, many of whom may go on to become immigrants."[15]

He goes on to identify a number of ministers who have come to England either as a foreign "reverse missionary" worker or as an immigrant, showing that the sheer quantity of such people is becoming important, and concludes that "increasingly the nature of faith in this country may be defined by immigrants".

Ethnicity by denomination

The proportion of churchgoers in different ethnic groups varies by denomination, as Table 5.2 shows[16]:

Table 5.2: Percentage of church attendance,
Ethnicity by Denomination, 2005

Denomination	White %	Black %	Indian %	Chinese %	Other Asian %	Other Non-White %	Base (= 100%)
Anglican	88.1	8.3	1.2	1.3	0.7	0.4	870,600
Baptist	87.8	7.7	1.1	1.6	1.1	0.7	254,800
Roman Catholic	82.6	7.6	3.3	1.9	2.8	1.8	893,100
Independent	86.6	6.3	1.8	2.9	1.5	0.9	190,500
Methodist	93.3	4.2	0.6	1.0	0.5	0.4	289,400
New Churches	89.2	5.1	1.5	1.5	1.5	1.2	183,600
Orthodox	91.8	0.4	1.6	2.7	2.7	0.8	25,600
Pentecostal	54.6	39.7	1.8	1.5	0.7	1.7	287,600
United Reformed	92.6	4.6	1.1	1.1	0.3	0.3	69,900
Smaller denoms.	66.9	19.8	2.2	7.8	1.7	1.6	101,100
Overall	**83.4**	**10.4**	**1.9**	**1.8**	**1.4**	**1.1**	**3,166,200**

Some features of this Table are of particular interest:

- Anglicans have the third highest percentage of black people in their churches.

- Roman Catholics have the highest percentage of churchgoers from the Indian sub-continent.

- The Independent churches have the second highest proportion of Chinese churchgoers, after the Chinese churches themselves, part of the Smaller Denominations group.

- Every ethnic group is represented in each denomination.

- One reason for the high percentage of black attenders among the Smaller Denominations is those attending the Seventh-day Adventists who have a considerable proportion of black people.

The percentage of black Roman Catholic churchgoers in Table 5.2, 8%, is nearly triple the 3% of black Catholic adherents in the United States[17].

Black churchgoers are not only the largest single Non-White ethnic group of churchgoers, but have also grown the fastest since 1998. Table 5.3 gives the specific numbers for them[18].

Table 5.3: Number of black churchgoers, by denomination, 1998 and 2005

Year	Anglican	Baptist	Roman Catholic	Independent	Methodist
1998	58,200	21,700	60,500	11,400	14,600
2005	72,700	19,500	68,100	12,000	12,000
% change	+25%	−10%	+13%	+5%	−18%
% of total	22%	6%	20%	4%	4%

	New Churches	Orthodox	Pentecostal	United Reformed	Smaller Denoms.	TOTAL
1998	9,800	100	69,500	5,200	17,200	269,000
2005	9,500	100	114,300	3,200	20,000	331,400
% change	−3%	0%	+64%	−38%	+16%	+23%
% of total	3%	0.03%	34%	1%	6%	100%

One-third of Black churchgoers are Pentecostal, and their numbers have increased by nearly 45,000 since 1998, an average of over 6,000 a year. In numerical terms the Anglicans follow behind the Pentecostals. Almost half of Black churchgoers are either Anglicans or Roman Catholics, both seeing substantial increases since 1998. However, some denominations saw their numbers of Black attenders decrease – the United Reformed, Methodist, Baptist and New Churches.

A similar Table for all the non-white ethnic groups is given in *Religious Trends*[19], and is illustrated in Figure 5.4. Against

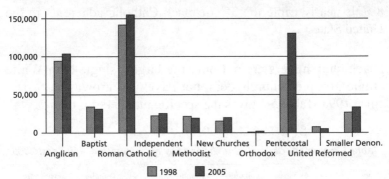

Figure 5.4: Total Non-White churchgoers, by denomination, 1998 and 2005

a universal picture of denominational decline, this chart shows that growth is not only possible, but has actually happened among non-whites since 1998 across all but three denominations.

Ethnicity by churchmanship

Tables similar to Tables 5.2 and 5.3 could easily be constructed for churchmanship rather than denomination, but they show few surprises. The basic Table is given in *Religious Trends*[20], and Figure 5.5 gives a comparison of how ethnicity by churchmanship has varied between 1998 and 2005.

The story is again of growth, this time in all churchmanships except the Liberals and those in the Low Church. The Charismatic Evangelicals have grown very considerably, consistent with the fact that it is largely the black churches which have secured that growth[21].

In some ways the multiplicity of churchmanship groups and ethnic diversity confuses the picture. Table 5.6 puts the figures in a simple way – the number of evangelicals and non-evangelicals broken down by white churchgoers and all non-white, for the years 1998 and 2005, and shows how the numbers have changed in that period.

Figure 5.5: Total Non-White churchgoers, by churchmanship, 1998 and 2005

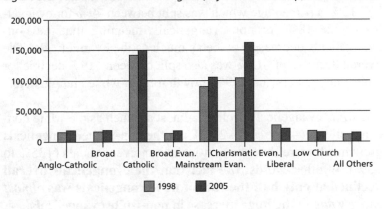

Table 5.6: Evangelicals and non-evangelicals, white and non-white,
1998 and 2005

1998	Evangelical	Non-evangelical	Total
White	1,182,800	2,091,800	**3,274,600**
Non-white	208,500	231,600	**440,100**
Total	**1,391,300**	**2,323,400**	3,714,700
2005	Evangelical	Non-evangelical	**Total**
White	978,800	1,661,800	**2,640,600**
Non-white	286,000	239,600	**525,600**
Total	**1,264,800**	**1,901,400**	3,166,200
Change 1998–2005	Evangelical	Non-evangelical	**Total**
White	*−17%*	*−21%*	*−19%*
Non-white	*+37%*	*+3%*	*+19%*
Total	*−9%*	*−18%*	*−15%*

The number of churchgoers between 1998 and 2005 decreased by −15%, a percentage which was split between −9% for evangelicals and −18% for non-evangelicals, meaning that the non-evangelicals decreased twice as much as the evangelicals. The overall decrease of −15% was also split between −19% decline for white churchgoers and +19% growth for non-white churchgoers.

The *white* evangelicals declined almost as much as the white non-evangelicals (−17% and −21%), but the non-white evangelicals grew much more than the non-white non-evangelicals (+35% to +3%). In other words, **the fact that the evangelicals overall declined at only half the rate of non-evangelicals was** *almost entirely due* **to the huge increase in non-white evangelicals**.

Ethnic change in Greater London

The change in Greater London can be broken down between Inner and Outer London; the basic figures are given in Table 5.7:

Table 5.7: Ethnic churchgoers in Inner and Outer London, 1998 and 2005

Year	White	Black	Indian	Chinese	Other Asian	Other Non-White	TOTAL
Inner London							
1998	117,100	89,600	8,600	6,700	9,800	7,900	**239,700**
2005	111,000	117,100	9,100	7,800	10,900	9,800	**265,700**
% change	*−5%*	*+31%*	*+6%*	*+16%*	*+11%*	*+24%*	*+11%*
Outer London							
1998	276,800	57,500	18,900	12,500	8,300	4,200	**378,200**
2005	245,500	63,700	18,900	12,400	10,800	6,000	**357,300**
% change	*−11%*	*+11%*	*0%*	*−1%*	*+30%*	*+43%*	*−6%*

All the non-white ethnic groups have grown across Greater London as a whole, as well as in Inner London itself. In Outer London, the Indians and Chinese have held their own. On the other hand, the white church attenders in both Inner and Outer London have declined.

The Black churchgoers have grown much more in Inner London than in Outer, by 27,000 to 6,000, reflecting where many live. There are more black people going to church in Inner London than white, despite several very large churches with substantial white congregations. Black churchgoers form almost half, 44%, of all Inner London church attendance (and are more than white churchgoers, 42%). The Black figures include churches like the Kingsway International Christian Centre (10,000 people) and Kensington Temple (Elim) (perhaps 3,000 Black people[22]). In an article the Bishop of London wrote, "The Church is being enriched by Black and Asian Christians. One of the most recent examples in London is the reception of a community of French-speaking Congolese Christians into the Diocese (of London)"[23]. Such examples could be multiplied.

The white attendance in Inner London in 2005 was two-fifths, 42%, of the whole, down from 49% in 1998. In Outer London the white proportion is two-thirds, 69%, down from 73% in 1998. This change is reflected in Figure 5.8:

Figure 5.8: Changing proportions of churchgoers by ethnicity, 1998 and 2005

While Greater London has the greatest percentage of Black churchgoers for any English county, 29%, it is not the only county where the percentage is above 10%. Other counties with such a proportion are West Midlands (19%), Bedfordshire (18%), Nottinghamshire (13%), Buckinghamshire and Leicestershire (both 10%). Leicester is expected to become the first UK city to have a non-white majority by 2010[24]. A further 13 counties have the percentage of Black churchgoers between 5% and 10%[25]. These variations are illustrated in coloured maps in *Religious Trends*[26].

The enthusiasm and entrepreneurial activity behind the growth is illustrated from an email we received which said, "I live in Colchester, Essex. There is a church on Greenstead led by two Nigerian doctors, and there's a rumour they may buy the church building on Harwich Road recently closed by the URC."[27]

The enthusiasm and excitement is not limited to black churchgoers; others from different nationalities are similar. A Messianic Rabbi, Moshe Laurie, said in an interview, "The Lord is saying to you, 'Tell them, NOW! . . . There is no tomorrow, only today. When Messiah comes it will be today.' . . . If you have to think about it, it's too late!"[28] The note of urgency is clearly there. No wonder the London City Mission, in recruiting for evangelists in 2006, headed their advertisement "Abandon the city, lose the nation. Reach London, touch the world."[29]

Ethnicity by age of churchgoer

We look at the ages of churchgoers in some detail in the next chapter, but while we are thinking about ethnicity it is worth looking to see the age variations that occur. The data for this purpose are not directly derived from the Census form, but from the slips that were sent out by Christian Research which are described in more detail in Chapter 7. The value of having the individual slips returned is that information relating to age by ethnicity could be extracted, which couldn't have been obtained in any other way.

The slips returned amounted to a sample of 1% of the churches giving us information, so the results are less robust than others, and require the four smaller ethnic groups to be combined.

The figures are shown in Figure 5.9:

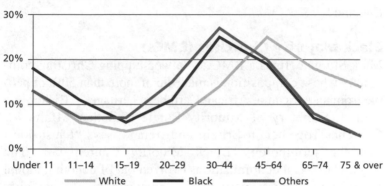

Figure 5.9: Age of churchgoers by ethnicity, 2005

There is a drop in the percentage of churchgoers in their teenage years which is common to all ethnicities. But there are greater proportions of:

• Black young people in church than for whites or others,

• Other ethnicities in church across ages 20 to 44, and

• A much greater percentage of white people in church after 45.

Black young people in church has been one of the strengths of the Black churchgoing population for several decades. Their numbers are helped by the fact that their fertility rate is higher than for white people[30]. However, the fact that the percentage of Black teenagers in church is little different from that of other ethnic backgrounds suggest that black churches leaders may be experiencing similar problems as white ministers in holding their young people.

Researcher George Barna notes the slow demise of the African-American church community in the United States. He writes, "The black community has traditionally been the people group that has been strongest in the Christian faith and lifestyle. There is an intriguing – and unfortunate – correlation between the economic rise of the African-American population and the deterioration of its faith in Christ."[31] Could the same happen in England?

Black Majority Churches (BMCs)

Mark Sturge defines a BMC as "a worshipping Christian community whose composition is made up of more than 50% of people from an African or African Caribbean heritage"[32]. Bishop Joe Aldred, Secretary of Minority Ethnic Christian Affairs for Churches Together in Britain and Ireland, says "I just don't like the terminology Black Majority Church! . . . The major Caribbean denominations evolved out of denominational expansion and missionary zeal . . . they continued their faith, liturgy and worship as practised back home."[33] Some of the ways in which they express their faith, however, attracts white people or those from other ethnic backgrounds, and so these churches are no longer just attended by Black people. Bishop Aldred's book, *Respect*, is very helpful in understanding Caribbean British Christianity[34].

Whether the term "Black Majority Church" is acceptable or not it is a useful expression in indicating that many churches have a mix of people from a whole variety of different ethnicities, cultures and backgrounds. In 2005, just over half the churches in England, 54%, had a white-only congregation. A much smaller percentage, 3%, of congregations were *entirely non*-white, and the remaining two-fifths, 43%, were mixed congregations.

Table 5.10 gives the detailed figures and compares the 2005 percentages with those from the 1998 survey.

Table 5.10: Percentage of ethnically mixed congregations, 1998 and 2005

Year	Percentage of churches with this percentage of non-white attenders									Base
	0%	1–5%	6–10%	11–20%	21–40%	41–60%	61–80%	81–99%	100%	
1998	58.9	17.0	8.3	5.7	3.3	1.7	1.0	1.4	2.7	9,830
2005	54.0	19.0	9.3	6.4	4.0	1.9	1.3	1.5	2.6	10,496

The Table shows that there has been a rise in the proportion of churches which have people from different ethnic backgrounds attending. If the proportions are true of all English churches, then nearly 2,000 churches have welcomed people from a different culture into their congregation over the 7 years 1998 to 2005.

There are still in 2005 over 20,000 churches who only see white people attending, even if some of these may in fact come from Europe, the United States or Australia. Many such churches are in rural areas. Likewise there are nearly 1,000 congregations which are entirely African, Caribbean, Chinese, Korean, Japanese, Tamil, Thai, or other nationalities. Some 16,500 congregations, however, have the added value of members from different ethnic backgrounds.

The Table shows that the proportion of people of different ethnicities are most likely to form up to 10% of the congregation. There are relatively few churches where the mix is between 11 and 99%. Even where they are, it doesn't necessarily mean a genuine multi-ethnic congregation.

One large Roman Catholic multi-racial 1,300 strong church[35] holds 5 Masses every weekend, one on Saturday evening, three Sunday morning and one Sunday evening. The priest of this church very kindly took details of all who attended at each Mass on 8th May 2005 and sent the details individually per service. This showed that 60% of those at the Saturday Vigil Mass were White, against only 25% at the 12.15 and 6.00pm Masses who were White. A third of the congregations at 10.45am and 12.15pm were Black, a quarter of the congregations on Saturday evening, 10.45am and 12.15pm were Indian, and Asians and Blacks each formed a quarter of the Sunday evening service. The various ethnicities tended to go at different times, so that although overall the church was 62% non-white, in reality the different ethnic groups were much more likely to go to some Masses than others[36].

The 35% where between 1 and 20% of a congregation is mixed breaks down into: 19% with between 1 and 5%, and 16% with between 6 and 20%. Therefore, of congregations which are not made up of either 100% white or 100% ethnic minority, almost half, 44%, have just a small number of people (1 to 5%) of different ethnic background, equivalent to 2 or 3 people (perhaps one family) in an average congregation of 84 people. These figures are illustrated in Figure 5.11:

Figure 5.11: Proportions of congregations of different ethnic mixes, 1998 and 2005

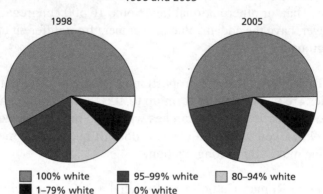

Congregations which are mixed tend to be smaller than average – 54 people against the overall average of 84. All white congregations average 106 people, and all ethnic average 128 people,

these figures including Roman Catholic churches where appropriate. Of the 54 in the mixed congregation, 49 would be white
and 5 would be non-white, on average.

Reasons for growth

In a detailed article about Black churches, Jonathan Oloyede,
one of the Senior Pastors of Glory House, a multi-cultural
church in East London, gives some of the reasons why Black
churches grow[37]:

- The Church is the hub for community life.

- Many Black churches have a cosmopolitan outlook, not a
  parish mentality.

- Black communities are very communal with a culture of visiting, socialising and regular personal interaction.

- Black churches are very evangelistic and outreach driven.

- The principle of tithe-giving helps financial buoyancy and
  independence.

- Bible-based sermons are relevant to the congregation.

- Services are vibrant, musical and worshipful.

- An emphasis on the Holy Spirit: many Black believers testify
  to experiencing healings and miracles.

- Many BMCs have a home cell network, which facilitates
  strong pastoral care.

- Sunday Schools are usually a norm and part of weekly
  worship.

- The dynamics of many BMCs facilitate lay leaders' training.

- Various departments and programmes allow large volunteer
  participation.

- Prayer is the key focus in many BMCs.

- BMCs lay good emphasis on business success and career prospects.

- BMCs have a culture of great respect and reverence for their pastors.

- Many BMCs have youth clubs/activities that retain young people within the Church community.

How many of these factors could be utilised in helping white churches grow?

Vision

While it is very likely that all these factors are relevant, I think he misses out one of the most important – the size of their vision. Matthew Ashimolowo is the Senior Pastor of Kingsway International Christian Centre, the largest church in the UK with over 10,000 attending most Sundays, and nearly all Africans. Their church had offered to build a complete Grandstand and Arena for the 2012 Olympic Games, providing it free while the Games are in progress, so long as they could have the use of it subsequently as a Worship Centre. However, this offer was not accepted. Few churches have the finance to source such an enormous vision, and the faith to believe that, if the plan had been accepted, God will provide the necessary resources.

Jesus House of All Nations in the north London Borough of Brent is a church of over 2,000 people who gather in a warehouse with ample room for their worship centre. But their Senior Pastor, Agu Irukwu, has a vision – along with a model to show everyone what it will look like – to rebuild and reshape their building to include a much larger worship centre, a swimming pool on the top floor, and a 24/7 Global Prayer Centre with a roof the shape of Greater London. He hopes the £10m project can begin by the end of 2008.

"How can white church leaders learn to have visions like black church leaders?" he was asked.

"You have to believe God will do the impossible," he replied[38].

You may feel that this is just two key black leaders. It is, but that kind of leadership encourages others, enthusing and helping to generate like visions among those who follow them. In one conference, Matthew Ashimolowo said, "Each church leader should have a vision – a vision the size they can believe God will honour." Believing God is not limited to black church leaders!

We need vision! But there is a huge confusion between indicating the reason for doing something and articulating what that something should be in concrete terms. "Getting involved in mission" is an excellent *purpose*, but it is not a *vision*. Building a £10m sanctuary is a superb vision, but it does not indicate the underlying motive – to reach people for Christ. Both elements are necessary: the purpose explains *why* we need the vision, the vision *how* it will be fulfilled. Lack of clarity of vision is perhaps partly because we get too encumbered with generalised statements of good intent. Black church leaders have learned to distinguish the two concepts.

Summary of main findings
What has this Chapter shown?

- The proportion of non-white attenders in English churches has increased from 12% in 1998 to 17% in 2005, an extra 85,000 people.

- Black people now account for 10% of English congregations and other ethnic minorities, in total, a further 7%. Thus only five-sixths are white.

- Over half, 54%, of congregations are all-white, down from 59% in 1998. 3% of congregations, in 2005 as in 1998, are 100% non-white. The remaining 43% of congregations are mixed; their average size is 54 people, of whom 5 would be non-white.

- Numerically the Pentecostals have most Blacks in their con-gregations followed by the Anglicans – 114,000 to 73,000. In 1998 the respective figures were 70,000 and 58,000.

- Roman Catholics have the highest percentage of those com-ing from the Indian sub-continent.

- The Independent churches have the second highest proportion of Chinese churchgoers, after the Chinese churches them-selves, part of the Smaller Denominations group.

- Only Liberals and those in the Low Church are seeing their numbers of non-white attenders decrease.

- Only two-fifths, 42%, of churchgoers in Inner London are white, a percentage down from 49% in 2005. Of the 58% who are non-white, 44% are black and 14% have other ethnic backgrounds.

- In Outer London, 69% are white, 18% black and 13% of other ethnic backgrounds.

- While almost a third, 29%, of Greater London's churchgoers are black, the percentage is 19% in the West Midlands and 18% in Bedfordshire.

- Black churches have a higher percentage of children, Asian churches a higher percentage of those aged 20 to 44, and white churches a higher percentage of those 45 and over.

- One of the key reasons why black churches grow is their huge relational emphasis in the church and community.

Looking beyond the detail

Some items of concern to church leaders are implicit in this analysis:

A) The growth of black attendance is impressive, especially in Inner London. Aside from immigration, are there factors here which white leaders can apply to their situation?

B) Equally there are concerns that black youth may be beginning to fall away similarly to their white counterparts. Are
there ways of combatting this? Do more black people return
in their 20s than white people?

C) Ministry among ethnic diversity often requires cross-
cultural communication. Are there elements of this which are
also applicable in mono-cultural situations? How can ministers best be trained to give them such communication skills?

D) Ram Gidoomal, Chairman of South Asia Concern and a former mayoral candidate for London, asked some relevant
questions in an article[39]: "Can we accept our own identity
and the identity of those who are different?" (That mixed
congregations are the smallest may suggest a problem here).
"Can we give each other freedom within a larger identity?
Can we help those alienated to re-discover a place within
our fellowship?"

E) "Where there is no vision, the people perish" is a well
known verse[40]. Where there is no vision, the leader perishes
and the church perishes. How can other church leaders
learn to envision and believe like some of the black church
leaders (and other ethnic minority church leaders)?

6 "Hallowed be Thy Game!"
[Age and gender analysis]

Football, and other sports, have a dominant place in the total output of television channels, especially if Sky TV is included. Sport is taught at young ages, and many a football match is played on a Sunday morning. After using the phrase captured in the heading, a conference speaker went on to say that "Football is more important than the difference between heaven and hell"[1] . . . to many young people. How true is this, and how much does sporting activity impact young people particularly (and their parents) in church attendance? In this chapter we look at age, gender and churchgoing.

The shrinking sands of time
The proportions of people going to church across the four English Church Censuses by age-group are shown in Table 6.1. In 2005, the youngest age-group of "Under 15" was split into two groups "Under 11" and "11 to 14" and the oldest age-group "65 and over" was divided into "65 to 74", "75 to 84" and "85 and over". Estimates for these sub-divisions have made been for earlier studies by using population proportions in order to give trend information.

Table 6.1 shows that the proportion of people under 45 in church has been steadily declining across 26 years, from a total of 62% of all churchgoers in 1979 to 47%, less than half, by 2005. Between 1998 and 2005 the largest proportionate drop has been among those in their twenties. Conversely, those 45 or over have grown in proportion from 38% in 1979 to 53% by 2005, with the largest proportionate increases between 1998 and 2005 among those aged between 65 and 74 and between 75 and 84.

Table 6.1: Age of churchgoers, 1979–2005

Age-group	1979 %	1989 %	1998 %	2005 %
Under 11	18	17	13	13
11 to 14	8	8	6	6
15 to 19	9	7	6	5
20 to 29	11	10	9	7
30 to 44	16	17	17	16
45 to 64	20	22	24	24
65 to 74	11	11	14	17
75 to 84	6	7	9	10
85 & over	1	1	2	2
Base (=100%)	5.4 mn	4.7 mn	3.7 mn	3.2 mn
Average age	37	38	43	45

Undoubtedly the biggest shift age-wise in the church in recent years was the huge decline in numbers of young people in the 1990s, when over that decade some 500,000 children stopped going to church. That was a huge loss which has not continued, partly because:

- The numbers of children of non-churchgoing parents who attend church have declined drastically to very small numbers and cannot reduce that much again. "Not only are we struggling to keep and care for young people from church families, we are making only negligible impact on the vast majority of the young people who are unchurched".[2]

- There has been an encouraging increase in the number of Children's Workers (as well as Youth Workers) employed by churches, particularly in the last five years – perhaps as many as a third of churches have one or other now, some on a part-time or shared basis.

- Much increased activity on behalf of many organisations working with young people, determined to *keep* youth as well as *reach* youth.

- A willingness by many churches, and the volunteer helpers in them, to organise young people's activities at different times both on Sundays and during the week.

- An increasing realisation of the importance of teaching their children the Christian faith by many churchgoing parents, perhaps helped by the apparent growing influence of grandparents.

However, the other major change in the 1990s, hidden somewhat by the alarm over the loss of young people, was the declining numbers of middle-aged (30 to 64) people. While the loss of young people has not continued at the same rate between 1998 and 2005, the decline in the number of middle-aged people has worsened. In addition the number of churchgoers 85 and over has increased – and at a faster rate.

The average age of a churchgoer has increased from 37 in 1979 to 45 in 2005, against an average population age of 37 in 1979 to 40 in 2005. The fact that the average age in the population has increased in this period indicates that the population in general has "aged", so an increasing proportion of older churchgoers is simply what might be expected. However, the "ageing" of churchgoers exceeds that of the general population, meaning that the church now has a far higher percentage of older people. Some take seriously the ageing of the population of Britain[3]; it is serious for the church as well.

Annual numerical change

These changes are reflected in Table 6.2, where the actual numbers for each age-group in the four Census years are given. The intermediate column gives the change per year that occurred between one Census and another, which is given on an annual basis since the period between each Census is different, and are illustrated in Figure 6.3. The final column shows the percentage change between 1998 and 2005[4].

Having trend figures is important to understand how the numbers are changing. Some churches[5] find this kind of assessment

Table 6.2: Annual numerical change, by age-group, 1979–2005

Age-group	1979	Change pa	1989	Change pa
Under 11	980,300	−18,000	800,400	−34,400
11 to 14	435,700	−5,900	376,600	−16,700
15 to 19	489,700	−15,200	337,300	−14,100
20 to 29	598,200	−11,700	481,200	−17,200
30 to 44	870,300	−6,100	809,400	−18,000
45 to 64	1,087,800	−4,500	1,042,500	−15,200
65 to 74	599,400	−7,100	528,400	−200
75 to 84	335,400	−1,600	319,900	−300
85 & over	44,200	+300	47,100	+1,900
Total	**5,441,000**	**−69,800**	**4,742,800**	**−114,200**
Age-group	1998	Change pa	2005	%98−05
Under 11	490,600	−9,900	421,300	−14
11 to 14	226,500	−3,400	202,700	−11
15 to 19	210,600	−8,200	153,300	−27
20 to 29	326,600	−13,700	230,600	−29
30 to 44	646,700	−21,500	496,200	−23
45 to 64	905,900	−21,600	755,100	−17
65 to 74	526,600	−300	524,400	0
75 to 84	317,000	−1,800	304,400	−4
85 & over	64,200	+2,000	78,200	+22
Total	**3,714,700**	**−78,300**	**3,166,200**	**−15**

Figure 6.3: Annual change in different periods by age-group

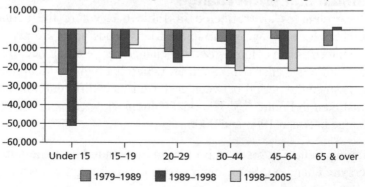

so useful that they undertake an annual survey of attendance, which can be very helpful in evaluating the consequences of major changes, such as when a minister leaves.

Table 6.2 and Figure 6.3 show:

- The catastrophic drop among those under 15 in the 1990s has slowed considerably to a much smaller annual rate of loss between 1998 and 2005. This may well be because a number of churches have started services outside the traditional times of 10.00am and 6.30pm, which are more convenient both to families and children. If children are involved in football on a Sunday morning with their school, or band practice, most parents find it difficult to get their children to church! A church in Finchley, North London, started a 4.00pm Sunday service and quickly found it attracted 60 people, three times its normal evening service. Tea follows – and the consequent fellowship lasts as long as the service!

- The combined rate of decline of those under 15 in the 1990s was much greater than the numbers leaving aged 30 to 44, suggesting that it was not just children leaving the church, but rather whole families with all their children dropping out.

...and now, here are the local Sunday-Attendance results: Fenbury United, 618, Fenbury Parish Church, 24

- There has been a decreasing decline in the annual numbers of those aged 15 to 19 leaving the church. Perhaps those who "make it" through the crisis years of 11 to 14 are more inclined to stay.

- The loss of those aged 20 to 29 has also decreased slightly since the 1990s. This ongoing loss, however, is important assuming that young people might wish to marry someone of their own faith. Research shows that just over a majority, 53%, of children follow their parents' churchgoing habits[6]. If the number of young people of marrying age are relatively very few, then the number of new Christian homes is likely to be small, and the number of future children who might come to church small also. On the other hand, "the family you come from isn't as important as the family you're going to have,"[7] and it may well be that past trends of children following parents' churchgoing habits may change in the days ahead.

- It may also be that the decreasing loss of those in their 20s is that some may have returned to church after having their first child, a phenomenon shown to have occurred in the 1990s by research published in the mid 1990s, but not updated since[8].

- A continuing increasing loss among those aged 30 to 64, which has *escalated* between 1998 and 2005, and now represents more than half the total loss in churchgoing numbers every year.

- A continuing decline in numbers aged 65 and over, although there is very little change since 1998 in the overall number aged 65 to 74, and only a modest decline in those aged 75 to 84. However, there is a continuing and slightly increasing number who are reaching 85 and over each year.

- The final column in Table 6.2 shows that the greatest losses *pro rata* are occurring among those aged 15 to 29, and the largest numbers dropping out are those between 30 and 64, with a higher percentage loss among those aged 30 to 44 than those aged 45 to 64.

There have been various studies suggesting that churchgoers live longer than those in the general population, partly because their lifestyle is healthier, with far fewer smoking, fewer drinking alcohol in large quantities (many older churchgoers are tee-total) and perhaps a more positive outlook on life. The actuaries behind the Church of England clergy pensions had to revise their calculations in 2002 when they realised that clergy had an average life span 3 or 4 years longer than average[9]. The increasing numbers in church aged 85 and older support this[10].

Figure 6.4 charts the percentages of the different age-groups between 1979 and 2005, for visual clarity, and compares these with national population proportions. It combines the two "Under 15" groups and the three "65 and over" groups to give comparability.

Figure 6.4: Percentage of churchgoers by age, 1979 and 2005

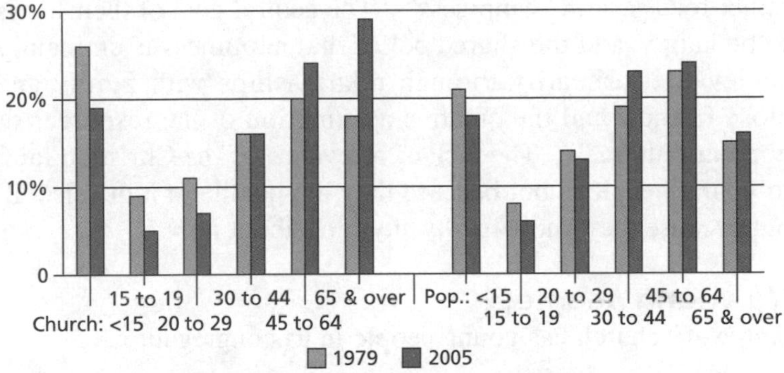

In 2005 the churchgoing percentage was only 1% different from the population proportions for those under 15 and aged 15 to 19. However churchgoers in their 20s were only half the percentage of that age-group in the population generally (7% to 13%), and likewise those aged 30 to 44 were less (16% to 23%). Churchgoers and population were in the same proportion, 24%, for those aged 45 to 64, but churchgoers were double the proportion in the oldest group (31% to 16%).

That young people are of a similar relative proportion in church in 2005 as they were in 1998 (even if the actual percentage is lower) indicates that a number of churches have been successful in incorporating into their activities those features which retain them: "the opportunity to express their thoughts, including their doubts and embryonic heresies. They need to be free to ask pointed questions about sex. They have to be able to openly discuss faith and life, without feeling that the script has already been written by paternalistic adults who know how the story has to end. And they have to be able to feel comfortable with how they dress and look."[11] Or, as the Government Green Paper on Youth declares, "Better information, advice and guidance about issues that matter to them, delivered in the way they want to receive it."[12]

Those in "Generation Y", defined by some as those born in the 1980s[13], have been found to have little spiritual interest, being rather focussed on "happiness". "The central goal of their life is to be happy, and the shared belief that happiness is eminently achievable, primarily through relationships with family and close friends, and the creative assumption of the resources of popular culture."[14] "The lack of relevance of the Christian faith to young people is not because they are hostile to it or reject it, but because they know hardly anything about it."[15]

No young people!

Not every church has young people in its congregation.

- 39% of churches had no-one attending under 11 years of age

- 49% of churches had no-one attending between 11 and 14, and

- 59% of churches had no-one attending between 15 and 19 years of age.

These are horrific figures and indicate the huge amount of work that churches have to do to reclaim the lost ground among young people today[16]. We may be emerging from the nosedive, but without the support of more young people, it will be exceedingly difficult to begin the climb back to a safe level.

It is interesting that these proportions are in complete contrast to the growing numbers of young people taking RE at GCSE or A Level and applications to read Theology at University[17].

Grandparents

The increasing proportion of older people in Figure 6.4 is obvi-ous, as are the decreasing proportions of teenagers and those in their 20s. As two-thirds, 68%, of churchgoers are married (very similar to American churchgoers of 69%[18]) and a further 13% are widowed, it is very likely that a good majority of those 65 and over (as well as some younger) will be grandparents[19].

In the UK as a whole there are 13 million grandparents, a quarter of the adult population, with an average of 4.4 grandchildren. Half of these still have a living parent (so many children know their great-grandparents) and a third of those under 60 still have a dependant child of their own at home. Some church children are brought up by their grandparents, not parents[20]. A third of grandparents spend 3 days a week caring for their grandchildren, and five-sixths, 82%, of children are cared for sometimes by their grandparents[21].

For 12% of Australian Protestant churchgoers, grandparents were the most significant people in showing what faith is about. Some 3% of children attending Sunday School in England are brought by their grandparents[22], and if grandparents go to church, 60% of their grandchildren will go to church with them when they visit[23]. Grandparents are key confidants, trusted people of influence. If a child's parents break up, their grandparents often have the role of holding the child's broken world together.

Grandparents therefore hold an important position in their families, and often in a church. Frequently they are asked to help with the Sunday School. Since there are so many of them in most churches, using their energies and family ties in the most strategic way is important. A few churches have experimented with holding "Being an Effective Grandparent" sessions.

Decadal change

The concern from Table 6.2 and Figure 6.3 thus focuses on the three age-groups where the decline since 1998 is over 20% – those aged 15 to 44, that is, older teenagers and those with young families. Part of this decline will be the inevitable consequence of the earlier losses of younger children, but Table 6.2 does not clearly identify this, as the Census years are different periods apart and the age-groups are of different sizes. Table 6.5 seeks to standardise both – by estimating the figures for 1985 and 1995 from the above, and making the age-groups into 10 year periods.

Table 6.5 looks complicated, but it is the final two columns which are of most interest. They show that the number of churchgoers declined more in the decade 1995 to 2005 than in the previous decade 1985 to 1995, but this is largely because of the huge loss of children. The large percentages on the lines "70 to 79" and "80 or over" are primarily because of people dying. It is the intermediate percentages which give us new information.

The higher percentages in the lines "40 to 49" and "50 to 59" than for the line "30 to 39" in the final column confirm that it is those in their 30s and 40s who are leaving more than those in their 20s. Furthermore, as these percentages are higher than in the previous 1985–1995 column, it tells us that the rate of loss in these two age-groups is increasing.

The Table also shows us that those in their 50s in both 1985 and 1995 are by far the least likely to leave. The increasing rates of loss among those in their 60s or above will be mainly due to normal mortality, though some may be people who re-locate when they retire and don't join a new church.

The proportion of churchgoers who are married is 68%[24], and while that information is not broken down by age, it is very likely that a majority, even two-thirds, of those in their 30s and 40s in church are married people. The loss is therefore occurring among couples, many of whom will have children. In other words, our prime loss continues to be families, although as the number of children dropping out is less, it may be that some parents drop out and their children continue to attend.

Table 6.5: Numbers attending church by ten year cohorts, 1985–2005

Age group	1985	1995	2005	Change 1985–1995	Change 1995–2005
0 to 9	773,700 ↘	565,000 ↘	383,000	–	–
10 to 19	863,500 ↘	612,900 ↘	394,300 →	–21%	–30%
20 to 29	520,900 ↘	376,700 ↘	230,600 →	–56%	–62%
30 to 39	545,500 ↘	448,700 ↘	330,800 →	–14%	–12%
40 to 49	534,400 ↘	454,100 ↘	354,200 →	–17%	–21%
50 to 59	523,400 ↘	459,600 ↘	377,500 →	–14%	–17%
60 to 69	544,600 ↘	499,000 ↘	451,000 →	–5%	–2%
70 to 79	446,800 ↘	427,600 ↘	414,400 →	–21%	–17%
80 or over	211,800	219,800	230,400 →	–51%	–51%
TOTAL	**4,964,600**	**4,063,400**	**3,166,200**	**–18%**	**–22%**

Why should the church be losing people in their 30s and 40s? Firstly, these are the age-groups when people attend less frequently; hence they are not necessarily leaving the church, but because they go less often, their numbers are less on any particular Sunday. Precisely the same was found in the 2002 Scottish Church Census[25].

Secondly, these are the age-groups when home pressures often get very high. In many cases both parents will be working, and need to continue to do so to pay the mortgage etc[26]. There will be young children and the home to look after, and church becomes one thing too many to fit into life, especially for the wife for whom initially the combination of husband, home, church and employment is sufficient but when children are added the load is too great. Some churches are responding to this by having services at more convenient times. The impact of weekend working on church life has been explored[27]; in the UK on Sundays 33% of women work compared to the EU average of 25%. Of those women who work on a Sunday who have children under 5, 55% work; when the youngest child is between 5 and 10, 73% are in the labour force, and this rises to 80% when the youngest child is 11 or more[28].

Cary Cooper, when Professor of Organisational Psychology at the University of Manchester Institute of Science and Technology (now part of the University of Manchester), wrote after a detailed survey, "The idea that parents can give quality time to their children or to each other when they are exhausted is a myth. Weekends filled with domestic chores increase the strain."[29] Hence "chilling-out" becomes an occupation sometimes taking preference to going to church. These people have not left the church; they simply haven't gone this week (or last).

Thirdly, these are the age-groups when many couples divorce. While it is thought that the percentage of Christian divorces is lower than for non-Christians[30], there are still many Christian divorces with the complications this causes. In a Focus Group I was conducting in Bristol, a woman explained, "I'm divorced, so I haven't attended church since." This result is not what the church desires, but it is commonplace. For the children of such families, Sunday often then becomes "Daddy's day", and Daddy unfortunately no longer goes to church at all, especially if his new partner is not Christian. Lest some feel this point is exaggerated, a survey undertaken by Christian Research early in 2005 found that nearly a third, 31%, of Secondary School age church children were *not* being brought up by their two natural parents[31].

Fourthly, these are often the age-groups when the relevance of the Christian faith to home life, to work and leisure becomes critical, both for parents and for children. Many find that the church is not relevant, and while some move to another church to "find something better" they do not always succeed in their quest. They are then likely to give up going to church altogether. Research has shown[32] that relevance is a critical factor for keeping people. It is one of the key reasons why the largest churches in the country tend to be growing churches, as the preaching in them is found to be relevant to the life of those who attend[33].

Fifthly, it is also a time of significant life changes that can be decisive decision moments about churchgoing – the birth of children, moving to new house and/or area, and settling down with a life-partner.

One night a father overheard his son pray, "Dear God, make me the kind of man my Daddy is." Later that night, the father prayed, "Dear God, make me the kind of man my son wants me to be."[34]

Age of churchgoers by denomination

We have already looked at the variation of age by church environment and ethnicity of churchgoer[35]; Table 6.6 on the next page gives the proportion in each age-group by denomination[36], and the average age for each also[37].

The variation by age across the different denominations is very great. Of the 10 denominational groups, three are within two years of the overall average age of 45 – the Baptists, Roman Catholics and the Smaller denominations, all being slightly younger. The Orthodox (40) and Independent (42) churches are younger still than the average, and the Anglicans rather older (49). Of the remaining four, two have an average age that is more than ten years younger, the Pentecostals at 33 and New Churches at 34, and two are ten years older than the average – the Methodists and the United Reformed Church.

The reason for this wide diversity is similar: the Pentecostals and New Churches have few elderly (10% and 8% respectively), while the Methodists and United Reformed both have nearly half, 47%, their churchgoers 65 years of age or over. Both the New Churches and Pentecostals have many young people (25%

Table 6.6: Proportion of churchgoers by age-group and denomination, 2005

Denomination	Under 11 %	11 to 14 %	15 to 19 %	20 to 29 %	30 to 44 %
Anglican	12	5	3	5	14
Baptist	17	5	4	7	17
Roman Catholic	13	6	6	8	16
Independent	12	7	6	10	19
Methodist	10	4	2	3	9
New Churches	17	8	7	14	23
Orthodox	8	7	10	12	19
Pentecostal	17	12	8	13	21
United Reformed	11	4	2	2	10
Smaller denoms.	10	9	6	8	15
Overall	**13**	**6**	**5**	**7**	**16**

Denomination	45 to 64 %	65 to 74 %	75 to 84 %	85 & over %	Average age
Anglican	26	20	12	3	**49**
Baptist	25	14	8	3	**43**
Roman Catholic	22	18	9	2	**44**
Independent	25	12	7	2	**42**
Methodist	25	24	18	5	**55**
New Churches	23	5	2	1	**34**
Orthodox	24	12	8	0	**40**
Pentecostal	19	7	2	1	**33**
United Reformed	24	23	18	6	**55**
Smaller denoms.	28	14	8	2	**44**
Overall	**24**	**17**	**10**	**2**	**45**

and 29% of their total attendance are under 15), and only the Baptists have a comparable percentage, 24%.

There is a close correlation between the average age and the rate of decline in denominations given in Chapter 2; if a graph of these were plotted, it would show a clear straight line. Statistically the correlation is very high, working out at –0.84[38]. How far this is cause and effect (older congregations tend to be declining) or effect and cause (declining congregations cause younger people to leave or not join) is unknown. One key way of breaking this cycle is the planting of new congregations.

As we shall see in Chapter 10, there is a considerable difference between the number of young people attending church, and those with whom a church is in contact through mid-week activities. While the Baptists, for example, are seeing a smaller number of young people in church, the total number of young people with whom the churches in the Baptist Union of Great Britain are in contact, is quite considerable[39].

The elderly

The disparity in the proportions of elderly are reflected in Figure 6.7 which shows how the percentage of those 45 and over has varied since 1979.

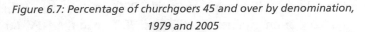

Figure 6.7: Percentage of churchgoers 45 and over by denomination, 1979 and 2005

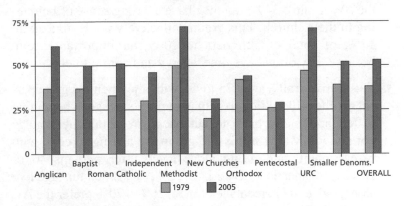

Figure 6.7 illustrates that all denominations have seen an increase in the proportion of older people over the 26 years up to 2005. The Orthodox and Pentecostals have changed least.

Those who are older fall into different groups, and should not be assumed to be a homogeneous category:

- The "younger old", those aged 55 to 64, are probably still employed, expecting to retire at 60 or 65, and despite current changes, may well have a final salary pension. Many church-goers of this age are in leadership positions within the church or local community; 30% help a voluntary or charitable organisation[40]. Four-fifths, 80%, use the New International Version (NIV) of the Bible, twice the proportion using the Authorised Version (AV) for preference[41]; about a fifth use both. Over two-fifths, 43%, say they have a strong sense of belonging to their church[42].

- The "Third Age", a Government term for those aged 65 to 74, are almost entirely retired, and, in many cases, "re-tyred" and ready to go! Appreciating relaxation, and being able to afford travel, they frequently go overseas with Saga or other travel companies. Some are still in church leadership, especially in more conservative denominations or smaller churches, while others play a willing supportive role. 30% of these also help a voluntary or charitable organisation. 70% read the NIV, 60% the AV. A third, 34%, say they have a strong sense of belong-ing to their church. This group collectively made up a sixth, 17%, of total churchgoers in 2005, an important group because they often have time, energy and commitment.

- The "active frail", aged 75 to 84, will enjoy being a grandpar-ent. While still willing to help organisations, age is beginning to tell and many have to cut back, the actual percentage not known. Many in this age-group are having to cope with bereavement, and living alone again after perhaps 40 or 50 years of marriage. Over half, 52%, of women this age live alone, twice the percentage of men, 26%[43]. 70% prefer the AV, 55% the NIV, again some using both versions. While making up one-tenth, 10%, of all churchgoers, some will need help to get there; they will see regular attendance as the norm. They form a greater proportion of smaller churches[44]. A quarter, 28%, have a sense of belonging to their church. They will be avid watchers of "Songs of Praise", and find spiritual nourishment through it[45].

- The "inactive frail", 85 and over, will generally mostly be confined to home, with increasing dependency on others, and may well only be able to attend on special occasions, like Easter and Christmas. Over half, 54%, of women this age will be living alone (men 37%), but a quarter, 23%, will be in a communal establishment (12% men). A fifth, 19%, have a sense of belonging to their church.

Smaller denominations

The "Smaller Denominations" category contains many small groups, as its title implies. It includes some, like the Church of the Nazarenes and Seventh-day Adventists which are strong in young people, and whose average age is 42 and 39 respectively. The Protestant Overseas Nationals are especially a younger group with half, 48%, of their churchgoers aged between 20 and 44, with a good number of children also, so that their average age is only 31. On the other hand, established denominations like the Salvation Army have an average age of 48 (a third, 34%, are 65 or over), while the Quakers have very few young people (only 12% are under 20) and a large proportion of elderly (45% are 65 or over), so that their average age is 56.

Emerging churches

The "Emerging Churches" are an especially important and encouraging group of churches. While total attendance in 2005 was almost 18,000 people, their average age was 29 against the 45 for all churchgoers. The overall percentage of attenders under 30 is 31% (Table 6.1), but in Emerging Churches the percentage is twice that: 61%. This would appear to confirm that their radical approaches are having the hoped-for impact – attracting those who would not go to traditional churches.

Age and churchmanship

The average age for each churchmanship is given in Table 6.8 together with comparison figures for 1989 and 1998;

the underlying figures for each individual churchmanship and the percentages for each age-group are given in *Religious Trends*[46].

Table 6.8: Average age of churchgoers by churchmanship, 1989–2005

Year	Anglo-Catholic	Broad Catholic	Broad Evangelical	Main-stream Evangel.	Charis-matic Evangel.	Liberal	Low Church	All Others	**OVER-ALL**
1989	42	43	38	41	35	31	42	43	43	**38**
1998	46	47	41	46	42	36	48	46	45	**43**
2005	49	48	45	47	42	38	50	49	46	**45**

The results fall into three groups, broadly determined by the number of children going to church in each group:

• Those which are above the average age: Broad (48), Anglo-Catholics and those in the Low Church (both 49) and Liberals (50);

• Those which are about the average: Broad Evangelical and All Others (both 47) and Catholic (45);

• Those which are below the average: Charismatic Evangelicals (38) and Mainstream Evangelicals (42).

In all groups, except the Mainstream Evangelicals, the average age increased from 1989 to 1998 and from 1998 to 2005.

Marital status of churchgoers

Some criticised the Census for not asking for a person's marital status, but this question was omitted because not every minister knows the precise marital status of every person in his/her congregation. Previous studies omitted the question for the same reason. However, a number of congregational studies have been carried out which did ask this question; these are put together to give Figure 6.9[47]:

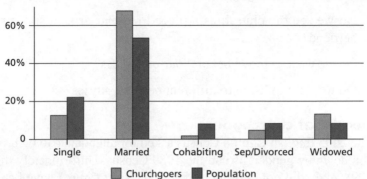

Figure 6.9: Marital status of English churchgoers and population, 2001

It is clear that *pro rata* there are far more married churchgoers compared with those who are cohabiting or lone parents (included with the "single" in the chart). These other groups are important as only 69% of church children are brought up with their two natural parents[48]. Across Britain the proportion of families consisting of married couples, with or without children, is decreasing rapidly, and the proportion of cohabiting couples and lone parent families (the very large majority being single mother families) is increasing, especially the latter.

Some churches have problems with these life-styles, and people in these categories may therefore have difficulty in finding acceptance should they venture into such a church. However, if they cannot find this acceptance, effectively the churches are disenfranchising a large and growing segment of the population, albeit unintentionally. How can church people be helped to welcome unconditionally both groups? How can the church, lovingly and sensitively, best impart to young people Biblical teaching on Christian marriage?

It is equally seen from Figure 6.9 that the church does not have as many single people proportionately as in the general population. An author of a recent book on this subject[49] suggested that part of the answer is resolving questions like:

- Do we want to engage with contemporary society?

- Do we see the church as a place to attend or as a space to befriend?

- Do we want to move beyond our prejudices?

- Do we want to listen to different people's stories?

Gender of churchgoers

The 2005 English Church Census asked for attendance to be broken down by gender, as had the 1989 Census. Unfortunately the 1998 study did not, although overall national figures have been estimated. The basic information given in Table 6.10 comes for the three years where gender has been measured, combining the "Under 15" and "65 and over" for ease of comparison.

Table 6.10: Gender of churchgoers by age-group, 1979–2005

Age-group	1979			1989			1998			2005		
	Male %	Female %	**Total %**	Male %	Female %	**Total %**	Male %	Female %	**Total %**	Male %	Female %	**Total %**
Under 15	13	13	**26**	12	13	**25**	9	10	**19**	9	10	**19**
15 to 19	4	5	**9**	3	4	**7**	3	3	**6**	3	2	**5**
20 to 29	5	6	**11**	4	6	**10**	4	5	**9**	3	4	**7**
30 to 44	7	9	**16**	7	10	**17**	7	10	**17**	7	9	**16**
45 to 64	9	11	**20**	9	13	**22**	10	14	**24**	10	14	**24**
65 & over	7	11	**18**	7	12	**19**	9	16	**25**	11	18	**29**
TOTAL	**45**	**55**	**100**	**42**	**58**	**100**	**42**	**58**	**100**	**43**	**57**	**100**

The 1998 gender split is completely estimated but is included because if the percentages for 1979 and 1989 are considered it would seem almost inevitable that the male percentage would decrease, and instead it has increased slightly. The reasons for this need examination.

The Table also shows the huge percentage drop in young people between 1989 and 2005, this occurring between 1989 and 1998 rather than 1998 to 2005, and occurring equally among boys and girls. It also shows a continuing decline in the proportion of those aged 15 to 29, again with both genders affected, with women declining in percentage terms the same as men (comparing 2005 with 1989). The proportions of both genders increase slightly in the (wider) age-group "45 to 64" with women increasing more than men.

The most noticeable increase, however, in Table 6.10 is the huge percentage increase in both genders among those aged 65 and over.

Changing gender proportions

Tables 6.11 and 6.12 may appear complicated, but they are the figures in Table 6.2, omitting 1979, but broken down by gender. In both periods, 1989–1998 and 1998–2005, the annual losses of women exceed those of men; the reason therefore why the percentage of men has increased is not because more men are beginning to attend church but because more women are leaving than men. The same phenomenon was observed in the 2002 Scottish Church Census, when the proportion of men attending church also increased[50]. The figures in Table 6.12 are important and the totals were the basis of Figure 6.3.

Table 6.11: Numbers by gender and age-group, 1989 to 2005

Age-group	1989		1998		2005	
	Men	Women	Men	Women	Men	Women
Under 15	569,100	607,900	334,300	382,800	292,700	331,300
15 to 19	142,300	195,000	105,000	105,600	78,000	75,300
20 to 29	189,700	291,500	148,600	178,000	103,400	127,200
30 to 44	332,000	477,400	260,000	386,700	218,200	278,000
45 to 64	426,900	615,600	371,400	534,500	316,200	438,900
65 & over	332,000	563,400	333,400	574,400	352,900	554,100
Total	1,992,000	2,750,800	1,552,700	2,162,000	1,361,400	1,804,800

Table 6.12: Losses by gender and age-group, 1989 to 2005

Age-group	Change per annum 1989–1998			Change per annum 1998–2005		
	Men	Women	**Total**	Men	Women	**Total**
Under 15	−26,000	−25,100	**−51,100**	−5,900	−7,400	**−13,300**
15 to 19	−4,200	−9,900	**−14,100**	−3,900	−4,300	**−8,200**
20 to 29	−4,600	−12,600	**−17,200**	−6,500	−7,200	**−13,700**
30 to 44	−8,000	−10,000	**−18,000**	−6,000	−15,500	**−21,500**
45 to 64	−6,200	−9,000	**−15,200**	−7,900	−13,700	**−21,600**
65 & over	+200	+1,200	**+1,400**	+2,800	−2,900	**−100**
Total	**−48,800**	**−65,400**	**−114,200**	**−27,400**	**−51,000**	**−78,400**

In the period 1998 to 2005 the annual loss of women is greater than the loss of men for every age-group, something not quite true for the period 1989 to 1998 (more boys under 15 left then than girls). The losses of women over men between 1998 and 2005 are not much higher in each age-group among those under 30, but this changes quite considerably for those 30 and over. Not only are the female losses between 1998 and 2005 at least twice the losses among men, they are also much more than the female losses between 1989 and 1998. A third, 30%, of the total annual loss of women to the church between 1998 and 2005 occurred among those aged 30 to 44, something which also occurred in the 2002 Scottish Census. As in Scotland, this is a very serious decline. More men in their 20s and aged 45 to 64 left each year between 1998 and 2005 than between 1989 and 1998, but fewer aged 30 to 44. Figure 6.13 is derived from Table 6.12, and shows the proportion of total losses in both periods which are women.

Figure 6.13 shows that the drop in numbers between 1989 and 1998 was especially among females aged 15 to 29. Between 1998 and 2005 this has changed, and is now much more likely to be women aged 30 to 44; 72% of losses in that age-group in this period were female. Furthermore the overall proportion of

Figure 6.13: Proportion of women in losses by age-group, 1989–2005

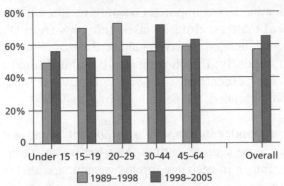

losses which were female has risen from 57% in the 1990s to two-thirds, 65%, overall between 1998 and 2005.

This loss therefore must be taken very seriously. Between 1998 and 2005 English churches saw 51,000 fewer women in church every Sunday per year, a cumulated loss of over a third of a million people, 357,000. Of these 51,000 lost each year, three-fifths, 29,000, were aged between 30 and 64, the years when many women are bringing up their families and also holding down a full-time job. More than half of this 29,000 loss occurred among women aged 30 to 44.

The number of men 65 and over attending church *increased* on an annual average between 1998 and 2005, but while women in this age-group had also increased between 1989 and 1998 they decreased between 1998 and 2005, some of which may have been normal mortality.

While men are leaving the church, they were doing so between 1998 and 2005 at only half the rate at which the women were leaving. That suggests that in some churches men are being made "to feel useful, to find solutions, to make a special contribution", factors found important for retaining male allegiance[51].

The fact that men are becoming a slightly increasing proportion of church attenders is important because research has found that in spiritual matters, children take their cues from Dad. When both parents attended church regularly, 33% of children grew up to attend regularly; if Dad went regularly but Mum only occasionally, the percentage was 38%; if Dad went regularly and Mum never attended, the percentage rose to 44%[52]!

Looking at gender in this way is important because it enables the losses to be seen over time. Another way is simply to say what percentage in each age-group are men, and this is given in Table 6.14:

Table 6.14: Percentage of men by age-group, 1979–2005

Year	Under 11 %	11–14 %	15–19 %	20–29 %	30–44 %
1979	<------ 50 ------>		44	45	44
1989	<------ 48 ------>		43	40	41
2005	*46*	*49*	*51*	*45*	*44*
2005 Pop	*51*	*51*	*51*	*50*	*50*

Year	45–64 %	65–74 %	75–84 %	85 & over %	**OVERALL %**
1979	45	<------------------- 39 ------------------->			**45**
1989	41	<------------------- 37 ------------------->			**42**
2005	*42*	*40*	*38*	*34*	***43***
2005 Pop	*49*	*48*	*41*	*29*	***49***

The percentage of men aged 15 to 19 and in their 20s has increased, which means that it is the percentage of women in these age-groups which has decreased. Men in fact are just in the majority in the 15 to 19 age-group, but remain in the minority in all others. Is this because so many young women aged 10 to 14 left the church in the 1990s?

The bottom line of Table 6.14 gives the population percentages of men in each age-group. Men are fewer proportionately in the church in every age-group except for those aged 15 to 19 and 85 and over.

Gender by denomination

The figures by age-group can also be broken down by denomination, but these are given in *Religious Trends* rather than here[53]. Table 6.15 does, however, give the percentage of men by denomination, the percentage of women being found by subtracting these percentages from 100%.

Table 6.15: Male percentage of attendance by Denomination, 1979–2005

Year	Anglican %	Baptist %	Roman Catholic %	Independent %	Methodist %	New Churches %
1979	45	43	46	47[1]	40	n/a
1989	39	40	45	49[1]	37	n/a
2005	40	41	45	48	36	50

Year	Orthodox %	Pentecostal %	United Reformed %	Smaller Denoms. %	OVERALL %
1979	45	44	43	44	**45**
1989	44	43	37	41	**42**
2005	45	49	35	42	**43**

[1] Includes New Churches

The three denominations with the smallest percentage of men are the United Reformed Church (35%), the Methodist Church (36%) and the Anglicans (40%), each substantially lower than the overall average. All three denominations have a lower percentage of men in every age-group, except for the URC and Anglicans among those aged 65 to 74, and Anglicans aged 75 to 84. Not every denomination finds itself able to keep men. Gender and age are related in the sense that women live longer than men, so older churches will tend to be more female.

The three denominations with the highest proportion of men are the New Churches (50%), the Pentecostals (49%) and the

Independents (48%), again well above the overall average. All three denominations have more than 50% of their children who are boys, and the Pentecostals have a majority of men among all age-groups under 45. The New Churches and Independents have a majority of men under 20 and aged 30 to 44.

Gender by churchmanship
Table 6.16 gives the proportion of men by churchmanship, with again detailed figures broken down by age-group being given in *Religious Trends*[54]. As can be seen there is virtually no change since 1989, other than a slightly greater proportion of male charismatics.

Table 6.16: Male percentage of attendance by Churchmanship, 1989 and 2005

Year	Anglo-Catholic %	Broad %	Catholic %	Broad Evangelical %	Mainstream Evan. %
1989	40	39	44	40	41
2005	41	40	46	41	43

Year	Charismatic Evan. %	Liberal %	Low Church %	All Others %	**OVERALL %**
1989	42	39	37	41	**42**
2005	45	39	37	42	**43**

Gender by environment
There is very little variation in the gender of churchgoers by environment. Those in City Centres are slightly more likely to be male (45% to the average 43%), and those on Council Estates slightly less (41%). Again details by age-group are given in *Religious Trends*[55].

How can this information be used?
This Chapter is full of data which can often be confusing. How may it be useful?

1) This Table illustrates one particular church which completed the Census, showing the proportions in the congregation broken

down by age and gender. Creating a similar Table for your church could be interesting.

Table 6.17A: Age and gender proportions of a Coventry congregation, 2005

Age-group	< 11 %	11–14 %	15–19 %	20–29 %	30–44 %	45–64 %	65–74 %	75–84 %	85/85+ %	TOTAL
Male	5	2	1	1	8	12	8	2	0	**39**
Female	6	2	0	2	16	20	10	4	1	**61**

2) Compare the figures thus obtained with the figures for a similar Table for (a) your denomination, (b) your churchmanship, (c) your environment, (d) your county, or (e) just generally for the whole country. The overall figures for England [the (e) option] are given in Table 6.17B:

Table 6.17B: Age and gender proportions of all English congregations, 2005

Age-group	< 11 %	11–14 %	15–19 %	20–29 %	30–44 %	45–64 %	65–74 %	75–84 %	85/85+ %	TOTAL
Male	6	3	3	3	7	10	7	4	0	**43**
Female	7	3	2	4	9	14	10	6	2	**57**

3) Compare the two Tables. Look at gender first: the 39% male in the Coventry church Table is less than the 43% overall in churches. Are there actions that the Coventry church could take to keep and/or attract more men? Some of the things that men like to do are given in this chapter. Why not ask some of the men who come what they would like to see the church do so that they could invite their friends or colleagues? Run an Alpha or other outreach course? Put on a quiz night in a local pub? Start a mid-week service at a relevant time? [One church in West Yorkshire has a 6.55am Tuesday Mass for those needing to catch their 7.35am train].

4) Next look at the totals of the percentages of those under 20. This Coventry church is especially low on teenagers, of both

genders. What kinds of activity might attract such young people? Are there those in the church who could lead a Teenage Group? What would be needed to resource them? Should a Youth Worker be employed?

5) Look next at those in their 20s. Again this church has a much smaller proportion than in churches generally. Could the minister meet with his Church Council and try and think strategically about what needs to be done to encourage more to attend? Ask those who already come what more might be done. Where is the church going? People in their 20s are often attracted by what the church does and what it aims to become.

6) Look at those aged 30 and above. This particular church has an above average proportion of those aged 30–64 attending. Since this is the group which generally is seeing much decline, that is good news! How can the church build on that strength? The Census shows that women in this age-range tend to drop out of church – are there any signs of that beginning to happen in this church? This church has about the same average of older people as in the overall church, which suggests that it needs to focus on those aged 15 to 30 as the key target area.

7) Finally, this Coventry church could compare its own experience with those of like denomination, churchmanship, environment and location. Take an overview asking where the church is likely to be in say 10 years time. What steps should be taken in the next two years in order that the church might fulfil its vision by 2015?

This is not meant to be a quick or easy process, but rather a time of the leadership thinking about the present situation, where it is going, and pondering what they would like the church to become in the days ahead. It may take a lot of discussion, but can generate excitement as risks are taken in order to move forward – and, who knows, attendance may grow since vision can be very attractive!

Summary of main findings

This is the longest Chapter in the book. What has it shown?

- *Child decline less.* The percentage of those attending church aged under 15, 19%, has not changed since 1998, the main losses of young people occurring in the 1990s. The drastic loss has therefore slowed to an average rate.

- *Young people declining most.* The percentage of those attending aged 15 to 29 has dropped to 12% from 15% in 1998. In part this is a consequence of the earlier huge loss, but nevertheless represents a serious fall. The overall drop in the 20 to 29 age-group was –29%, the highest of any age-group and double the overall decline of –15%.

- *Middle-age decline is especially female.* The proportion of people attending aged 30 to 44 has declined 1% to 16% since 1998, relatively small overall, but more serious when broken down by gender since it is the women in this key age-group who are leaving much much more than men (72% of leavers are women). At an overall decline of –23%, this age-group saw the third largest decline since 1998.

- *Pressure for women.* Aside from young people and those 75 and over, it is those in their 40s who have declined most in the last decade in absolute numbers. This is the age when many women are returning to work after having a family so that home, work and family pressures become intense. Sunday working in Britain is particularly high among women of this age. How can the church be supportive and relevant to people in this situation? Should services be held at more convenient times, or during the week? The rate of decline of women aged 30 to 64 is of similar crisis proportions as the number of children leaving the church in the 1990s.

- *Proportion of women.* Women are leaving the church twice as fast as men, 51,000 a year to 27,000. As a consequence the proportion of men in the church has increased to 43% against 42% in 1989 and 1998.

- *Older people increasing.* The proportion aged 45 to 64 is unchanged since 1998 at 24%, and hence declining at the same overall rate, while the proportion of older people has increased from 25% 65 and over to 29%, especially those in their "Third Age", 65 to 74. The number of men 85 and over has increased in numerical terms.

- *Grandparents vital.* There are many grandparents in church, many of whom are already being used effectively in keeping the church running, teaching and reaching others. Could more be done in training and using this important group?

- *Average age up.* The overall average age of churchgoers has therefore increased to 45 from 43 in 1998, against a population average of 40.

- *Youngest denominations.* Those in Pentecostal Churches are the youngest (average age is 33), followed by those in the New Churches (34) with their special focus on young people. These two denominations also have the highest percentage of men in their congregations.

- *The oldest denominations* by far are the Methodists and United Reformed Church both of whose average age is 55, and who both have 47% of their overall attendance 65 or over, and almost a quarter (23% and 24% respectively) 75 and over. These two denominations also have the smallest percentage of men in their congregations.

- *Marital status.* The number of married people in church is greater than in the population as a whole. Single people, those cohabiting and lone parents are under represented, key groups which are growing in the population and somehow need to be included more in the life of the church.

Looking behind the detail
Of all the numbers what are the key trends here?

A) The decline in the age-group 15 to 29 is serious, but was probably inevitable given the enormous losses of younger people in the 1990s. This cohort of church people will be smaller in every subsequent age-group as they get older. The decadal analysis in Table 6.4 shows that those in their 20s have actually declined less than those either younger or older, confirming that the current drop is more of a consequence of past decline than present dissatisfaction.

B) While it is in some ways comforting to know that the decline in young people has stabilised, it should be noted that girls are leaving more than the boys. 46% of those under 11 were boys; thus 54% are girls. But only 51% of those aged 11 to 14 are girls, and just under half, 49%, of those aged 15 to 19 are young women. As overall, 57% of church-goers are women, these percentages suggest an increasing disillusionment in church by young women, perhaps because they see the pressure their mothers are under and react accordingly, or because their lifestyle is deemed incompatible with the church (nearly a sixth, 15%, of girls aged 15 to 18 attending church more than once a month have had sex[56], as against 6% of boys that age[57]). "For young people, sexual activity and the use of alcohol and other drugs are entwined"[58].

C) However, the decline in women aged 30 to 64 is extremely serious, not simply because many such women are the field force for many a church activity, but because the key reason is the clash of priorities they face in their general life-style. That this has happened elsewhere (in Scotland) confirms the analysis, but does not solve the problem. The overall numbers dropping out are large and thus will have severe repercussions a generation ahead. On the other hand, few of these women are actually *leaving* the church; as the next chapter will show, they are in many cases simply attending less frequently.

D) The increasing proportion of older people, 65 and over, with their actual number virtually unaltered since 1998, is good for numbers now, but in a decade or so, will leave a big hole in the church. It is important to use them while they are able, especially as the proportion of those in their Third Age, 65 to 74, has increased, those who are of grandparent age if not necessarily actually such. These still have energy and enthusiasm for the church, and, more importantly, have the time to help, train and host events.

E) In the context of age and gender, denominational variations proved much more important than churchmanship or environment. What can other denominations learn from the youthful Pentecostals and New Churches, the one growing with its influx of ethnic diversity, and the other declining although parts are growing through church planting? The two denominations, Methodists and URC, which have virtually half their attendance 65 or over, and a quarter 75 or over, are in serious trouble, and possibly even terminal decline. How can those individual churches within each group which are bucking the trend be encouraged and enabled?

F) Those absent from the church, the singles, lone parents and those cohabiting, also need serious strategic evaluation as to how they might be attracted. If friendship and acceptance are needed to attract them, is this something that larger churches, big enough to have a number of people in each category, should especially focus on? Are there ways in which groups of churches could work together for this purpose?

7 Prayerful sunbathing
[Frequency and size analysis]

The phrase "prayerful sunbathing" is attributed to the Archbishop of Canterbury in a *Church Times* article which summarised the results of a survey on how the general public regarded church buildings[1]. Five-sixths, 86%, claimed "to have been in a place of worship in the past year", which would include attendance at baptisms, weddings, funerals, remembrance and memorial services, and other times. Since "in a consuming society an alternative consciousness is surely difficult to sustain"[2] this is encouraging. In this chapter we look at regular worship attendance.

Fewer people are attending church on an average Sunday, but those who do go are going more frequently. That is the conclusion that emerges from asking for the numbers attending individual churches on one particular Sunday in 2005, and requesting those attending to say how frequently they usually came, or if they were visiting.

Visitors
Overall, 5% of those attending church services in May 2005 were visitors to the church, the same percentage as in 1998. How this varied by denomination, churchmanship and environment is shown in Table 7.1 on the next page.

The Orthodox and the Anglo-Catholics had the highest percentage of visitors (9% each) and churches on Council Estates the lowest (3%). One large Evangelical church in Nottingham attended by a substantial number of students computerised all its data and sent Christian Research a copy of the print-out. That Sunday they had 7% of their congregation who were visitors, the large majority of

Table 7.1: Percentage of Visitors (V) in 2005

Denomination	V%	Churchmanship	V%	Environment	V%
Anglican	6	Anglo-Catholic	9	City Centre	5
Baptist	4	Broad	5	Inner City	5
Roman Catholic	4	Catholic	4	Council Estate	3
Independent	5	Broad Evangelical	4	Suburban	5
Methodist	5	Mainstream Evan	5	Separate Towns	5
New Churches	4	Charismatic Evan	4	Other built-up	5
Orthodox	9	Total evangelical	4		
Pentecostal	7	Liberal	6	Commuter Rural	6
United Reformed	4	Low Church	6	Remoter Rural	7
Smaller denoms.	5	All others	7		
				Overall	**5**

whom said they read their Bible regularly. That does not prove they were all necessarily habitual churchgoers, but it does suggest that the bulk of them were churchgoers who normally attended other churches and that Sunday were visiting friends or relatives or just wanted to try a different church. If that is true of most visitors in most churches, then "visitors" will not normally mean less-than-regular or non-churchgoers, and the percentage of visitors is not a means unfortunately of reliably estimating the evangelistic opportunity these people may represent.

Nevertheless the numbers are important: 5% of 3,166,200 people is just under 160,000, and if, say, 75% of these are regular churchgoers attending elsewhere on a particular Sunday, that leaves 40,000 non-regular churchgoers every week, or an average of say 1 per church per week. How do churches best spot their non-church visitors, and welcome them? Two large churches both of which I visited in July 2001 (a Baptist Church in Torquay and an Anglican Church in Norwich) happened to have at least one identical feature – two places at the rear of their church which served coffee or tea after the service. One was labelled "Church members" and a charge was made; the other was labelled "Visitors" and the coffee there was free. Visitors could thus choose – pretend to be a member, pay for your coffee, but remain anonymous; or get free coffee and a welcome from someone deliberately standing nearby.

Some churches held a baptism service (as part of their regular activities) on Census Sunday and specifically included the number of extra visitors on their form. One church in St Albans saw its Sunday attendance of 168 increase by a quarter with an extra 44 people, for this reason[3].

Frequency of attendance

If those who attend monthly or more frequently are deemed "regular", then of regular attenders:

1998

- 18% attend twice a week   [15%]
- 65% attend once a week   [59%]
- 11% attend once a fortnight, and [14%]
- 6% attend just once a month.   [12%]

Thus, two-thirds, 65%, of regular churchgoers in 2005 went on a weekly basis, with the other third split virtually evenly between more frequently and less frequently. The 1998 percentages are given in square brackets, and show that in the seven years since then, regular churchgoers are attending *more* often, not less. The difference is not huge; perhaps regular churchgoers are attending four more services over a year in 2005 than they did in 1998[4].

Many churches used the "slips" described on page 147 in order to obtain precise information on the frequency with which people attended church; other churches estimated the figures. Three times more churches actually counted the answers than estimated them. These two streams of data are amalgamated in the above answers as a statistical test showed they were not significantly different[5]. The counted figures mean that almost 350,000 people personally described their church-going frequency, a very high number. It suggests that the above percentages are as accurate a portrait in 2005 as one is likely to get.

Frequency of attendance by denomination

These percentages varied greatly by denomination, but not very much by churchmanship: Charismatics attended most frequently, with 25% going twice on Sundays, and Liberals least often, with 12% going twice. These two churchmanship variations are similar to churchgoing in the United States[6]. Figure 7.2 shows denomination frequency in order of that frequency:

Figure 7.2: Frequency of church attendance by denomination, 2005

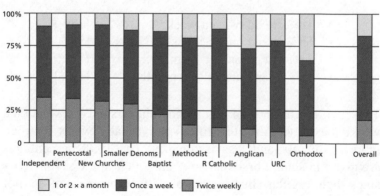

Four denominations have a much higher attendance commitment than others: the Independents, New Churches, Pentecostal and Smaller Denominations, all of which have at least 30% of their regulars attending twice a week. (This is a higher percentage of New Church attendance than reported in the United States[7]). In contrast there is the Orthodox of whom more than a third, 36%, attend less frequently than weekly, and the Anglican church where over a quarter, 27%, attend fortnightly or monthly (17% and 10% respectively).

Roman Catholic weekly attendance is higher than in some Catholic countries on the continent. In Belgium, for example, some 33% of the population say they are practising Catholics, but only attend Mass once a month[8].

The two denominations with the highest average age, the Methodists and United Reformed Church, have the next highest percentages of those who attend least frequently (19% and 21% respectively fortnightly or monthly).

Slips

In order to help churches count the number of people by age and gender, and to ascertain the frequency of attending, their ethnicity and Bible reading habits, a page of 5 "slips" of paper was supplied along with the questionnaire. It was suggested that this be photocopied by the church, and then cut up into individual slips and given out to those attending the services.

It was the intention that the person completing the form would count the ticks on these slips and put the resulting totals in the relevant places on the questionnaire. Most were kind enough to do this, but some returned the slips to us as well. Other churches returned their slips *without* completing the form. A few of those returned showed they had been completed by people with humour: one person, for example, ticked they were both white (and added "in the winter") and non-white (and added "tanned during the summer")!

These returned slips, however, gave rise to an unexpected opportunity for analysing the results in more detail than had been expected. So we are very grateful to the 160 churches, virtually 1% of the churches replying to the Census, which between them returned nearly 8,500 slips, a substantial number which reasonably allows extra analysis[9].

Here we look at how these individual slips show the frequency of churchgoing by age, gender and ethnicity[10].

Frequency of attendance by age

How often do different aged people attend church? Figure 7.3
shows, not surprisingly that children under 11 are very unlikely
to attend twice on a Sunday, and that while two-thirds of
children, 70%, attend every week, one in seven, 15%, attends
once a fortnight, and 8% attend only monthly. Older young
people go more often and the fact that those under 11 on average
attend church least frequently of all almost certainly reflects the
lesser frequency of those aged 30 to 44 which is seen very
clearly in the diagram.

Figure 7.3: Frequency of church attendance by age-group, 2005

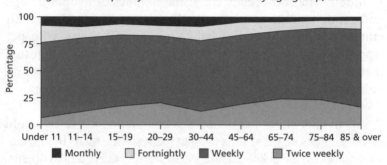

The last chapter showed that those aged 30 to 44 had declined very
sharply in numbers attending since 1998. However, the drop is not
because they have left the church but mostly because they are coming less often. If parents come less often so do their children. Thus
part of the child decline in attendance is not children leaving the
church but coming less frequently. Of those aged 30 to 44, 13%
attend fortnightly and 9% monthly (against overall percentages of
11% and 6%). Part of the pressure for many in this age-group are
the combined pressures of home, family and work, with church
one pressure too many. One answer is to hold church services at
more convenient times. St Nicholas', an Anglican church in
Sevenoaks, Kent, started a 4 o'clock service in a local school
in 2006 so that, in part, parents could come after their
children had played football in the morning[11].

The frequency of attendance for those either side of the 30 to 44 age-group, those aged 20 to 29 and 45 to 64, is greater. While the number of those in their 20s attending church is relatively few, those who do come attend very regularly. Those who are in their Third Age (65 to 74) and those aged 75 to 84 attend the most regularly of all, this regularity falling among those aged 85 and over presumably because of frailty, lack of transport or living in a residential home.

Some American research on the frequency of adolescent attendance at church has shown that, in part, it depends on their personality. Thus 54% of those who went to church every week agreed they like to take risks against 60% who went less often than once a month[12]. Such research if replicated and undertaken across more age-groups might help in understanding better the frequency with which people attend.

Frequency of attendance by gender

Calculating the average attendance per year by age-group and gender allows the graphs of Figure 7.4 to be drawn:

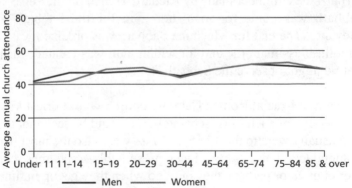

Figure 7.4: Average annual attendance by age and gender, 2005

Figure 7.4 shows that boys under 15 attend church more frequently than do girls of the same age, but young women aged 15 to 29 attend more than young men. Women are slightly less

regular than men in the 30 to
44 age-group, suggesting that
while fewer women come
regularly, most often it is a
joint decision of a couple and
not the woman opting out
alone. Women aged 75 to 84
are more frequent than men.
Overall, women attend weekly
services more frequently.

Frequency of attendance by ethnicity

Five-sixths, 83%, of non-white churchgoers attend church just once
on a Sunday[13], compared with three-fifths, 62%, of white people.
White people are more likely to attend twice – almost one-fifth,
19%, do so, compared with a tenth, 10%, of non-white[14]. White
people are three times more likely to go to church fortnightly or
monthly, 19%, compared with 7% for non-white churchgoers.

This all adds up to saying that for non-white churchgoers,
church attendance is essentially a once-only weekly event.
Perhaps the comment made by Richard Trench on the verse "the
Sabbath was made for man, not man for the Sabbath"[15] is
relevant: "The end for which the Sabbath was ordained was that
it might bless man; the end for which man was created was not
that he might observe the Sabbath"[16].

In one multi-racial Roman Catholic church whose priest kindly
sent details for each Mass separately[17], it could be seen that those
who usually went to the 12.15pm Mass were also the most likely
to attend less than weekly – lunch presumably sometimes scored
over church, or perhaps they only go when they get up in time!

Attending less frequently than monthly

The questionnaire asked those completing it to estimate
the additional numbers of people who came to the church on a

quarterly, half-yearly or annual basis. Naturally these increase the percentage of people attending church during the course of a year. Adding in these extra people and expressing the results as a percentage of the population, we get the following percentages for Sunday attendance (these figures will be modified when those coming mid-week are added; details are in Chapter 10):

It should be noted that the 6.3% of the population in church on an average Sunday is made up of two groups of people: the core who attend weekly (5.2% in 2005 against 4.4% in 1998) and variable attenders who were present when the count was taken (1.1% in 2005 against 3.1% in 1998).

Over 2 weeks, attendance is the same 5.2% who come weekly and another 1.7% of variable attenders who happen to be in church on a particular Sunday, giving a total of 6.9%. The 1.7% is a larger proportion than the 1.1% because it is spread over a fortnight. The numbers below show how the numbers build up to a total of 14.5% who attend at least once a year.

- 5.2% attend weekly + 1.1% that week   =   6.3%
- 5.2% attend weekly + 1.7% in 2 weeks   =   6.9%
- 5.2% attend weekly + 2.1% monthly   =   7.3%
- 5.2% attend weekly + 2.8% quarterly   =   8.0%
- 5.2% attend weekly + 4.7% in six months =   9.9%
- 5.2% attend weekly + 9.3% annually   = 14.5%

The percentages which have slipped most between 1998 and 2005 are those who attend monthly (down 2.9%) or quarterly (down 3.3%). This suggests that churchgoing has moved in two directions:

A) Those who go regularly have, if anything, *increased* their regularity;

B) Those who don't attend regularly (weekly or fortnightly) have, if anything, *decreased* their regularity.

It should be noted that the percentage attending once a year, which, for the huge majority, will be at Christmas, has dropped a relatively small percentage. More than twice as many people go to church at Christmas than are in church each Sunday: the 14.5% means some 7.3 million people attend church at Christmas, one person (adult or child) in 7 in England. Figures published regularly by the Church of England[18] show that almost two-fifths, 37%, of these, 2.7 million, will be at Anglican churches[19]. The 7.3 million people in church once a year is made up of 2.6 million in church every week, and a further 4.7 million who go to church at least once a year.

For many people "going to church" is part of their Christmas activity, whether this be one of the increasingly popular Christingle services which draw young people, the more traditional carol services or the Christmas Eve midnight communion or eucharist. A number of churches in the south east of England known to the author now have two carol services rather than one to accommodate all who wish to come.

Not attending at all

What is not known from these percentages, and indeed not known at all, is the percentage of people who used to be regular churchgoers and who no longer attend, except perhaps at Christmas, not because they have lost their faith, but for other reasons. They are still Christian believers, with other regular overt religious behaviour such as praying or reading the Bible, but not going to church.

It is possible, though debatable, that stopping-going-to-church for preventable reasons is something which has only really developed over the last 25 years. There are 2.3 million fewer churchgoers in 2005 than in 1979 (Table 2.2). If a third, 32%, of these have chosen to stop altogether[20], then some 730,000 churchgoing people have stopped attending. This represents some 1.4% of the population, somewhat less than the 3.5% estimated of the United States population who are "self-proclaimed born-again Christians in the USA who have not been to church in the past 6 months, other than Christmas or Easter"[21].

Size of church

We turn now to the second topic of this Chapter. The smallest churches in England have congregations in single figures and the largest have congregations in five figures. Table 2.17 gave the average size of a congregation across all denominations as 84 people in 2005, and Figure 7.5 shows the percentage of churches of different sizes and the percentage of the total churchgoers who attend them.

Figure 7.5: Size of English churches, 2005

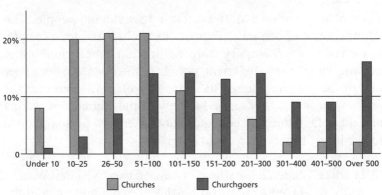

There is a massive imbalance.

- 25% <-> 70%. Those attending the smallest churches which have a congregation of 100 or fewer people amount to a quarter, 25%, of all churchgoers, but they attend more than two-thirds of churches, 70%.

- 50% <-> 26%. The middle band of 50% of churchgoers attend 26% of the churches with congregations between 101 and 400.

- 25% <-> 4%. The final quarter of churchgoers, 25%, attend just 4% of churches, those with congregations of over 400.

Larger churches

The numbers attending churches classified as "Over 500" include many large Roman Catholic churches whose collective Mass attendance on a Sunday (and Saturday Vigil Mass) is frequently in four figures, as well as the very large Pentecostal churches mentioned in Chapter 2 and the large Anglican churches, especially in Greater London. There are perhaps 500 churches (1.3% of total) with four-figure congregations, 90% Roman Catholic, who collectively account for perhaps a fifth, 20%, of all church attendance[22]. These large churches are invariably heavily involved with their local communities, providing many needed services.

They also often have staff available to welcome people. The administrator of one large Baptist church in Kent, for example, answered a casual enquiry from a Christian couple thinking of moving into the area by giving details of the town. An hour later one of the pastors phoned the wife to welcome them into the area; by post next day arrived a copy of the church's magazine and other literature; a week later another church person phoned to ask if any further help could be given.

St Thomas' Church in Sheffield organised two "Visitors' Weeks" in 2006, produced a colourful leaflet to explain them, and the special events visitors could attend if they wished. The leaflet gave a photo and brief biography of the church senior leaders whom a visitor might expect to meet.

The vicar of an expanding Anglican church in south London heard that a Christian family was moving into his Borough not far from his church. He personally called on them on the very day they moved in, said, "I'm not stopping; I know you are busy. I just wanted to welcome you to this town. God bless you. Contact me if I can help further," and left his card. That two-minute encounter was the mechanism by which the family felt they should visit that church, and later joined, staying as members for over 35 years.

The Anglican church in the village of Oxshott, Surrey, has a team which visits everyone who moves into the village within a couple of weeks to provide help with practical information on locating doctors, dentists, etc. and, of course, to give a personal invitation to one of the church services. "Most people change churchgoing habits when something else is changing in their lives."[23]

Different church sizes

The proportions of churches of different sizes is changing as shown in Table 7.6[24], with the percentage which have under 26 people more than doubling since 1989 (13% to 28%):

Table 7.6: Size of church, 1989–2005

Year	Under 11 %	11 to 25 %	26– 50 %	51– 100 %	101– 150 %	151– 200 %	201– 300 %	301– 400 %	401– 500 %	Over 500 %	BASE (=100%)
1989	3	10	22	23	17	10	6	3	2	4	38,607
1998	5	16	19	24	11	7	7	4	2	5	37,717
2005	8	20	21	21	11	7	6	2	2	2	37,501

Although not in the period 1998–2005, the churches between 101 and 200 have shrunk in proportion from 27% to 18% of the total since 1989. The proportion of large churches (over 300) has reduced also from 9% to 6% between 1989 and 2005, although the percentage went up to 11% in 1998 – there are still many large Roman Catholic churches but their sizes are reducing.

The United States uses different size bands for measuring church size, but in 2000 they had 35% of their churches with fewer than 75 people (against our 2005 percentage of 38%), 20% between 75 and 125 (against our 37%) and 45% in excess of 125 (against our 25%), showing that their churches, on the whole, are somewhat larger than ours[25]. Canadian churches are, respectively, 35%, 30% and 35%.

Other research on the size of church has shown that the smaller the church, often the greater the commitment to it. If this is measured in annual giving, then per capita giving in churches with less than 26 people is more than half as much again as per capita giving in churches with 200 or more[26]. However, it is the smaller churches which are most likely to close.

Size of church by denomination

Church sizes also vary hugely by denomination, as the figures in Table 7.7 indicate.

Table 7.7: Percentage for each grouping of churches of different sizes, by denomination, 2005

Denomination	Under 11 %	11 to 25 %	26– 50 %	51– 100 %	101– 150 %	151– 200 %	201– 300 %	301– 400 %	401– 500 %	Over 500 %	BASE (=100%)
Anglican	10	27	24	22	7	4	4	1	½	½	16,247
Baptist	4	10	17	21	13	16	14	3	1	1	2,386
Roman Catholic	½	4	9	13	19	7	10	7½	12	18	3,656
Independent	6	9	18	27	20	15	3	1	½	½	2,281
Methodist	14	21	26	21	9	7	2	0	0	0	5,999
New Churches[27]	½	3½	13	29	19	12	10	5	3	5	1,307
Orthodox	7	26	21	13	11	9	7	4	2	0	317
Pentecostal	2	12	18	17	14	12	11	9	3	2	2,227
United Reformed	7	18	29½	29	12	4	½	0	0	0	1,470
Smaller Denoms.	9	27	15	24	11	7	5	1	½	½	1,611
Overall %	**8**	**20**	**21**	**21**	**11**	**7**	**6**	**2**	**2**	**2**	**100**
Base	3,040	7,403	7,886	8,064	4,096	2,550	2,072	862	636	892	37,501

Five denominations have more than half their churches with congregations of 50 or less: Anglicans and Methodists (both 61%), United Reformed (55%), Orthodox (54%) and the Smaller Denominations (51%). It should be noticed that the combined number of churches with 50 or fewer in their congregations totals over 18,300, virtually half, 49%, of all the churches in the country. More than half of these, 54%, are Anglican.

The percentage of Anglican churches which are over 400 on a Sunday is small but because the number of Anglican churches is large, these represent over 150 places of worship. These will include some cathedrals. Separate studies of the churches in this group[28] show that the majority (54%) are growing and that five-sixths, 83%, were evangelical[29]. The average age of their incumbents (vicars) is slightly younger than average; half have been appointed in the last 10 years; five-sixths, 83%, were appointed to a church that was already large. Their importance is seen in that this 1% of churches accounted for 5% of total Church of England attendance in 1989, 7% in 1998, 9% in 2005 and could be 13% by 2015.

The Roman Catholics have fewer church buildings, preferring greater efficiency in using people and plant. They therefore tend to have much larger congregations and a consequent high proportion of the country's very large churches.

An article looking at size in public services said there were arguments for and against large-ness[30]. Arguments for big organisations were that they usually had better quality leadership, more specialist services, were more professional and more strategic in their operation. Arguments against them were loss of accountability, less attentive to local need, less democratic because there were fewer representatives and that leadership was more distant. The positive arguments will be true of most larger churches, but apart from the loss of accountability most of the arguments against may be less true of these churches.

Size of church by churchmanship

As might be expected, churches of Catholic persuasion have the largest congregations, averaging 206 in 2005. The next largest

are the Charismatic Evangelicals averaging 104 people on a
Sunday, followed by other Evangelicals at 70[31]. The smallest
congregations are those in Low Churches, averaging 36,
followed by Liberals at 46 and Broad and Anglo-Catholic
churches both at 54. These results are in line with earlier
findings. Full details are in *Religious Trends* for those interested
in them[32].

Size of church by environment

However the variations in church size when looking at environment are considerable. Of all the City Centre churches 7% are
over 300 in size; less than 1% in Remoter Rural areas. Two-
thirds, 64%, of Remoter Rural churches have congregations of
25 or fewer against 11% or fewer in Towns, Suburban areas or
Inner City areas. Table 7.8 gives the details.

Table 7.8: Size of church by environment, 2005

Environment	Under 11 %	11 to 25 %	26– 50 %	51– 100 %	101– 150 %	151– 200 %	201– 300 %	301– 400 %	401– 500 %	Over 500 %	BASE (=100%)	Aver- age[33]
City Centre	3	16	21	23	15	10	5	2	2	3	**1,662**	98
Inner City	2	8	24	28	12	8	6	3	4	5	**3,110**	118
Council Estate	3	12	30	26	9	7	4	4	3	2	**2,463**	91
Suburban	1	8	16	26	17	9	10	5	3	5	**8,550**	131
Separate Towns	2	9	17	27	16	11	9	4	2	3	**4,797**	115
Other built-up	4	10	24	29	13	7	6	2	2	3	**1,498**	93
Commuter Rural	9	24	26	21	10	5	4	1	1	*	**6,142**	55
Remoter Rural	23	41	20	10	3	2	1	*	*	*	**9,279**	28
Overall %	**8**	**20**	**21**	**21**	**11**	**7**	**6**	**2**	**2**	**2**	*100*	84

* = Less than 1%

The largest churches are Suburban churches. These are followed
by Inner City and Town churches which also average over 100
per congregation, the former because this is where many Roman
Catholic churches are situated. Commuter Rural churches are

two-thirds the size of an average church, and Remoter Rural churches average half that, 28 people, per congregation.

The frequency with which people attend church varies by size only insofar as the smaller churches, with services held less often, have less frequent attendance.

Size of church by age of attenders

Do people of different age-groups tend to go to churches of different sizes? The answer is shown in Figure 7.9 which gives the proportions of people of different ages in various size of churches.

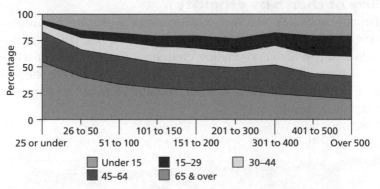

Figure 7.9: Age-group of churchgoers by size of church, 2005

The proportion of young people in a church depends on the size of its congregation. There is an increasing percentage of young people under 15 ranging from 6% in churches under 25 to 21% in churches with about 200 on an average Sunday; thereafter the percentage remains much the same. Likewise there is an increasing proportion of people aged 30 to 44, in many cases the parents of the children. Almost certainly this is due to the availability of youth activities, and shows their importance in attracting young people.

The proportion of older people decreases as church size increases. In small congregations (under 26) they are more than half, 55%, of the total, but this reduces gradually to 20% in the largest churches of all, albeit with a slight "hiccup" increase in churches with congregations between 201 and 300. For some reason also there is a higher proportion of people aged 45–64 in churches with between 301 and 400 (19% to 15%).

This finding (that the proportion of older people decreases as the church gets larger) is not new. It has been previously found in research among the Christian Brethren[34] and the FIEC[35]. Presumably older people are loyal to a declining church which they have attended for a long time, whereas younger people are more likely to leave and go elsewhere.

Size of church by ethnicity

Broadly speaking, the larger the church the greater the proportion of non-white attenders, as Figure 7.10 shows. However this is less true of the very smallest churches (where more non-white attend than might be expected), and also the very largest churches where fewer non-white attend than might be expected from the general trend.

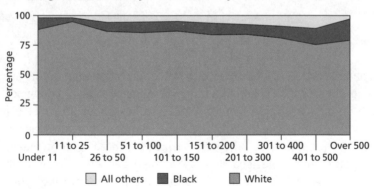

Figure 7.10: Ethnicity of attendance by size of church, 2005

The proportion of non-white attenders increases from 5% in churches with between 11 and 25 in the congregation to 25% in churches with between 401 and 500, reducing to 21% for those churches with over 500. Could this be because there is a greater welcome in these larger churches, or because non-white people feel more at home in a crowd? Perhaps, but some non-white people indicated that they like to go to "successful" churches, and as large churches are seen as successful, they are more attracted to these.

Summary on frequency of attendance

So what has this Chapter found?

- *Population proportions (cumulative).* 6.3% of the population are in church each week, 7.3% attend monthly, 9.9% twice a year and 14.5% once a year. Those who attend church less often than once a month are attending less frequently than previously.

- *Regulars go more often.* Fewer people are attending church on an average Sunday, but those who do go regularly are going more frequently. 18% of churchgoers attend twice a week, 65% once a week, and 17% once or twice a month.

- *Visitors* make up 5% of the average congregation, more in Anglo-Catholic churches (9%) and fewer in Council Estate churches (3%).

- *Variation by denomination.* Frequency did not greatly differ by churchmanship, but they did by denomination. Independent, New Churches, Pentecostals and those in the Smaller denominations attend more frequently and the Orthodox and Anglican less often.

- *Variation by age and gender.* Children under 11 attend church less often than others, and those aged 30 to 44 fall in regularity of attendance by 5% from those in their 20s or those aged 45 to 64, suggesting that the pressure of looking after home and family, as well as working, is sometimes too great. Women attend church more frequently than men.

- *Variation by ethnicity.* Non-white people are more likely to attend church regularly, but only once every week, not twice.

Summary on size of church

This Chapter has also shown:

- *Imbalance between attenders and congregations.* 70% of smaller churches account for only 25% of churchgoers, and, at the other end, 4% of churches account also for 25% of churchgoers.

- *Basic numbers.* While 28% of churches have 25 or fewer people (doubled from 13% in 1989), 42% have between 26 and 100, 24% between 101 and 300, and just 6% are larger than 300 on a Sunday. There are perhaps 500 churches, 90% Roman Catholic, with attendance of over 1,000, who collectively account for perhaps 20% of all church attendance.

- *Variation by environment.* Rural churches are much smaller than average, and City Centre churches much larger. Remoter Rural average 27 on a Sunday, City Centre 154 against an overall average of 84.

- *Variation by age of attenders.* The smaller the church the greater the proportion of older people in the congregation; the larger the church (up to 200 people) the greater the proportion of young people.

- *Variation by ethnicity.* Generally, non-white people form a greater proportion of the congregation the larger the church.

Looking behind the detail

A number of key issues arise from this chapter:

A) If the core are going more often, and the fringe are going to church less often, does this say something about the way churches are currently involved in mission? Should that be changed?

B) *Smaller churches.* Mostly these are in the Remoter and Commuter Rural areas, with far fewer than average attendance. There are huge numbers of such churches, especially Anglican, yet their attenders are the more committed (as measured financially). How viable are they in the long run? This issue keeps on emerging. They have a greater proportion of older people.

C) *Larger churches.* These are found in City Centres, Inner City areas (many Roman Catholic churches there) and Suburban Areas and Towns. They are an increasingly important group, especially among the Anglicans, in that they are attracting a greater percentage of total church attendance. They have a greater proportion of younger people, and a greater proportion of non-white people. They are invariably immersed with community activity, and offer a warm welcome to visitors, Christian and non-Christian.

D) *Middle-sized churches* are literally caught in the middle! A slowly reducing proportion of the whole.

E) Christmas is emerging as an important phenomenon for church attendance. What can churches do to bridge the gap between Christmas attendance and more regular Sunday attendance?

F) One of the more worrying elements is the smaller proportion of those aged 30 to 44 attending church. Will their experience of lesser attendance continue as they get older? How can the churches help alleviate the pressures this age-group faces? How can they make church relevant amidst such pressures? How can they maintain good relationships with them so that when the pressures reduce they feel happy to come more often again?

8   In the Country, Ma'am!
[Age and gender of ministers]

This chapter looks at church leadership, and, as the title might suggest, focusses on the environment where ministers serve (especially rural areas), and their gender. There were an estimated 28,977 ministers across all denominations in England in 2005[1], mostly ordained, male and female, full-time and part-time.

This number includes senior leaders in administrative positions and retired ministers still exercising pastoral responsibility, but what proportion these are of the total is not known: in the Church of England 23% of clergy were not incumbents in 2004[2]. If half that percentage applied for other denominations then in 2005 there would have been an estimated 24,600 ministers responsible for church congregations in England[3], two-thirds, 66%, of the number of churches, or 2 ministers for every three churches.

The English Church Census asked for age, gender and duration of current position for the (senior) minister in each church. 10,113 replies were given, a response rate of 41%, two in every five, and possibly the most extensive study to date obtaining such details. That this response rate breaks down between 36% for male ministers and 75% for female ministers immediately indicates that female ministers are (we are very grateful to note) much more likely to complete census forms, or glad to have been counted! The proportion of female ministers as a percentage of all ministers, allowing for this differentiation in response, was 12.3%, virtually identical to the 11.9% already published[4] which would include all the senior clergy.

Church leaders

There are many leaders in most churches, paid and unpaid, ordained and lay, part-time and full-time, men and women. The questionnaire asked for the number of *paid* staff, and the gender, year of appointment and age of the senior leader. This Chapter focusses on the latter, the person who is frequently the ordained (or at least recognised) minister of a church, the person as some would see it at the top, even if part-time or shared between several churches. It does not include non-stipendiary ministers (to use the Anglican term), that is, those who are unpaid, but would include part-time people who doubled their responsibilities to the church with another job (as in many black churches). Most of the analysis excludes full- or part-time staff, paid or volunteers, ordained or not, who are leaders of the church but simply not the most senior person.

Nearly three–quarters, 72%, of churches had just one full-time, ordained or recognised, leader/minister. One church in ten, 10%, had a part-time leader or minister (sometimes sharing with another church), and the remaining sixth, 18%, of churches had more than one ordained leader of which the very large majority (14% of this 18%) was a full-time second person.

Five-sixths of churches, 84%, have no other full-time non-ordained member of staff. Of the 16% who do, most have just one person (10%) and 3% have two people. Half the churches, 53%, have part-time staff, ordained or not, to help lead them, half of these (52%) having just one person, and a fifth, 22%, having two people, most of the rest having 3 or more.

Number and age

We now turn to the senior minister of the church. Table 8.1 shows the basic proportions by age-group of currently serving church ministers in England and Figure 8.2 how these vary by gender. The average age of churchgoers over 20 is 55, virtually identical to the average age of a minister at 54, which in turn is

Table 8.1: Age of Ministers responsible for congregations in England, 2005

Under 30 %	30–39 %	40–49 %	50–59 %	60–69 %	Over 69 %	Base (=100%)	Average age[6]
1	7	24	45	18	5	10,113	54

very similar to that of a recent earlier study[5] giving it as 53.

Figure 8.2 shows that there is a greater proportion of female ministers in their 50s than men, and smaller proportions at older ages. To one decimal place, the women are a year younger on average than men (53.6 years to 54.8) but the difference is not statistically significant[7].

Figure 8.2: Ministers by age and gender

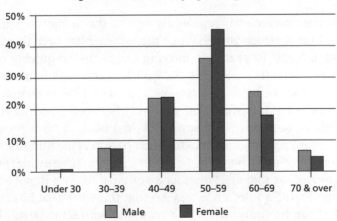

Duration of current appointment

How long had ministers been in post in their present position?
Table 8.3 shows:

Table 8.3: Ministers by number of years in current appointment, in 2005

Year appointed	2001– 2005	1996– 2000	1991– 1995	1986– 1990	1981– 1985	1980 or earlier		
Years in post	Under 5 %	5 to 9 %	10–14 %	15–19 %	20–24 %	Over 24 %	Base (=100%)	Average length
Male Female	43 64	31 28	14 5	6 1	3 1	3 1	7,232 1,581	7.4 yrs 4.8 yrs
All	47	30	12	5	3	3	8,813	6.9 yrs

Nearly half, 47%, of current ministers had been in their post for
under 5 years. Some denominations move ministers on at regular
intervals, like the Salvation Army who usually do so every
5 years. The initial appointment for a Methodist minister is
5 years, but it can be renewed for up to 5 years at a time and
frequently is. Some Methodists stay in a post for 15 years; 10 is
common. Others, like the Church of England, allow ministers to
stay as long as they wish if they have the freehold, although
plans are in hand to begin awarding 5 year contracts.

However, research has repeatedly shown that a church is most
likely to experience growth when the minister has been there for
between 5 and 10 years[8], so moving clergy on too quickly may
be a self-defeating exercise. As Bob Jackson says in his most
recent book, "better to give clergy . . . a 10 or 12-year contract"[9].
Only a third of ministers were currently between 5 and 10 years
in their present post, and some 3% had been in their present
church for 25 years or more. One such person is the minister of a
United Reformed Church in the north east who is an evangelical.
"If I move," he told me, "my successor most likely will not be an
evangelical. So I prefer to stay so that the work that has been
started can be continued in the way that we feel is best." The
church he leads agrees.

It would appear from Table 8.3 that female ministers are perhaps more likely to move more quickly. This may be true, but it might also be because the proportion of female ministers who have been serving one particular church for 15 years or more is very low (3% compared with 12% for male ministers). The Church of England only ordained its first female ministers in 1994, but have ordained many since, so that in 2005 Church of England women ministers were more than a third, 37%, of the total female work-force, but could not have been serving in an incumbency position with the same church for more than 11 years in 2005.

Leadership by denomination

The Church of England is the only denomination which regularly publishes the age-groups of its clergy[10]. There was no significant difference between its proportions, for either male or female incumbent clergy and the sample received in the Census.

There was relatively little variation in age by denomination. The New Churches had the youngest average age for male ministers of 51, and the Roman Catholics and the Orthodox had the oldest, at 59 and 63 respectively, against the overall average of 54. For female ministers, Independent churches averaged 60, with all the others close to the overall average.

There was, however, a distinct variation in the proportion of women ministers by denomination with the Smaller Denominations (incorporating especially the Salvation Army, 57% of whose officers are women), United Reformed, Methodists and Anglicans having the highest percentages – in that order. Figure 8.4 on the next page illustrates.

It will be seen that the percentage of women in Pentecostal churches is about half the overall percentage. This reflects the fact that women are less frequently the senior minister in black or other ethnic diversity churches. It is in white, or largely white, churches that they are more likely to have that responsibility, although not in Independent churches.

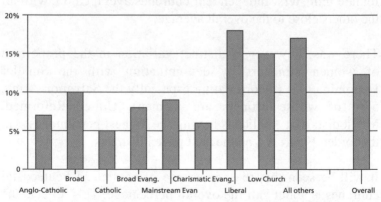

Figure 8.4: Percentage of Female ministers by Denomination, 2005

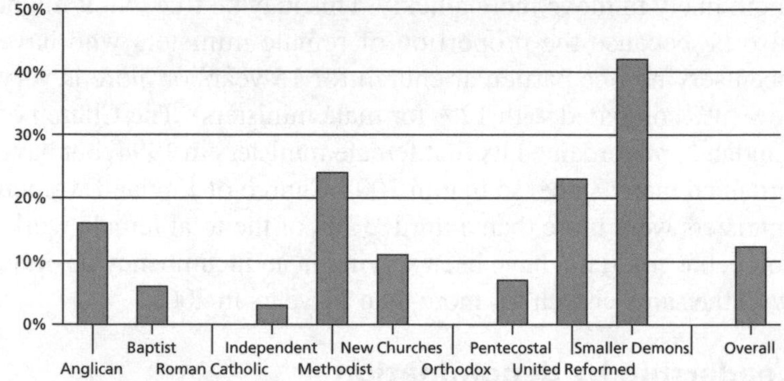

Leadership by churchmanship

Likewise the variations by age-group of ministers by churchmanship were very small, but they did vary by gender. The
Liberals, Others and Low Church have the highest percentage of
female ministers (in that order) and the Catholics, Charismatics
and Anglo-Catholics having the lowest (in ascending order).
Figure 8.5 illustrates.

Figure 8.5: Percentage of Female ministers by Churchmanship, 2005

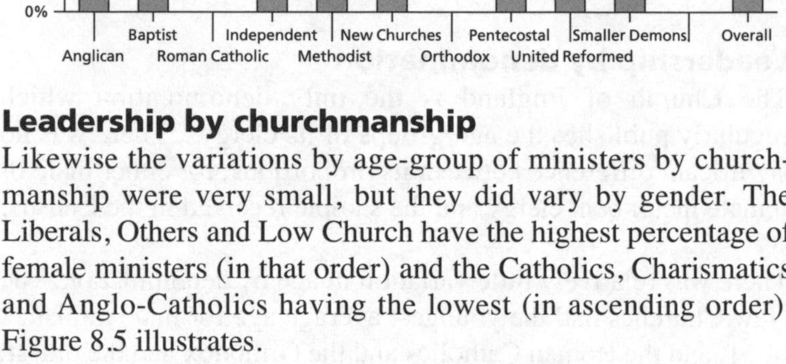

The high proportion of Liberal churches who have women
ministers has been seen in other research: the 2003 Cost of

Conscience survey showed that this was reflected also in basic theological beliefs[11]. The Census showed that just over half, 51%, of women ministers were either Broad or Liberal, and a further third, 30%, either Low Church or "All Others". Collectively, 13% were Evangelical.

Leadership by environment

At a seminar Christian Research was taking on rural ministry in the autumn of 2004, one male minister was heard to say, "Well, of course, they send all the women to rural parishes." Is this true? The Census question gave the opportunity to find out. Like most generalisations, there is some truth in it. More than twice the proportion of churches in Remoter Rural areas are led by a female minister to those in City Centres (16% to 7%), and the difference was statistically significant[12]. This means, like the variations seen across denominations and churchmanships, the variations are important, even though they are smaller. They are illustrated in Figure 8.6.

Figure 8.6: Percentage of Female ministers by Environment, 2005

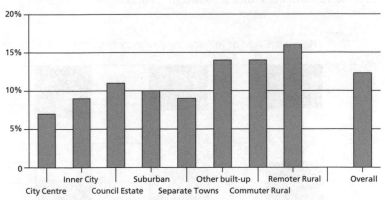

Female ministers are most likely to be serving in Remoter Rural, Commuter Rural, Other Built-up areas. They are also less likely to be responsible for churches in Separate Towns as well as

Inner City and City Centre churches. This could be partly because a slightly higher percentage of Town Churches are Independent than in other environments (16% to 13%) and Independent churches have fewer women ministers.

There is therefore some truth in the statement that "Women look after rural churches" as over half, 56%, of female ministers are responsible for a church in a rural environment. However, another third, 34%, look after churches in suburban, other built-up areas or in separate towns. It is in the city centres where women ministers are far fewer – in the City Centre churches (some of which are very large) and the Inner City areas, perhaps because these are areas of greater violence where personal attack is more likely[13] – but not the Council Estates.

Older ministers, whether male or female, were slightly more likely to be responsible for rural churches and younger ministers, those in city areas, as Figure 8.6 indicates. One eighth, 12%, of ministers under 40 look after a church in a city area, but only 7% of ministers under 40 are in a rural area.

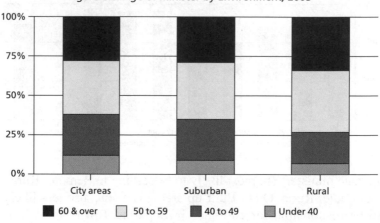

Figure 8.6: Age of minister by Environment, 2005

Leadership by size of church

It is equally possible to examine the age and gender of ministers by the size in 2005 of their present church. This shows three broad trends:

- For churches with 150 or fewer, the smaller the church the older the minister, whether that person be male or female. Thus a church with between 101 and 150 would, on average, have a minister aged 52, whereas a church with fewer than 11 people would have a minister of average age 57.

- Churches with congregations in excess of 150 have in general ministers, male or female, of the overall average age of 54.

- The smaller the church the greater the likelihood of it having a female minister. 2% of churches with between 201 and 300 people have a female minister. This proportion increases gradually until for those fellowships with fewer than 11 people 19% of their ministers will be women.

These trends are important. It may be thought that "the older you are, the smaller your church" is not a philosophy that rewards greater experience, but large firms such as Marks & Spencer are characterised by a retirement pattern not totally dissimilar. The manager of a large store is asked what his/her preferred retirement location will be, and if there is a suitable, but smaller, store in that vicinity, he is invited to become the new manager a few years before retirement. The smaller store thus gains from the experience of having a person used to a more complex operation being at its helm. The same might broadly be said of some church appointments.

In one instance known to the author, the minister of a large (250+) church in Kent asked his Bishop if he would like him to take responsibility for a smaller church in the Diocese whose previous minister had been asked to leave. "I'll turn it round," he said, "before I retire in 5 years time." The Bishop was very willing so to do, and after much hard and strategic work the 60 year old minister increased the congregation of that failing church from 25 to 330 in his final five years.

Figure 8.7 illustrates the proportions of ministers serving different size churches by age.

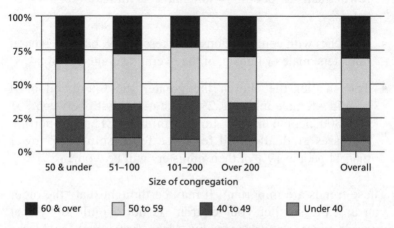

Figure 8.7: Size of church in 2005 by age of minister

The chart shows that older ministers (60 and over) may be more likely to be in the smallest (50 and under) and the largest (over 200) churches. Younger ministers are more likely to be looking after congregations with between 51 and 200 people.

The largest church in England for whom a female minister was responsible, as identified in the Census, was an Anglican church in North Yorkshire, whose total attendance was given as 297 people. This particular minister was in her 50s. Two women ministers had regular access to 350 or more young people, one of whom was a school chaplain in Durham and one a College chaplain in Reading.

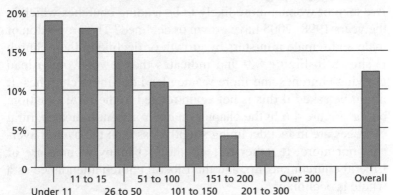

Figure 8.8: Percentage of Female ministers by Size of Church in 2005

It appears that women are appointed to smaller churches, demon-strated by the fact that more than two-fifths, 43%, are responsible for churches of 25 or fewer people, and a further quarter, 26%, lead churches with between 26 and 50 people. Thus two-thirds, 69%, of women ministers look after churches of 50 and under compared with just under half, 47%, of male ministers.

There is some degree of overlap. More female ministers are responsible for rural congregations, which are much smaller than average. Hence it is to be expected that women minsters look after small congregations. At the same time, a fair percent-age of women look after suburban congregations which gener-ally are not small. However, statistically, it is the *environment* rather than the size of the church which is the more significant. That women **tend to be appointed to rural congregations** is the dominant finding rather than that they are asked to be responsible for smaller churches.

This has other consequences. Rural churches often have less reg-ular services, so women ministers are also associated with less frequent church attendance, but again it is the rural connection rather than frequency *per se* which is significant.

Leadership by growth of church

Are men or women more likely to be leading churches which in the years 1998–2005 have grown or declined? The proportion of male and female ministers by growth or decline in their church is shown in Figure 8.9 and indicates that fewer women lead growing churches and more women lead declining churches. It might be asked if this is not again related to the rural situation, but, as Figure 4.6 in the chapter on environment indicates, rural churches are in fact declining slightly less than the overall average, not more. It rather reflects the fact many women are of Liberal churchmanship, and the Liberal church attendance as a whole is declining.

Figure 8.9: Change in Church 1998–2005 by gender of minister in 2005

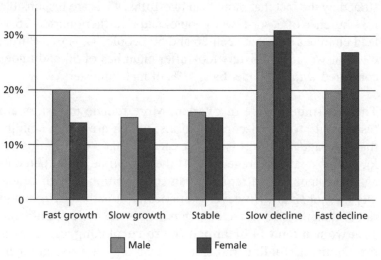

The evidence from Figure 8.9 is very clear. The data relates only to the period between 1998 and 2005 and for those churches which gave information for both those years. The year 1998 was chosen rather than 1989, the year of the second Census, as the Church of England only first ordained female ministers in 1994. Male ministers are more likely to be looking after fast growing churches and less likely to be looking after fast declining churches, and vice versa for women ministers.

It is also possible to identify whether churches were growing or declining in the period 1989 to 1998 (when there was data for both years), and therefore possible to ascertain whether churches which in 2005 had a woman minister were growing or declining in 1998. Not every church with a female minister in 2005 necessarily had a female minister in 1998, and unfortunately we do not know the gender of ministers in 1998, but the question is still worth asking as giving an indication as to whether female ministers simply inherited declining churches or in fact have turned them round. Table 8.10 shows the proportion of churches led by a female minister in 2005 which grew between 1989 and 1998 and grew, became stable or declined between 1998 and 2005, and so on:

Table 8.10: Percentage of female ministers in 2005 by
how their church changed in earlier periods

| | | 1998 to 2005 | | | |
		Grew %	Stable %	Declined %	Overall %
1989	Grew %	11	11	15	13
to	Stable %	10	9	14	12
1998	Declined %	13	15	18	16
	Overall	12	12	16	14

This Table may be read as follows: Between 1989 to 1998 13% overall of churches now led by a female minister grew. This 13% is an overall average of 11% which continued to grow between 1998 and 2005, 11% which became stable, and 15% which declined. 12% of churches led by a female minister in 2005 were stable between 1989 and 1998; this is a combination of 10% which grew between 1998 and 2005, 9% which remained stable and 14% which declined. Between 1989 and 1998 16% of churches now led by a female minister declined, a percentage which is an amalgam of 13% of churches which grew between 1998 and 2005, 15% which remained stable and 18% which have continued to decline.

One sixth, 18%, of churches which saw decline 1989 to 1998 and also declined between 1998 and 2005 were led by a woman minister in 2005. That percentage is higher than the 13% who turned a declining church in the 1990s into a growing church 1998 to 2005. Likewise 11% of churches which grew in the 1990s and have continued to grow since had a woman minister in 2005. But 15% of churches which grew in the 1990s but have declined since were led by a woman minister. Some women have taken on the challenge of a declining church, and, like any minister, male or female, have sometimes succeeded in reversing that trend, and sometimes have failed to do so. Thus although a greater proportion of women ministers in 2005 were responsible for declining churches, given the history of these churches, this was a factor which existed at their appointment and the change experienced between 1998 and 2005 is not necessarily a direct factor due to their gender.

The churches which have changed in terms of their congregations growing or declining are those in the shaded boxes in Table 8.10. The three in the bottom left hand corner are "good" in that their condition has become more positive, while those in the upper right hand corner have become more negative. The balance in female leadership in these two groups is reasonably similar, and such differences as exist are not statistically significant. This shows that the growth or decline of a congregation has much less to do with *gender* of the minister than with his or her *gifting*. Vision and leadership are the key characteristics of growth; lack of vision is a common feature of declining churches. It is the gifts that women deploy which can help a church to grow, and this is equally true for male ministers. Gender is neutral in terms of growth factors.

Age of leadership and growth

Finally it is worth asking if the age of a minister varies with whether a church is growing or not. Previous research, based only on Anglicans[14], showed that the best time for growth was when the minister was in his or her early 40s or early 60s. The Census, taking the findings across all denominations, did not find an ecumenical equivalent to the boost in the 60s, but did show that two-fifths, 40%, of ministers in their 30s were in charge of growing churches, more than those in their 40s, 36%, in turn more than those in their 50s or older, 33%. These findings are illustrated in Figure 8.11.

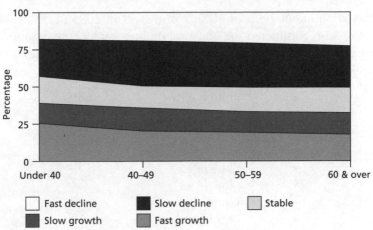

Figure 8.11: Change in church 1998–2005 by age of minister in 2005

A quarter, 25%, of ministers under 40 were responsible for churches which had seen fast growth between 1998 and 2005, against 17% of those 60 and over. It probably takes more energy to lead a fast growing church! Are age and vision correlated? Joel says that "old men shall dream dreams, your young men shall see visions,"[15] so perhaps they are. Among fast growing UK companies, 42% of leaders are under 50, as opposed to 39% overall[16].

Leadership by number of churches

If there are 24,600 clergy for 37,501 congregations, that is an average of 1.5 each. While the majority are responsible for one church, many look after several. This is especially true in rural areas, where, for Anglican clergy at least, "five or six is common and some have as many as 14"[17]. A 1989 survey found that those looking after more than four churches at that time tended to find the strain too great[18]; it may be that with greater lay leadership, more non-stipendiary leadership and different structures the ability to look after more without undue stress has increased. However, other research suggests that "an unacceptably high number of rural clergy show signs of emotional exhaustion from their ministry."[19]   .

Based on an analysis of 10,097 ministers in 2005 (41% of the total) who completed the question on how many congregations they were responsible for, the number of ministers who said they looked after:

•	1 church was	68%
•	2 churches	10%
•	3 churches	7%
•	4 churches	6%
•	5 churches	3%
•	6 churches	2%
•	7 churches	2%
•	8 or 9 churches	1%
•	10 or more churches	1%

giving an average of 1.9 churches per minister, higher than the overall average.[20]

The number varies significantly by denomination[21]. Some denominations have very few ministers responsible for more than one church: the average for the Baptists was 1.0; Independent and New Churches were 1.1 each; Pentecostal and Roman Catholic clergy were 1.2 each; and Smaller Denominations 1.3. The Methodists, whose ministers often look after a circuit, averaged 3.0 churches each. The averages for other denominations, where clergy are often part of a team ministry where, say, three ministers are responsible for 5 churches (so that the above figures do not necessarily mean *sole* responsibility) were between these extremes. Thus Anglicans averaged 3.3 churches each, United Reformed 2.1 and the Orthodox 2.0 each. In many cases, there will also be non-ordained staff who are part of the leadership team, taking some of the burden and stress of accountability.

Nevertheless, the overall percentages are still quite high. One tenth, 10%, of clergy equivalent to 2,500 ministers, are responsible for 5 or more churches; in some of these situations at least the stress level of responsibility is likely to be excessive[22].

The average number of churches for which a minister is responsible did not vary by churchmanship, but not surprisingly it did by environment. Those in rural areas on average looked after twice as many churches as those in non-rural areas (2.7 to 1.4). In Remoter Rural areas, 45% of ministers were responsible for one congregation, 31% for between 2 and 4, and a quarter, 24%, for 5 or more.

Something of the strain of looking after multiple congregations can be seen in the fact that 60% of ministers appointed to what was their current responsibility in May 2005 had been looking after at least two congregations in the previous 5 years. This contrasts with 56% of those appointed 5 to 9 years before, 47% 10 to 14 years before, 39% appointed 15 to 19 years before and 31% who had been in their post for at least 20 years. In other words, multiple responsibilities leads to shorter periods of service. However, it might also be that older ministers seek Remoter Rural appointments before they retire.

Summary

Leadership is a complex of multiple factors, and the Census only focussed on the age, gender and length of appointment of leaders. Issues such as motivation for leadership and calling were not considered in this study, nor how these might vary by age or gender. However, this chapter has found that:

- *Average age*. The average age of a minister in England in 2005 was 54, very similar to the average age of an adult member of their congregation, 55. There were more female ministers in their 50s than male ministers, but smaller percentages in other age-groups.

- *Supporting staff*. Nearly three-quarters, 72%, of churches have just one minister, and five-sixths, 84%, have no other full-time ordained staff. Half the churches, 53%, however, do have the help of part-timers, paid or volunteer, ordained or not, and half of these, 52%, have one such person, and a fifth, 22%, have two.

- *Not enough younger ministers*. Almost half, 45%, of ministers were in their 50s, a quarter, 24%, were in their 40s and a quarter, 23%, 60 or over. There is a dearth therefore of younger leaders.

- *Age of minister by location and growth*. Younger ministers were more likely to be in City Centres; older ministers in Rural areas. Younger ministers are more likely to be responsible for a growing church. 40% of those in their 30s lead such a church against 33% of those 50 or over.

- *Age of minister by size of church*. The smaller the church the older the minister, whether that person be male or female, for churches with congregations of 150 or fewer. The average age of a minister of a church with fewer than 11 people was 57, and 52 for a church with between 101 and 150 people.

- *Length of appointment*. On average ministers had been in their current post for 7 years, men longer than women.

- *Number of churches looked after*. Ministers are responsible on average for 1.9 churches; 68% have one church, 23% have 2 to 4 churches, and 9% have 5 or more. The number varies by denomination, and by location. Those more recently appointed look after more than those who have stayed longest.

- *Women ministers by denomination*. There were more women ministers in percentage terms among the Smaller Denominations (42%), (Methodists (24%), and the United Reformed Church (23%) than generally (12%). There are no female priests serving in either the Roman Catholic or Orthodox churches.

- *Women ministers by churchmanship*. There were more female ministers in churches which were Liberal (18%), Low Church (15%) or Other Churchmanships (17%) than average. Catholic (5%) and Charismatic Evangelicals (6%) had the smallest percentage of female ministers.

- *Women ministers by environment*. There were more women ministers in Remoter Rural (16%) areas than in City Centres (7%). Well over half, 56%, of women ministers serve in a rural area. Rural churches have smaller congregations on average, but it is the environment of the church and not the size of its congregation which is the most significant factor for female ministers.

- *Women ministers by size of church*. The smaller the church the greater the likelihood of it having a female minister. 2% of churches with between 201 and 300 people have a female minister. This proportion increases gradually until for those fellowships with fewer than 11 people 19% of their ministers are women. Two-fifths, 43%, of female ministers have congregations of 25 or less.

- *Women ministers by growth or decline*. Female ministers are often associated with declining churches but when the history of the church is considered this relates more to the state

of the church at their initial appointment than current performance. Churches both grow and decline under both male
and female ministers; it is gifting not gender which is the
key factor.

Looking behind the detail

There is a mass of numbers in this chapter. What are the significant elements?

A) *Female ministers*. More likely to be Methodist, URC or
   Salvation Army (39% are in one of these three), Liberal,
   Low Church or Other churchmanship (65% are in one of
   these three), serving in a Rural area (56% of all) with a
   small congregation, often declining, whose members attend
   church less frequently. Many (45%) are in their 50s. With
   Churchmanship and Denomination very highly correlated,
   the key factors of significance are Churchmanship and
   Location, in that order. Many people would quail at working
   within such a set of constraints, and it must take huge
   courage to keep going when there is so much discourage-
   ment. The very high order of commitment among female
   ministers needs to be noted.

B) *Male ministers*. While all Roman Catholic and Orthodox
   priests are male, there is a significant proportion of ministers
   who are male: Independent (97%), Baptist (94%) or
   Pentecostal (93% each), against the overall percentage of
   88%. They are likely to be Catholic (95%), Charismatic
   (94%) or Anglo-Catholic (93%). They are more likely to
   be serving in the City Centres (93%) or Towns (91%). All
   churches with congregations in excess of 300 people are
   currently led by men.

C) *Growth or decline*. Male and female ministers are equally
   likely to experience growth or decline in their congregations.
   The skill of leadership, the building of vision, increasing the
   size of the congregation are traits which are not primarily

gender related, but God-given gifts and skills developed through training and experience.

D) *Age of ministers*. Younger ministers are more likely to be in growing churches, in larger churches, and in City Centre churches. While statistically age proved less significant when compared with gender, that does not stop age being highly important. It must be a concern that only one minister in 12 is under the age of 40. Existing ministers have to work with, train and help younger ministers or else their ministry fails to have long term effect. If that does not change over the next 20 years there will be a crisis of too few leaders, and, one imagines, an increasing proportion of part-time lay people taking responsibility. Denominations need to have "a solid strategy to train, encourage and release younger leaders at all levels" as one church leader of 50 wrote.

E) *Potential clash*. The percentages given here suggest future pressures. The number (and proportion) of women ministers is increasing[23] and the proportion of evangelicals is also increasing. Given that many women ministers are not evangelical, how far will the placement of women ministers in those locations where non-evangelicals tend to be strong continue? On the other hand, if the type of church that women ministers are likely to be leading is unlikely to change from that described above unless something radically alters, could this prove a problem for future appointments?

F) *Stress level*. The responsibility of multiple ministry can be huge, and the stress level of such accountability very high. Is the process of one person being asked to look after yet more and more churches really the best answer for encouraging growth and local responsibility? This is especially relevant if the average term of service for those in multiple ministries is shorter than those with a single responsibility.

G) *Lonely job*. It has always been known that leadership is a lonely position, but the amount of supporting staff is still surprisingly low. There is a difference between having effectively a managerial position (such as a volunteer looking after the youth work, or acting as church secretary) and having some overall *leadership* responsibility. It is the latter which is in short supply.

Resources

There are many leadership resources available. There is a plethora of books on leadership, numerous websites, many magazines (including the British *Church Leadership*[24] and the American *Leadership*[25]) and a whole range of resources available from various agencies. The *how* of leadership is obviously crucial, but the *who* of leadership and the *where* of leadership are perhaps even more significant items which are less frequently addressed. The conclusion of this Chapter is to suggest that these latter two elements are going to become much more important in the days ahead for the future of the church in this country.

Selection, training and careful placement will therefore become even more vital.

9 Building Churches without Buildings
[Growth and decline]

"More new churches than Starbucks" was the headline of a press release issued for the Mission 21 Conference on church planting held in Sheffield in March 2006. Between 1998 and 2005 481 Starbucks branches started, while the organisers knew of at least 500 new churches which had started in the same period[1]. As Table 1.1 in this volume shows there were actually over 1,000 new churches started in this period, as we were able to count many of the independent, black and other ethnic diversity churches. Behind the headline, however, is an exciting story of growth. Newly planted churches invariably suggest growing churches, but as the heading to this Chapter[2] suggests not every church is necessarily in a building.

I think you should come to an arrangement with Starbucks and offer your growth methodology in exchange for their coffee making expertise!

There is good news and bad news. The **good** news is that a higher percentage of churches have grown in the last 7 years, 34%, than grew in the previous 9 years, 21%. More churches growing has to be encouraging! Furthermore this increase has been taking place over the entire period: a survey which measured Anglican growth separately in both the early 1990s and late 1990s showed that 30% of those churches which grew or were static in the early 90s saw growth in the later 90s[3].

The **bad** news is that overall attendance continues to decrease, despite more growing churches. This is essentially a problem of size. A "growing church" is a single unit, and its growth may be from 10 to 20, or 150 to say 180. If there are many small churches growing, like a lot of small swim-  ming pools filling up, that is good, but if some larger churches are declining, like large swimming pools emptying, then overall levels of attendance (or water) decrease. So if 100 small churches (say a 100 strong) grow by 10 people each (or 10%) that increases attendance by 1,000, but it only takes 40 large churches (say 250 strong) to lose 50 people each (20%) to cancel out the growth.

Measuring growth

Altogether 11 out of every 12 churches in England, 92%, have been kind enough to complete a Census form for Christian Research in either the 1989, 1998 or 2005 surveys. Two-fifths, 42%, of these completed the form in just one of these years[4]; another third, 36%, completed forms in two of the three studies[5], which leaves a seventh, 14%, completing forms in all three Censuses. This 14% is 5,157 churches, more than sufficient as an adequate sample through which growth may be ascertained[6].

Churches which replied to more than one Census had their answers to total attendance compared and the most recent one expressed as a percentage of the earlier one. "Growth" was defined as churches which grew in attendance at least 1% per year on average across the 9 years 1989 to 1998; and because many churches grew more than this their growth rates were divided into four groups: 10% to 24%, 25% to 39%, 40% to 59% and 60% or over. Churches which declined were measured in equivalent steps, but negatively. Churches growing between

1998 and 2005 were measured at the same rate of growth but the percentages for the break points were slightly different because it was a shorter period[7]. Churches whose change was between ± 9%[8] were described as "Stable". Likewise churches which only answered the 1989 and 2005 studies were analysed for growth, with different percentages for the same breakpoints.

A nine-point scale was thus created, four stages of growth, one of stability, and four stages of decline. Statistical tests were applied across all nine points where numbers permitted, but for presentation here for simplicity this scale is reduced to five elements: fast growth (40% of more), slow growth (10% to 39%), stability (9% to –9%), slow decline (–10% to –39%) and fast decline (–40% or over), except for Table 9.1 which gives the overall figures:

Table 9.1: Percentages of churches in various growth/decline rates

Period	Fast growth		Slow growth		Stable
	Growth 60% or more %	Growth 40–59% %	Growth 25–39% %	Growth 10–24% %	Stable +9 –> –9% %
1989–1998	7	<– – – –	14[9]	– – – –>	14
1998–2005	14	5	6	9	16
1989–2005	7	5	6	10	23

Period	Slow decline		Fast decline		
	Decline –10 to –24% %	Decline –25% to –39% %	Decline –40% to –59% %	Decline of 60% or more %	Base (=100%)
1989–1998	16	17	18	14	8,681[10]
1998–2005	15	14	14	7	7,182
1989–2005	21	17	9	2	11,908

This Table may be read as follows: Between 1989 and 1998, 21% [7% + 14%] of churches grew at least 10%, 14% remained stable, and 65% [16% + 17% + 18% + 14%] declined. While this is *churches*, not *people*, it was nevertheless true that those

dropping out in the declining churches more than compensated
for those joining through the growing churches.

Between 1998 and 2005 (the most recent 7 years), a third of
churches, 34% [14% + 5% + 6% + 9%], grew at least 10%, 16%
remained stable, and precisely half, 50%, declined. Again the
declining attendance in the declining churches outweighed the
increased numbers in the growing churches.

Across the 16 year period, 1989 to 2005, a quarter, 28% [7%
+ 5% + 6% + 10%] of churches grew (at least 19%), a quarter,
23%, remained stable, and virtually half, 49% [21% + 17%
+ 9% + 2%] declined. Clearly there were some which grew in
the first period and declined in the second, and vice versa. There
were very few churches declining at 60% or more (which over
16 years compounds to more than 80%) left to be counted,
which is why the final box has just 2% in it.

Consistent growth in churches?

Not all churches which grew between 1989 and 1998 saw continued growth between 1998 and 2005. Table 9.2 shows, overall,
how the different patterns of growth changed or continued
during the two periods.

Table 9.2: Growth and decline, 1989–1998 and 1998–2005

		1998–2005					
		Fast growth %	Slow growth %	Stable %	Slow decline %	Fast decline %	**Overall %**
1989 to 1998	Fast growth	1	1	2	3	3	**10**
	Slow growth	2	1	2	3	3	**11**
	Stable	2	2	2	5	3	**14**
	Slow decline	6	5	5	10	7	**33**
	Fast decline	9	5	5	8	5	**32**
	Overall	**20**	**14**	**16**	**29**	**21**	**100**[11]

This Table says that:

- 5% of churches grew 1989–1998 **and** 1998–2005 [top left hand box of 4 numbers added together];

- 4% grew 1989–1998 and were stable 1998–2005 [top middle box];

- 12% grew 1989–1998 but declined 1998–2005 [top right hand box];

- 25% declined 1989–1998 but grew 1998–2005 [bottom left hand box];

- 10% declined 1989–1998 became stable 1998–2005; and

- 30% declined 1989–1998 and continued to do so 1998–2005 [bottom right hand block of 4 numbers added together].

Thus 37% of churches stayed in a growth, stable or decline mode [5% + 2% + 30%], and exactly the same percentage, 37%, either switched from decline to growth or from growth to decline, while the remaining quarter, 26%, either became stable or moved from stability to growth or decline (10% moving from decline to stability). It is clear that a history of growth or decline is no predictor of continuing growth or decline. Growth is not dependant on history, but, under the sovereignty of God, on other factors, especially the leadership and vision of the minister.

This gives hope! Just because a church has been declining, it does not mean that it has to go on declining; if 25% of declining churches can become growing churches a few years later, this has to be a possibility for any church. While some people like to join a church they consider "successful" because it is already growing, others will join a church which has the determination to change (that is, they are willing to participate in the adventure of trying). While the 25% percentage is based on a sample of 5,000+ actual churches, if that applied to all the churches in

England, then in the last few years more than 9,000 churches have actually stopped declining and begun to grow. It can be done!

Churches and churchgoers

The average size of a congregation in 2005 which was:

- Fast growing was   119 people
- Slow growing   93 people
- Stable   87 people
- Slowly declining   73 people
- Fast declining   60 people,

compared with an overall average of 84 people. The fast growing congregations are thus double the size of fast declining congregations. The proportions of churches and churchgoers in the different groups is shown in Figure 9.3:

Figure 9.3: Proportions of churches and churchgoers by growth categories

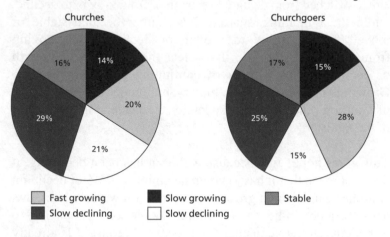

More than a quarter, 28%, of all churchgoers are in fast growing congregations. How far this lends support to the suggestion that some churchgoers are attracted to "successful" churches is not certain, as fast growing churches might be expected to have larger congregations as one factor of their growth, but there is a much greater proportion of churchgoers in fast growing churches compared to the proportion of fast growing churches (28% to 20%) than of churchgoers in slowly growing churches (15% to 14%).

On the other hand, it may be seen that two-fifths, 40%, of all churchgoers are in the 50% of churches which are experiencing decline.

The age of churchgoers varies by whether the church is growing or declining, with a slightly greater proportion of those in their 20s and 30s in growing churches than in declining ones (27% to 19%)[12].

Growth of churches by denomination

Some denominations have seen more growth than others over the seven years to 2005. Details are in Table 9.4:

Table 9.4: Growth and decline, by Denomination, 1998–2005

Denomination	Fast growth %	Slow growth %	Stable %	Slow decline %	Fast decline %
Anglican	21	15	17	27	20
Baptist	18	14	16	31	21
Roman Catholic	10	13	21	39	17
Independent	23	17	18	22	20
Methodist	15	10	15	33	27
New Churches	28	16	17	21	18
Orthodox	32	11	12	11	34
Pentecostal	36	15	16	22	11
United Reformed	10	12	14	32	32
Smaller denoms.	23	14	15	26	22
Overall	**20**	**14**	**16**	**29**	**21**

More than half, 53%, of the Pentecostal churches grew between 1998 and 2005, as did 44% of the New Churches, 43% of the Orthodox and 40% of Independent churches (which include some Fresh Expression churches). On the other hand, 64% of United Reformed churches, 60% of Methodist, 56% of Roman Catholic and 52% of Baptist churches saw decline. The Catholic decline is in line with the drop in the number of priests[13].

Between these two groups are the Anglicans and Smaller Denominations both of which saw slightly more than average proportions of growing churches (36% and 37% respectively) and slightly fewer declining (47% and 48%).

The Pentecostal and the Orthodox saw considerable proportions growing quickly, both partly because of planting new churches and through growing larger congregations. The danger for the Orthodox, however, is that they have the highest percentage of fast declining congregations – not all their new churches with newly ordained ministers are working.

While these results broadly match the overall findings in Chapter 2, which looked at denominational attendance change between 1998 and 2005, they may also be looked at another way by taking the numbers behind the percentages in Table 9.4 (which are given in *Religious Trends*[14]) vertically instead of horizontally. Doing this would show that virtually half, 47%, of the growing churches in England are Anglican, which presumably is part of the reason why they have not declined as fast as had been expected. However, Anglicans also have two-fifths, 41%, of all the declining churches.

How have these percentages changed since the 1990s? For ease of comparison, we have combined the two growth categories into one, and just focussed on growth by denomination between 1989 and 1998 and 1998 and 2005 in Table 9.5.

Table 9.5 shows that all denominations have had growing churches in both periods. It also shows that in the latter 7-year period there was a considerable increase in the percentage of

Table 9.5: Growing churches by Denomination, 1989–1998 and 1998–2005

Period	Anglican %	Baptist %	Roman Catholic %	Independent %	Methodist %	New Churches %
1989–1998	17	21	18	39	13	61
1998–2005	36	32	23	40	25	44

Period	Orthodox %	Pentecostal %	United Reformed %	Smaller Denoms. %	**Overall %**
1989–1998	n/a	43	24	32	*21*
1998–2005	43	51	22	37	*34*

growing Anglican, Baptist, Methodist and Pentecostal churches despite the considerable decreases in attendance in some of these. On the other hand, the proportion of churches which grew dropped considerably for New Churches and slightly for United Reformed Churches. Could this suggest a growing disparity between "successful" and "unsuccessful" congregations, some being winners, others losers?

Growth and decline by churchmanship

Similar figures for churchmanship can be produced as for denomination, the detail being given in *Religious Trends*[15]. The key variation which makes the overall numbers highly significant is among the Catholics, as there are proportionately far too few fast growing Catholic churches compared with other churchmanships and more which are declining[16]. The reverse is true of the Charismatics, who have more fast growing and fewer declining. There are growing, even fast growing, churches in all churchmanships, as well as declining churches in every one. However, it is also true that half, 46%, of the growing churches are evangelical, as well as 36% of the declining churches.

Growth and decline of churches by environment

While fuller details are given in *Religious Trends*[17], there were three areas of especial significance when analysing by church environment:

- There was a higher percentage of fast declining Suburban churches (25% to an estimated 21%);

- There was a lower percentage of fast declining churches in Separate Towns and Commuter Rural areas (15% and 16% respectively against an estimated 21% and 21% respectively);

- There was a higher percentage of fast growing churches in the Remoter Rural areas than estimated (24% to 20%).

The last of these re-inforces previous statements that the Remoter Rural areas are seeing in some places a renewal of church life. However, the fact that so few really significant variations were observed indicates that of all the factors leading to growth, environment is not one of them, something that other research has also found[18].

Growth and decline by size of church

How much do churches grow or decline with respect to their size? Figure 9.6 shows that there is a definite relationship between size and growth.

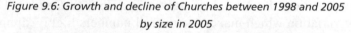
Figure 9.6: Growth and decline of Churches between 1998 and 2005 by size in 2005

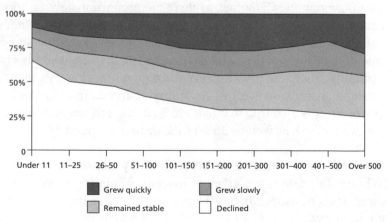

Several things are obvious from this chart, which may be considered under the four groups shown.

Declined. The smaller the church the much more likely it was to have declined; virtually three-quarters, 74%, of the smallest churches did so, and as 53% of them declined very fast, more than 40% over 9 years, it is likely that perhaps 2,000 of these will close in the next few years. The association of decline with size stabilises in churches with congregations of 150 or larger – about a third of these had declined.

Stability. The larger the church, the more likely it was to have remained stable, but this goes in phases. This was very true for churches up to 100 in size, where only 8% of those with congregations under 11 are stable, compared with 20% of those with congregations between 51 and 100. Stability then keeps at about this level until congregations get over 300 in size, when they become much more likely to be stable. Thus 18% of churches with congregations between 201 and 300 remained stable, compared with 23% of churches over 300. Could this suggest a danger of "resting on one's laurels" so to speak?

Slow growth. The larger the church the greater the likelihood it had grown slowly (from 8% in the smallest churches rising continuously to 21% for churches with between 401 and 500), until churches over 500 are reached when the percentage drops.

Fast growth. This percentage is the most interesting of all. The proportion of churches which grew quickly rises continuously from the smallest churches (10%) to churches of between 201 and 300 (27%), but then declines to 24% for churches with between 301 and 400 and 20% for churches with between 401 and 500, but then suddenly jumps to 29% for churches with more than 500 in their congregation. The denominational factor in these larger churches cannot be excluded – the rapidly growing Pentecostal churches of this size, and many of the Anglican churches, offset by the less buoyant Roman Catholic churches, many of which are over 500.

Figure 9.7 shows the proportion of churches growing by actual number of churches in each size-group[19]. It shows that churches are growing whatever their size, and that while the larger churches may have a higher proportion of growing churches there are many smaller churches experiencing exactly the same phenomenon. Size may be important in *encouraging* growth, but size is not a prime determinant in *causing* growth. That depends on other factors entirely.

Figure 9.7: Number of churches by size in 2005, and the number which grew 1998–2005

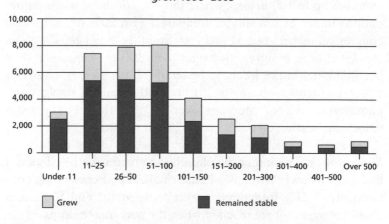

"Churches" in this diagram includes Cathedrals, a special instance of a large church, true both physically and in many cases congregationally. Furthermore, Cathedral church attendance is growing. The 43 Anglican cathedrals in England collectively had 15,800 adults and 2,500 children attending them in 2004, a 21% growth since 2000[20], an average congregation of 430 each, although the percentage of children attending is low compared with normal churches (14% to 19%). During the week a further 8,500 adults attend and 4,100 children. "Cathedrals are success-fully attracting all sorts of people, the young and those older, to explore the spiritual story they offer," said Rev Lynda Barley, Head of Research and Statistics Department, Archbishops' Council of the Church of England[21].

The five values of a "mission shaped church" are suggested in Graham Cray's report as a focus on God the Trinity, an incarnational church, involvement in transformation, making disciples and being relational. In a paper on the future of the church, the Bishop's chaplain in the Diocese of St Edmundsbury and Ipswich commented: "My experience of visiting churches and talking with local church leaders over the years is that these are frequently the values of *growing* churches."[22]

Reginald Bibby shows that churches with more than 150 in their congregation tend to have different priorities from smaller churches[23]. While "meaningful worship services" are top priority whatever the church size, churches with more than 150 focus on youth activity, while "providing a sense of community" and "trying to keep the church going" become the priorities of churches with less than 150 people.

Growth and decline of churchgoers by ethnicity

Figure 9.3 gave the overall proportions of churchgoers attending churches by various rates of growth or decline; a chart in *Religious Trends* shows how this varies by ethnicity of churchgoer[24]. Most of the non-white churchgoers are involved with growing, successful, churches. Almost half of Black and Chinese churchgoers (45% and 48% respectively) are attending churches which are growing fast – increasing at least 40% over a nine year period. Less than a quarter (24%) of white people are doing the same. What can the one group learn from the other, and is it willing to do so?

Growth and decline by frequency of attendance

Do churches which are growing attract less frequent attenders? The answer is a powerful YES, they do! Figure 9.8 shows very

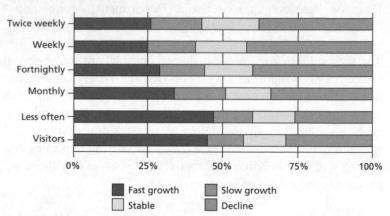

Figure 9.8: Frequency of attendance in growing and declining churches, 2005

clearly that those who attend less frequently than fortnightly are much more likely to go to a fast growing church.

This gives some support to the suggestion that growing churches are seen as successful churches – they seem to be successful in attracting those who come to church less frequently, the group that some have called the "fringe". Perhaps it is the attractiveness of a lively congregation that draws them or the warmth of the welcome or the friendliness of the people. "Friendship does not need hierarchies or paid positions for it to flourish, . . . although it will always be costly"[25]. Perhaps the "fringe" feel less conspicuous in a successful church and less likely to have to become "involved" in any way.

All these are important factors, but behind them are the key factors of leadership and vision. If churches have a sense of knowing where they are going, that sense of purposefulness is often of itself attractive, and communicates itself to those who come less frequently. Growing churches therefore would not seem to be an optional extra for the benefit of the church community but a key mechanism in reaching out to outsiders.

Overall numbers

Some may say that "growth" is really "the saints moving around", and there is much truth in this. Some switch church without moving their home, while others change their church because they have moved. Britain has become a mobile society and many people – of the order of 10%[26] – move home in the course of a year. Some of these are bound to be Christian and churchgoers. The evidence is scanty, but perhaps four in five people moving to a new church do so because they have moved home as well.

In 1998 there were 3.72 million churchgoers and in 2005 there were 3.17 million, a drop of 550,000.[27] This number is the difference between those who started (about 850,000) and those who left (about 1,400,000). It is possible to give rough breakdowns of these two groups by estimating the numbers of people who were added to growing churches or left declining churches.

Started going

In the 7 years 1998 to 2005 roughly 850,000 people joined a church, that is to say, started attending. No recent comprehensive survey breaks down the reasons why people join a church, but a survey for the Anglican Diocese of Rochester[28] showed that in 2002/2003 34% of those who joined their local church were from a non-church background. This broad percentage is similar to the percentage found in Canada (30%)[29], and to some Focus Groups undertaken by Christian Research in 2001, but very different to Australian experience where the percentage is closer to 67%[30].

The other two-thirds or 70% therefore include those who move (the majority), some who come back to church after being away, and some who are children either newly born and coming with their parents or old enough to join in their own right. If the number of women in the church given in Table 6.11 have the same number of children as the population generally[31], making due allowance for their age and marital status[32], then over the seven years about 100,000 children were born to churchgoing mothers.

From the figures for the number of Alpha courses held by churches given in Chapter 11, and the estimated number of people who have joined these churches because of these courses (which the churches themselves estimate at 10%[33]) then perhaps some 100,000 people have started attending church (with many coming to faith also) because of Alpha in England in the years 1998 to 2005. Other courses are known to be as effective as Alpha in seeing people come to faith[34], but collectively only half as many courses have been held[35], so perhaps another 50,000 have started church through these. Added to these numbers would be those coming to faith for other reasons than attending teaching courses.

Perhaps some 50,000 people came back to church having been some 8 to 10 years before[36], maybe because they started a family, or a personal crisis, or some other reason. The remainder were people who moved into the area or changed church, forming over half, 53%, of newcomers. So the numbers would be:

+ 100,000 new primarily through Alpha courses
+ 50,000 new primarily through other courses
+ 100,000 joining for other reasons
+ 100,000 children starting to attend
+ 50,000 returning to church
+ 450,000 moving home and/or church
_____
+ 850,000 people joined a church in 7 years

Stopped going

The same Diocese of Rochester survey puts deaths at about 35% of all leavers. This figure is broadly confirmed by 29% of churchgoers who are 65 and over (Table 6.1), which equates to more than 900,000 people. Given a mortality rate of 31% over 7 years that is 300,000 people[37].

Not all those churchgoers who move home find another church they like, and so stop going to church altogether. That leaves two groups: some 250,000 who ceased church attendance because they found it not relevant to their lives (the key reason given for dropping away), although a few of these will return after being away for several years. This lack of relevance is as true for young people as those who are middle-aged. This number will include older people no longer able to attend because they move to an institutional home, lack transport or are in poor health. The other group are those who begin to attend less frequently, perhaps because other demands take priority or they find church less relevant, but don't stop entirely. The less frequent attendance of these people is equivalent to a loss of 350,000 over the seven year period. Thus the overall numbers might look like:

-   300,000 people dying
-   250,000 stopping entirely because church seems irrelevant
-   350,000 coming less frequently
-   450,000 moving home and/or church
-     50,000 movers who don't find a church they like

- 1,400,000 people leaving a church in 7 years

These numbers are obviously very approximate, but if they are about the right order of magnitude then several things follow:

- A large part of the growth and decline of churches is from people simply moving church and/or house, especially if those who do move are attracted to the more "successful" (that is, growing) churches. This is the "moving deckchairs on the Titanic" phenomenon; on a national scale, much of the "growth" is illusory.

- More people die than come to faith. When one Diocesan Bishop asked Holy Trinity Brompton[38] where were all the new people converted through Alpha located the answer in part is that twice as many churchgoers die as are converted through teaching courses!

- Despite the combined evangelism of churches, the lack of relevance in many churches is a key reason for their decline. People come less frequently initially before stopping altogether, and the large majority will not return.

- It is important to encourage "movers" to find another church (maybe the church they are leaving could help?), and to have a church with a warm welcoming process. "People don't want a friendly church, they want a friend."[39]

We may be coming out of the nosedive, but on these figures we lack the pulling power to climb again – we simply are cruising downwards more gently.

Relevance

Most churchgoers who stop attending give as their reason "church was irrelevant to my life" or words to that effect. Over two-thirds, 70%, of 14,000 people who answered an advertisement to explain why they had stopped church gave this as their reason[40]. There is no doubt that relevance is hugely important, but it may be the easier explanation when there could be another.

Jill Garret, Director of Caret, but with extensive research experience of assessing leadership gifting, indicated in a lecture that in commercial life, "70% do not leave their job, they leave their manager"[41]. Could such be true in churches also? A church without an effective leader will discourage rather than encourage attendance. What then is an effective leader? Jill went on to say that "Effective leaders create a culture and talent base where others can flourish". What inspires someone to follow a leader?

- The ability to manage and engage people

- Their personal makeup: whether they are honest, open, committed, focussed, humble, patient, vulnerable and energised

- The novelty of their outlook: do they bend rules, love pressure, are they highly accessible, strongly visionary?

- They create the future

- They grow, appreciate and enthuse others

- They turn ideas into action: they get results, take risks, think laterally, manage themselves well, are reflective in their learning

- They clarify values, and are consistent with them[42].

Could it be that some church leaders do not have these qualities and thus put people off the churches they lead? If that should be, how can ministers be appropriately trained and given experience to enable them to have some of such qualities?

So what is growth?

"Growth" is a complex variable not readily reduced to single factors. An important study looking at this phenomenon was undertaken by Christian Research in 2003 on behalf of the Salvation Army but going across all denominations. We wrote to churches which we knew had been growing in the 1990s and those which we knew had declined, and analysed the answers to every question by this criteria. It was surprising how many factors did NOT make a statistically significant difference whether a church grew or declined[43]:

- Did *parking facilities* make a difference to church growth? NO! Half the churches, 46%, had a car-park and street parking, 3% no immediate parking, with the remainder a variety of arrangements.

- Did *other churches* in the catchment area make a difference? NO!

- Did *church location*, whether it be in a rural, suburban or inner city area make a difference? NO!

- Did the *distance people had to travel* to get to the church mean that some churches grew more? NO!

- Did churches which were *well located by bus routes* tend to grow more than those less well connected? NO!

- Did the *attractiveness of the church building* mean the congregation was more likely to grow? NO!

- Did a greater percentage of the *congregation with degrees* mean a church was more likely to grow? NO!

- Did the *income of a church* make a difference to its likely growth or decline? NO!

- Were certain types of evangelism, like Alpha courses, likely to make a church grow? While Alpha certainly aids growth, as do other courses, overall the answer is: NO!

- Was the size of the congregation important in making a church grow? As we have seen, size does correlate with growth, but it is not the cause *per se* of growth, so NO!

- Do cell groups help make a church grow? NO!

- Does the provision being made for young people help make a church grow? This may attract more families, but ultimately activities of any kind are not the prime factor. So NO!

- Does having students nearby in a College or University help make a church grow? NO!

- If the church happens to have an associated school linked with it, does that help the church grow? NO!

Churchgoers sometimes cite one or more of these 14 factors as the reason why their church can or cannot grow. The Salvation Army survey showed that such "reasons" were actually excuses! What then makes a church grow? *Strong Leadership and Clear Vision!* These are not just the prime factors, but were proved statistically in the study to be the key reasons.

Strong leadership may result in many different kinds of action, one result of which could be growth. One of the most popular forms of church growth is seen through the phenomenon of church planting, which is not discussed here, as it has been well documented elsewhere[44]. Alternative forms of worship are increasingly popular, as is involvement with the local community.

So what has this chapter shown?

There is much detail in this chapter, the key points of which are:

- A sophisticated method of measuring growth and decline was possible owing to the high number of churches which had responded to the 2005 English Church Census as well as earlier studies.

- A greater percentage of churches grew between 1998 and 2005, 34%, while between 1989 and 1998 only 21% did so.

- This translates into more churches: Nearly 8,000 churches grew in the 1990s, but more than half that number again, over 12,500, saw growth between 1998 and 2005.

- At the same time, it is equally true that 50% of all churches declined between 1998 and 2005, and the loss from these churches is sufficiently large collectively to offset the increases in the growing churches, so that the overall numbers decrease.

- Churches which grew in the 1990s did not necessarily grow between 1998 and 2005, and some which declined in the 1990s have started to grow again. Past performance is no indicator of future potential.

- Fast growing churches have twice the congregation of fast declining churches (119 to 60; average 84).

- Growing churches have a higher percentage of people aged 20 to 44 in their congregations than declining churches (27% to 19%).

- Over a quarter, 28%, of all churchgoers are associated with fast growing churches. In other words, this is their current experience of church life.

- More than half, 53%, of the Pentecostal churches grew between 1998 and 2005.

- More than half the churches in some other denominations declined: United Reformed (64%), Methodist (60%), Roman Catholic (56%) and Baptist (52%).

- Nevertheless all denominations had some growing churches, and most had a higher percentage than in the 1990s. The main exception to this was the New Churches which had 61% of its churches seeing growth in the 1990s, but only 44% which did so between 1998 and 2005.

- Variations by churchmanship and environment were much less significant.

- Churches are growing whatever their size: while the larger churches may have a higher proportion of growing churches there are many smaller churches experiencing the same phenomenon. Size may be important in *encouraging* growth, but size is not a prime determinant in *causing* growth.

- Non-white churches have seen explosive growth!

- Growing churches attract more people who attend less frequently.

- Twice as many churchgoers die every year as come to faith through teaching courses.

Looking behind the detail

There is much encouragement in some of these figures.

A) It is important to look not only at the immediate causes for growth in terms of physical elements, or a church's well-being. Growth is related to many variables, but the key factors behind growth relate to leadership, and this is the prime motivator.

B) It follows that it is critical to train ministers in leadership, and ensure they get the necessary experience[45]. It is also important to align a person's key motives with mission, evangelism and growth.

C) It is also equally clear from this chapter that some churches of all denominations, churchmanships, environments, and sizes have seen growth between 1998 and 2005. Every church has the potential for growth, wherever it is located and whatever background it has, and this is irrespective of its past record. A forthcoming book[46] highlights a number of churches with most unlikely backgrounds which have grown significantly. This echoes Tony Campolo's comment "The idea that the Church in Britain is somehow in terminal decline is simply not true."[47]

D) The implication behind past growth is that it will continue into the future. Therefore because nearly half, 46%, of evangelical churches *have* grown the expectation is that they *will* continue to grow. Likewise the Anglican and Methodist churches which have seen a much greater proportion of their churches growing 1998–2005 than previously. The same assumption prevails for larger churches, non-white churchgoers, less frequent attenders. These are but implications!

E) If growing churches attract more people in the crucial 20 to 44 age range, is this because they are seen as "successful" churches, or because they offer more facilities, or because the vision of the church's leadership is especially attractive for this age-group? It may be helpful to find the answers to this, but they cannot be ascertained from this Census.

F) While the recycling of the saints may confuse the pattern of growth, that twice as many die every year as are converted through courses constitutes an urgent call to evangelism. Somehow also, churches need to be more relevant to the lives people lead to stop this key attrition factor.

G) Likewise, urgent attention needs to be given to those who feel the pressure of church life to be too great, or church not as attractive as it was, and begin to attend less often. New or differently-timed services, are perhaps a key opportunity here.

10   Open seven days a week?
[Midweek activity]

People who come to a midweek church service add to the basic number involved. Churches have been holding such meetings for centuries! What is new in the 21st century is the way in which the number, nature and nuance of these meetings has changed. So, for example, it may be that:

- More churches are holding a midweek meeting, that is, the number of basic units is increasing;

- More churches are holding more midweek meetings, that is, the average number of meetings per unit holding them is increasing;

- More people may be coming to any particular midweek meeting, that is, the number per occasion is growing;

- These meetings are increasingly reaching people who are not a regular part of the Sunday programme;

- The *type* of meeting is becoming more diverse – while some are explicitly worship meetings, others are much less formal;

- The *purpose* for such meetings is becoming more focussed; not just a meeting for meeting's sake, but a gathering in order to fulfil some overall underlying aim in the church's programme.

One example of the last is a church which stopped its Parents' and Toddlers' group in order to begin a Family group with the intention of later inviting the adults to an Alpha Course. Research has shown that where midweek meetings exist to help fulfil the church's overall vision, that church (not just the midweek meetings) is much more likely to be a growing church[1].

Are midweek meetings significant in the life of the church? Yes! "Today, at least 40 million Americans are in religiously based small groups, and the growing ranks of small-group membership have caused a profound shift in the nature of American religious experience."[2] They are important in Britain also. One church in Cheltenham, Holy Trinity, reported at the NEAC Conference in September 2004 that it had 76 small groups[3] which fed into a weekly congregation at that time in excess of 1,500.

Midweek meetings vary enormously from the Catholic daily Mass, through small groups, cell groups, Bible Study meetings and Home Groups to clubs for a wide range of ages. Whether the ones for youth are uniformed (such as Boys' Brigade) or not is less important than whether they exist.

Research in Scotland showed that midweek meetings often scored over church attendance for young people because they are fun (church is not perceived to be fun – "no-one laughs in church"[4]), there is frequently food around, and they are free from knowing that their parents are close by[5]!

Church of England counts

The Church of England is one of the few denominations which seeks information about numbers attending midweek services on a regular basis. Since 2001 totals have been published alongside Sunday attendance, for adults and children, showing the numbers coming midweek. These are graphed in Figure 10.1.

The overall weekday attendance is substantial, averaging about one-sixth, 17%, of the Sunday attendance. How many of these attend on a Sunday? One survey carried out for the Church of England Diocese of Rochester showed that their midweek attendance, 2001–2003, attracted men more than women at a time when the Sunday services were losing men. Were they "switching"? The report said, "If men are switching then at best only a quarter, 23%, are doing so, and that assumes that *all* who drop

Figure 10.1: Numbers attending Church of England services,
Sunday and midweek, adults and children, 2001–2004

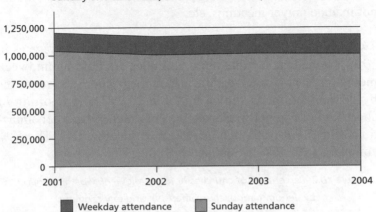

out of Sunday start in the weekday which is unlikely to be true"[6].
It may well be that the majority of people attending on a weekday are not involved on a Sunday. If so, the weekday attendance
therefore adds to the number of people who regularly attend
church. The overall 6.3% attending church on Sunday is thus
enhanced.

Census questions

The actual questions about midweek activity were previously
used in the 2002 Scottish Church Census, when they were well
answered, so they were repeated with only minor changes
for England. They had also been used in the 1998 English
Church Attendance Survey. One question asked about midweek
worship, one question asked specifically about youth meetings
midweek, and the third asked about attendance at other midweek
church-run activities. In each case it was requested that the
overall numbers be broken down by age and gender.

Midweek worship

The actual question asked was "Do you have regular midweek
worship, such as services, cell groups, etc.?" In the covering

notes this was explained as "By midweek worship we mean activities which attenders might consider as 'church', so it does not include prayer meetings, etc."

Two-fifths, 42%, said YES they did, the same percentage as in 1998, so the hearsay that more churches are holding midweek meetings is not true overall, although the percentage varies by denomination, as shown in Table 10.2. The proportion of churches holding midweek meetings has *reduced* in 5 denominations since 1998, although increased in the other five. The 42% compares with 56% in Scotland in 2002[7].

Table 10.2: Percentage of churches holding midweek worship services, by denomination, churchmanship and environment

Denomination	1998 %	2005 %	Churchmanship	1998 %	2005 %	Environment	2005 %
Anglican	51	45	Anglo-Catholic	78	55	City Centre	48
Baptist	45	41	Broad	36	57	Inner City	44
Catholic	31	24	Catholic	51	30	Council Estate	47
Independent	59	51	Evan: Broad	36	68	Suburban areas	51
Methodist	22	39	Evan: Mainstream	52	32	Separate Towns	50
New Church	23	50	Evan: Charismatic	41	35	Other built-up	53
Orthodox	46	50	Liberal	42	49	Commuter Rural	46
Pentecostal	66	51	Low Church	26	31	Remoter Rural	28
URC	19	42	Others	10	30		
Others	34	36	**OVERALL**	**42**	**42**		

Altogether the total numbers attending amount to 460,000 people, compared with 335,000 in 1998, up a third, 37%, so it is true that more people are going midweek. This was not because there were more meetings for them to attend but because more are attending the same number of meetings. Two-fifths, 40%, of this total are in Anglican churches, a very similar number to that reported by the Research and Statistics Department at Church House[8].

The 460,000 represents an additional 0.9% of the population. However, some of those attending midweek also attend on

Sunday, and the census form asked for that percentage. Half, 46%, the churches said that all 100% of those attending their midweek meeting attended on Sunday, and overall the percentage worked out at 72.4%. Thus, the percentage of the population attending church in the course of a week is an extra 0.9% × 0.276 = 0.3%, giving a total of 6.6% for church attendance, rather than the 6.3% on Sunday.

Table 10.2 shows that it is the Independent, Pentecostal, New and Orthodox denominations where a majority of churches have a midweek service, as it is with the Broad Evangelical, Broad and Anglo-Catholic churches. There is little variation by environment, except the much smaller number of such meetings in Remoter Rural areas. Apart from the New Churches these are the three denominations seeing a measure of ethnic growth, or at least are not declining as much as others. Is it the need to disciple new people, welcome them to the UK, learn English, meet others of your own nationality, etc. which is behind these extra services where there is ethnic growth in attendance?

The average size of these midweek worship services was 29 in 2005 compared with 21 in 1998. This supports the larger numbers given above and, as the proportion of churches holding such services has remained the same confirms that the average number attending each service has increased rather than churches are holding more services midweek than they used to.

How do those attending midweek compare with the usual Sunday attenders? 58% are female, identical to the 58% of those on Sunday. The age-variation (excluding those under 15) is shown in Figure 10.3 on the next page.

Those attending midweek worship services are more likely to be in their later teens and 45 to 64 than those coming on Sunday, and less likely to be 65 or over, presumably because many midweek services are in the evenings, when older people would rather not

Figure 10.3: Age of those attending midweek services and on Sunday, 2005

Sunday attendance · Midweek attendance

venture outside. Those coming midweek are on average about 5 years younger than those attending church on Sunday.

Churches which are completely made up of those from non-white backgrounds are only half as likely as other churches to have midweek worship services, or youth meetings or other kinds of church-run activities. Churches led by male

It all started with a midweek meeting!

ministers are more likely to have midweek services than female (68% to 53%), and regular youth activities (45% to 34%).

Youth meetings

"Do the young people in your church attend a regular youth activity(ies) (eg Rock Solid Club, Youth Club, etc.)?" was the question on the form. YES said 27% of churches, which compares with the 47% of Scottish churches which have a midweek youth activity[9].

The percentage of churches holding youth activities is low, and 4% of this 27% hold them in conjunction with other churches, suggesting a lack of necessary resources.

As before, the percentage varies by denomination, churchmanship and environment, as shown in Table 10.4. It may be seen that only 27% of Anglican churches have midweek youth activity, supporting the statement in the 2005 report that "half the Church of England parishes had no work among young people"[10], with presumably some of the rest having a Sunday School but no midweek activity.

Table 10.4: Percentage of churches holding midweek youth activities by denomination, churchmanship and environment, 2005

Denomination	2005 %	Churchmanship	2005 %	Environment	2005 %
Anglican	27	Anglo-Catholic	23	City Centre	27
Baptist	34	Broad	42	Inner City	26
Roman Catholic	8	Catholic	12	Council Estate	29
Independent	36	Evan: Broad	57	Suburban areas	38
Methodist	31	Evan: Mainstream	23	Separate Towns	37
New Church	41	Evan: Charismatic	29	Other built-up	38
Orthodox	16	Liberal	31	Commuter Rural	31
Pentecostal	34	Low Church	23	Remoter Rural	15
URC	37	Others	18		
Others	22	**OVERALL**	**27**		

The highest percentage in Table 10.4 is the 41% of New Churches holding a midweek youth activity, which re-inforces the traditional emphasis on young people by the New Churches, and the high percentage of their attenders who are under 15 (25% in Table 6.5).

More than half, 57%, of Broad Evangelical churches have midweek youth meetings, but less than a quarter, 23%, of

Mainstream Evangelical churches have such. Midweek youth activities are more likely in Suburban areas and Towns and much less likely in Remoter Rural areas.

The overall 27% is based on *all* the churches, but not every church has people who are under 20. One third, 33%, of churches have no-one attending who is under 20 either on Sunday or midweek (Chapter 6). So of churches with at least one person attending under the age of 20, 40% have a midweek activity.

Numbers attending

The overall total number of young people attending a midweek activity is 329,000, of which a third, 36%, are Anglican (the largest single denomination). A fifth of churches, 20%, said that their young people who came midweek came on Sunday as well, and a quarter, 27%, indicated that less than 5% of those coming midweek came on Sunday.

Overall, the percentage who came both midweek and on Sunday was 45%, which obviously means that 55% of those coming midweek do *not* come on Sunday. This 55% is equivalent to 181,000 young people, representing an additional 0.3% of the population. If coming to a midweek youth activity can be equated to "attending church", then altogether 6.9% (the previous 6.6% + 0.3%) of the population are involved in church.

The average size of these youth activities is 31, with the Baptist and Independent Churches being higher, and the Anglicans and Orthodox being the smallest on average. This is smaller than the 43 reported at youth services in 1998, and only half the average size of 59 reported in Scotland[11], which are of course, very different types of event. It emphasises the value and importance of having a Youth or Children's Worker. More than 10% of Baptist churches now employ a Youth Worker[12]. In a 1968 study, over a quarter of those who are converted to Christianity came to faith before they were 14[13], a percentage which a later study suggests could well have more than doubled by 2005[14].

There is an even balance in gender among the young people attending midweek activities, 47% being boys and 53% girls, identical to the percentages given in Table 6.13 for young people. Figure 10.5 breaks the figures down by age-group, and compares them with those under 20 attending church on Sunday[15]:

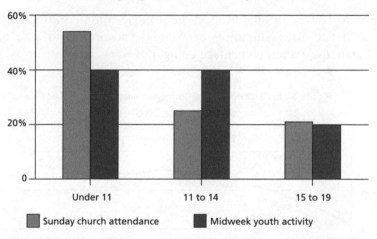

Figure 10.5: Age of those attending midweek youth meetings and going to church on Sunday, 2005

Figure 10.5 shows that a greater proportion of those coming midweek are in the important 11 to 14 age-group than those who attend on Sunday. This is the age range when young people are most likely to leave the church[16], so the fact that some 132,000 young people are still involved with a church in one way or another is important, and shows that holding such youth activities is worth while.

Those attending on Sunday will include many very young children who would not be old enough for any midweek activity, so the fact that the proportion of Sunday attenders among those under 11 is much higher is no surprise. Some of the older teenagers might be helpers for the younger activities, but in the event the proportion coming midweek is virtually the same as those going on Sunday. In other words, midweek youth activities are especially important for the key 11 to 14 age-group, but have less impact on older young people. It was the same in Scotland[17].

Ministers in their 30s and 40s were more likely to be leading a church with regular youth activities than ministers in their 60s or 70s (54% to 33%). Given that only 32% of ministers are under 50 (Table 8.1) this is potentially very important.

Figure 10.6 shows the proportion of those coming to midweek youth activities attending on Sunday, according to size of church, the overall percentage being 45%.

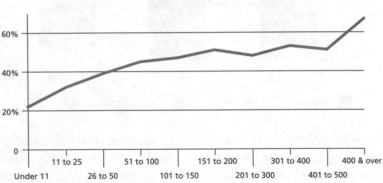

Figure 10.6: Percentage attending midweek youth activity and on Sunday, 2005

Figure 10.6 indicates that the larger the church the greater the proportion of its young people attending midweek who also attend on Sunday. This is probably a logical consequence of the fact that the larger the church the more likely Christian people are to attend so that their children can take advantage of the youth activities. It means however that a smaller proportion of children in midweek youth groups in large churches are from non-church backgrounds, although in numerical terms this number will be more than in smaller churches, even though the percentage of such children is greater.

Midweek church-run activities

The final question in this section asked: "Please could you estimate how many people usually attend midweek church-run activities like Drop-in Centres, Lunch Clubs, etc. but do not normally attend worship services at any church. Please exclude those organisations that may hire or make use of your church premises."

Altogether 20% of churches replied to this question and gave details of the ages of those attending their midweek activities. In 1998 the percentage of churches indicating they had such activities was 45%, and the smaller percentage in 2005 almost certainly reflects not that the percentages of churches with midweek activities has drastically dropped but that many churches did not readily have the age and gender information requested[18].

Numbers attending

The number attending such activities across all denominations totalled 412,000 people, 0.8% of the population. If this number was increased pro rata to the 45% of churches with church-run activities midweek reported in 1998, then the total would be 930,000 (1.8% of the population), about three-quarters of the 1.2 million attending in 1998. In other words, either the number of church-run activities midweek are fewer than they were, or that smaller numbers are attending them, or both.

Average attendance at these meetings was 55 per church, against 70 in 1998, with New Churches, Roman Catholics and Baptist churches averaging over 60 per meeting. With fewer people attending church (and therefore presumably a smaller supply of helpers and organisers of activities) it is perhaps inevitable that fewer outside people come. This suggests that activities run by churches to reach "fringe" people are being less successful (in terms of numbers being reached). Is this primarily because of the church's inability to support them as necessary, or an increasing

lack of relevance or usefulness of such activities for the local
community or just pressure of life?

Attenders at these activities are 37% male and 63% female,
proportions quite different from the 42%:58% split for church
attendance. The possible reason is the dominance of Parent and
Toddlers' groups (which despite the generic "parent" are predominantly mothers and grandmothers) which 65% of churches
hold[19], and the many Lunch Clubs and Coffee Mornings run by
64% of churches, when more women, especially widows in the
older age-groups, are available[20].

Figure 10.7 again compares the ages of those coming to these
church-run activities with Sunday church attendance.

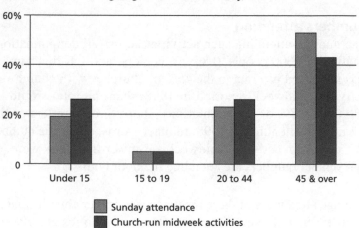

*Figure 10.7: Age of those attending midweek church-run activities
and going to church on Sunday, 2005*

Church-run midweek activities reach proportionately more
children and those aged 20 to 44, reflecting the dominance of
Parent and Toddlers' groups. These groups thus provide opportunities to encourage people to either attend church or courses like
Alpha or Emmaus.

That the proportion of those 45 and over is so much less may reflect older mothers returning to work and infirmities of ageing senior citizens, or simply that churchgoing proportions in this age-group are increasing (up from 25% in 1998 to 29% in 2005 in Table 6.1).

Variation by church size

The proportions of churches holding midweek worship services or youth activities varies by the size of the church, as shown in Figure 10.8:

Figure 10.8: Midweek services and youth activities by size of church, 2005

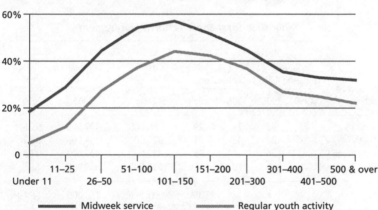

Figure 10.8 shows that up to about 150 in the congregation, the larger the church the more likely it is they will run midweek activities of some kind. Given that the larger the church the more helpers will be available, this is logical. What is more surprising perhaps is that as churches get above 150 in the congregation a smaller proportion run midweek activities.

Is this because leadership is under too great a pressure to organise such activities, or that the committed are too over-committed, especially as Figure 7.3 shows the decreasing frequency of attendance by those aged 30–44? If larger churches are less likely to run youth activities, this suggests they would find it hard to help other local churches in similar activities (one of the implications if they were to follow the so-called "Minster Model" of ministry). Or could it be that the larger churches are more eclectic and while their congregations are willing to travel a distance to attend on Sunday they are less likely to do so during the week?

Putting it all together

This chapter has looked at three types of midweek meeting; the findings may be summarised as follows:

Table 10.9: Total English church involvement

Mid-week activity	% of churches having this		Average attendance		Total attendance in England	Of whom attending midweek only	% of population
	1998	2005	1998	2005	2005	2005	2005
Services	42	42	21	29	460,000	127,000	0.25
Youth	~	27	43	31	329,000	181,000	0.36
Church-run 05	~	20	~	55	412,000	412,000	0.82
Church-run 98	45	~	70	~	930,000	930,000	1.85
				TOTAL midweek 2005	720,000	1.4 or
				using 45% in 2005	1,238,000	2.5
				Sunday attendance	3,166,200	6.3
				GRAND TOTAL 2005	**3,886,200**	**7.7 or**
				using 45% in 2005	**4,404,200**	**8.8**

Taking the total of the first two percentages in the final column – 0.6% – means that midweek services and youth activities add about another 10% of people involved with the church on a regular basis but who do not attend on a Sunday[21], which is about the percentage that the Church of England have identified through their more detailed measurements, Diocese by Diocese.

The Census data shows that this Anglican data is applicable in the same broad proportions to the other denominations also.

In addition, however, there is the "fringe" of people who regularly attend church-run activities but who do not normally attend church on Sunday. This number, in total, varies between 0.8% of the population who answered the question in detail in 2005 and 1.8% who answered the question in general in 1998. It might be assumed that they form part of the extra 8.2% of the population identified in Chapter 7 who attend church with a frequency between fortnightly and once a year.

So what does all this say?

This chapter has shown:

- More people are attending midweek church events: the number attending midweek services has increased by 37% between 1998 and 2005, largely because the average number attending each service increased.

- The proportion of churches holding such services has not increased, however: two-fifths, 42%, of churches held midweek services in 2005, the same percentage as in 1998.

- The average size of a midweek worship service was 29 people in 2005, compared with 21 in 1998.

- Midweek services attract the same percentage by gender as those who attend church, but are slightly younger (by 5 years).

- Just over a quarter, 27%, of churches run a regular midweek youth activity.

- 45% of these young people come to church on Sunday.

- 47% of these are male, and there is a higher proportion aged 11 to 14 midweek than there is in church on Sunday – a key age-group.

- The average number coming to a youth activity is 31, smaller than in 1998 and much smaller than in Scotland.

- 20% of churches gave an age breakdown of those coming to their midweek church-run activities, down from 45% who answered this question in 1998 probably because many respondents did not have all the information needed to answer the question.

- Even if the true response would have been 45%, the number attending is still considerably less than in 1998 (0.9 million to 1.2 million).

- Regular midweek activities drew an average of 55 per church in 2005, compared with 70 in 1998.

- As a church increases in size beyond 150 the less likely it is to have a midweek service or a regular midweek youth activity. On the face of it, this seems an extraordinary finding; perhaps the larger churches don't count house groups, only central meetings.

- Midweek services and youth activities add about 10% to the overall numbers who are involved with the church but who do not attend on a Sunday.

Looking behind the detail

Certain facets of these findings are important for further consideration:

A) There is still a desperate absence of work with young people. While it may be presumed that a midweek worship service in some ways replicates a Sunday worship service, it is by no means as certain that a midweek youth club activity is the same as Sunday School. The teaching element in a midweek youth club is presumably less than in a church or Sunday context. While it is good that there are many young people who come to a church youth activity midweek, how are they to be taught the Christian faith in depth if so few attend on Sunday?

B) Midweek worship services are increasing the number of people coming to church each week, so that the percentage of the population worshipping each week is 6.6% not 6.3%. While this excludes those coming to youth activities, it is still good news!

C) There are more people attending midweek services, but fewer coming to youth activities and fewer coming to church-run activities. Have churches got their priorities correct? If the "fringe" of people that the churches are already in contact with is decreasing, how can that be rectified? Are church-run activities just activities for the sake of tradition or social involvement, or are they purposeful happenings designed to increase worship attendance (and by implication, commitment to Christ)?

D) It seems very odd that the larger the church, over 150 in the congregation, the smaller the percentage holding midweek activities. Is this really reflecting lack of people to help, or are there other reasons?

11   Beyond the Numbers
[Church and Mission]

We are very grateful to the different organisations who helped to sponsor this fourth English Church Census, without whom it simply would not have been possible. A complete list of them is given on the title page. Those who gave a substantial donation were able to have one or more questions included on the Census form. The overall answers to these questions are given in this chapter as they will be of interest to a wider audience, although a more detailed analysis will be made for these sponsors.

Alpha courses
Holy Trinity Church, Brompton (HTB), the home of the very popular Alpha course sponsored a question. By the end of 2005, 2 million people in the UK and 8 million worldwide had attended an Alpha course, of whom 25,000 had attended at HTB itself[1]. Two-fifths, 38%, of the churches replying to the Census said they had undertaken an Alpha course at some time. If applied across all the churches in England that would be some 14,000 churches which had used Alpha, double the active number to which HTB regularly send news and information. A negligible number of ministers said they had never heard of Alpha, 110 in total, a tribute to the very extensive advertising that HTB undertakes every September about forthcoming Alpha courses, as well as the coverage it receives in the media.

Length of time holding Alpha
Churches using Alpha had held the course on average 5.6 times, which will be a combination of some which have used it just a

few times and others which have been holding Alpha courses regularly for more than a decade. As the average number of courses held per church was 1.7 in 2005[2], this suggests that churches have been holding Alpha courses for just over 3 years. This is the length of time that other research has shown to be effective[3] in bringing in new people; existing church members often attend the first Alpha course a church runs, and their friends the next time. It is only when their friends' friends are invited that the church begins to grow.

The most popular months for starting Alpha courses are September and January, and the year a church first started them is shown in Figure 11.1. The diagram shows that the peak period of beginning to use Alpha was in the latter half of the 1990s. As many of the churches using Alpha run a course at least once a year this length of holding Alpha courses means that in many cases these are now genuinely reaching out beyond the church's membership and immediate fringe, and could explain the increase in numbers attending Alpha in 2004 and 2005[4].

Figure 11.1: Year that a church started using Alpha courses

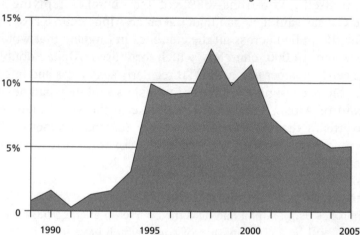

Numbers attending

On average churches said that they had had 28 visitors and 40 church members attend Alpha courses, which works out at about 20 people per year, very similar to the overall average reported in the surveys undertaken by HTB for the past 4 years[5]. The ratio of visitors to members is also the same as HTB finds in its annual surveys, if those helping to run Alpha are excluded[6]. HTB records indicate that 1,980,000 people in the UK have attended Alpha courses in the period 1992 to 2005. These include helpers at the courses, and cover the whole of the UK, not just England[7].

Other courses

Alpha is the best known course in the UK teaching about Christianity according to MORI surveys undertaken by HTB each year, but it is not the only one. The main other courses mentioned in the Census returns by at least 1% of respondents were: Emmaus (7%), Christianity Explored (3%), CAFÉ & RCIA (Roman Catholic), Lent courses, Start (CPAS) and the Y Course (each 1%)[8]. A considerable number of churches, however, 7%, used their own course. In all 24% of churches indicated they had tried a course other than Alpha. Some will have tried more than one, but of the order of three-fifths of churches have held a course.

Bible reading

The Bible Society sponsored questions on Bible reading and church involvement in society. The Bible reading question was included on the slips that individual churchgoers were asked to tick, as it was thought ministers would not be able to answer it on behalf of their attenders. This enabled a much more detailed response.

Altogether, some 27% of churchgoers in England in 2005 claimed to read the Bible personally at least once a week, outside of church services. This percentage is between the 45% of adults reading the Bible weekly in the United States[9] and the 12% of Finns who read it at least once a month[10].

The English 27% varied across the country with the highest percentages in Avon (40%), Cumbria (38%), and Norfolk and Wiltshire (37% each), and with the lowest in Inner London and Greater Manchester (20% each), Gloucestershire and the Channel Islands (19% each) and the Isle of Man (18%). It varied considerably by two of the 3 major control factors as shown in Table 11.2:

Table 11.2: Percentage reading the Bible personally at least weekly, 2005

Denomination	%	Churchmanship	%	Environment	%
Anglican	24	Anglo-Catholic	25	City Centre	23
Baptist	27	Broad	42	Inner City	23
Roman Catholic	4	Catholic	9	Council Estate	30
Independent	64	Evan: Broad	45	Suburban areas	27
Methodist	27	Evan: Mainstream	24	Separate Towns	30
New Church	66	Evan: Charismatic	25	Other built-up	31
Orthodox	21	Liberal	32	Commuter Rural	27
Pentecostal	62	Low Church	27	Remoter Rural	26
URC	31	Others	20		
Others	29				
		OVERALL	**27**		

It was those attending churches in the more evangelical denominations that read the Bible most – New Churches, Independent and Pentecostal churches – and those in churches describing themselves as Broad or Broad Evangelical rather than Charismatic or Mainstream Evangelical. Evangelicals as a whole were 29%, slightly above the overall average[11]. Environmental variations were not significant.

Variation by other factors

Women read the Bible slightly more than men – 28% to 26%. Those from a non-white ethnicity read the Bible much more than those who were white – 40% to 25%. The proportion who read the Bible at different ages is shown in Figure 11.3, and shows that those under 20 read it least of all, while those aged 20 to 29 read it most, followed by those aged 85 and over. In between these two groups, those aged 30 to 44 read it least, presumably because of the same pressures as have already been identified for

Figure 11.3: Percentage reading the Bible weekly by age-group

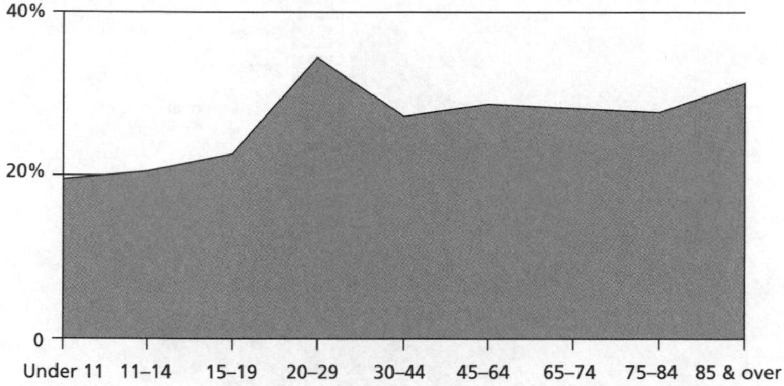

this age-group, indicating that other behavioural characteristics of Christianity are affected as well as church attendance.

Figure 11.4 on the next page shows the variation in Bible reading across England. Churchgoers in the western Midlands read it most with a few other scattered more rural areas, while those who read it the least are the counties where Catholics and Evangelicals are strongest, and much of the north and east, with some southern counties in between.

The proportion who read their Bible at least weekly is shown broken down by size of church in Figure 11.5. Apart from the smallest churches, in general the larger the church, the smaller the percentage of the congregation who read the Bible regularly. This is mainly because many of the largest churches are Roman Catholic, where fewer read the Bible personally. If these are excluded, as shown in Figure 11.5 on the next page, it can be seen that the larger the (Protestant) church when the congregation exceeds 300 the greater the proportion who read the Bible[12].

Priorities of Church Resources
A question sponsored by Tearfund asked respondents to indicate the order of priority placed on their church resources by six

Figure 11.4: Percentage of churchgoers reading the Bible at least weekly

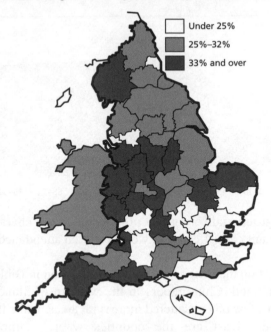

Figure 11.5: Percentage reading the Bible weekly by size of church

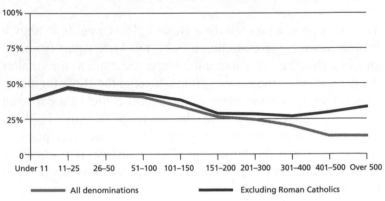

aspects of church work, indicating both their own personal view and what they felt would be their congregation's collective view. Some indicated on their form that they had replied according to the financial resources allocated by their church to the different topics[13], and nearly 500 forms did not have the congregation's views expressed as some ministers felt unable to say what it might have been. Overall, the priority order was as follows:

Priority	Minister	Congregation
1	Preaching/teaching	Preaching/teaching
2	Evangelism	Church Fabric
3	Children/Youth Work	Children/Youth Work
4	Church Staff	Church Staff
5	Church Fabric	Evangelism
6	Poverty	Poverty

On four of these, the minister's viewpoint was much the same as that of the congregation: Preaching/teaching, Children/Youth Work, Church Staff and Poverty (in that order). On the other two, ministers felt more strongly that Evangelism was important, but the congregation felt the Church Fabric was more important, to be in second place in their overall priorities. The difference in position between the minister and the congregation was greatest on using resources for the Church Fabric rather than for Evangelism.

Table 11.6 gives the detailed percentages of each who indicated their priority as 1 (which was top) through to 6 (the lowest); the figures in bold indicating the highest percentage in each column.

Table 11.6: Priorities of different aspects of church resources

Priority	Children/Youth work		Church Fabric		Church Staff		Evangelism		Preaching/teaching		Poverty	
	Own %	Ch'h %	Own %	Ch'h %	Own %	Ch'h %	Own %	Ch'h %	Own %	Ch'h %	Own %	Ch'h %
1	14	16	11	**28**	20	19	20	12	**48**	**34**	5	5
2	23	24	17	23	11	15	**25**	15	21	21	7	7
3	**30**	**25**	14	15	10	12	20	18	14	20	15	15
4	17	16	15	12	15	14	15	20	8	13	**25**	21
5	9	11	19	10	21	17	12	**21**	5	8	23	23
6	7	8	**24**	12	**23**	**23**	8	14	4	4	**25**	**29**
Average	**3.1**	**3.1**	**3.9**	**2.9**	**3.8**	**3.6**	**3.0**	**3.6**	**2.1**	**2.5**	**4.3**	**4.4**
Base	7,539	7,134	7,739	7,461	7,211	6,832	7,673	7,180	7,843	7,356	7,504	7,087

Ch'h = Church or Congregation

Support for the Third World

A question about giving was a combination of questions sponsored by the Bible Society, Tearfund and World Vision. It was in two parts, in each of which 7 statements were listed and respondents were asked to tick one out of the first 7 statements and as many as applied in the second set.

The first set asked which description best fitted how a particular church gave to the Third World. Answers were:

- 28%   We split our giving evenly between long-term projects and one- off gifts
- 23%   We give mostly to long-term projects with which we like to have an active relationship
- 14%   We give mostly to long-term projects, but we don't have much involvement with them
- 10%   We prefer to make lots of smaller gifts throughout the year
- 9%   We only give occasionally or through a few smaller gifts

- 7% We encourage people to give direct to agencies
- 4% We do not give regularly to projects in the Third World, and
- 5% Did not answer the question.

Churches which give to the Third World clearly find long-term projects more attractive; it was preferred by two-thirds, 65%, of churches answering this question. The 1989 Census asked churches if they gave to Third World projects, and 2% then said they did not do so[14]; the penultimate 4%, plus presumably some of the 5% who chose not to answer rather than tick "no" suggests this dis-engagement has increased.

Which factors were the most important in choosing which agency to support? Answers were as follows, each respondent ticking 2.4 boxes on average:

- 44% Their work fits with the vision of the church
- 43% A tradition of long-term support
- 41% We give in response to appeals received
- 35% The personal relationship between church members and the agency
- 29% We receive regular information on where our money goes
- 25% Someone comes to speak at the church
- 21% It is our denomination's agency

The three which are most important are the vision of the church, a tradition of support, or the receipt of an impressive appeal. These might be summarised as: internal direction, past history, and current need. This suggests that agencies need to help churches find their vision, consolidate their support with those who already donate, and communicate in an arresting manner to as many churches as they can.

The personal relationship between church and agency is also important, though how far this implies the value of local representatives (but not always wanting them to speak!) or the relationship between the church and someone known to the congregation serving with a particular agency is not clear. Loyalty to the church's denomination was at the bottom of the list!

Areas of engagement

Another Bible Society sponsored question consisted of 6 potential programmes in which a church might be involved. Again respondents were asked to tick as many as applied. Their answers were:

- 46%   Local or national politics
- 32%   Popular or higher Arts
- 10%   Local or national media
- 9%   Social action
- 8%   Primary/ Secondary/ Tertiary education
- 5%   Sport

Virtually half the responding churches said they were involved in political action, either nationally or locally. One Anglican church in south London for example vigorously (and successfully) opposed the possible opening of a sex shop nearby. Another, a New Church, distributed leaflets to local households highlighting their Borough's discriminatory policies, some of which the Borough was forced to discontinue because of the reaction generated. Not every such action, however, is of course successful.

A third of churches said they were involved with "popular or higher Arts". Many churches hold concerts regularly, or provide nativity plays at Christmas. One Pentecostal church, again in south London, publicly put on an Easter play in 2005 as an experiment, with church members undertaking the action. This was very popular, and several people subsequently joined the church.

That only a tenth of churches are involved with the media, locally or nationally, seems a huge wasted opportunity. Likewise the proportion saying they are involved in social action seems very small when some 30% of churchgoers indicate they are involved with several kinds of community work[15], although some of this is undertaken outside of the church. Perhaps the church leaders, who largely completed the questionnaire, were unaware of the extent of their congregation's involvement in such activities.

The Chief Executive of one Midlands Local Authority wrote to Christian Research after the publication of the results of the 1998 English Church Attendance Survey saying he was distressed to learn that church numbers were declining, as his Authority greatly depended on church members for community support. Was there anything he could do to encourage more people to attend church?

Altogether there are 6,300 church primary schools and 600 secondary schools[16], making a total percentage of 18% of churches with a linked school; why less than half that proportion ticked the education option is not known, but perhaps the church leadership did not see their church as really involved in their local school in a significant way, which again seems a lost opportunity. Of the six areas of engagement listed in the question, education emerged as the fifth. The Prime Minister, Tony Blair, talks much about faith schools and the importance of sponsored school academies, so it is especially sad that so few churches are involved in any active way.

The image of mission
The Church Mission Society sponsored the final question. Some respondents found our phrasing of their question confusing and Christian Research had many emails, letters or phone calls asking for clarification[17]. Twelve words or phrases were given and respondents were asked to select up to five of these in answer to two statements: (A) "Christian mission movements generally" and (B) "The ideal agency that your church would like to support". Answers are given in Table 11.7, and the positive replies are graphed in Figure 11.8 on the next page.

In Table 11.7, the replies have been listed in order of the difference between the responses for the two statements. The key

Table 11.7: The phrases associated with two statements

Word or Phrase	Mission movements generally %	Ideal agency church would support %	Difference %
Transforming	26	38	+12
Empowers people	36	47	+11
Spirit-led	20	30	+10
Gets me involved	14	22	+ 8
Fights for justice	34	40	+ 6
Faithful	36	30	− 6
Out of date	5	0	− 5
Out of touch	5	0	− 5
Evangelistic	42	38	− 4
Obsessive	3	0	− 3
Stuffy	3	0	− 3
Multicultural	20	19	− 1
Average	**20**	**22**	**+ 2**

Figure 11.8: Proportions associating with the positive statements of existing and ideal mission agencies

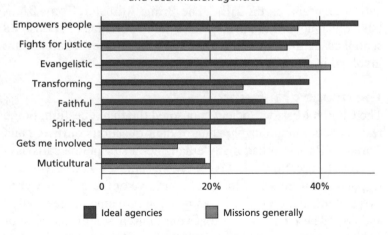

characteristics of Christian mission movements generally in the opinion of respondents were that they were (in order): Evangelistic, Empowering people, Faithful and Fighting for justice. Respondents largely rejected the four negative words or phrases in the list: Out of date, Out of touch, Obsessive and Stuffy.

In other words, the perception of mission movements is generally positive, but not as positive as people think it ought to be. However, they *don't* want them to be more evangelistic, faithful or multicultural.

The key characteristics that respondents would like to see in the ideal agency were (in order): Empowering people, Fighting for justice, Evangelistic, Transforming, Faithful and Spirit-led. The order of importance has changed from how mission movements are seen, but two additional phrases were scored by at least 30% of respondents: Transforming and Spirit-led.

These two phrases, together with "Empowering people", were the three where the difference was greatest between how mission movements are currently seen and what respondents would ideally like them to be. Transforming, Empowering people, Spirit-led are all relational, active, powerful phrases, indicating the kind of movements that people are more likely to support in the 21st century, or at least these are the emphases that potential supporters would like to hear expressed.

The two phrases not mentioned thus far in Table 11.6 are "Gets me involved" and "Multicultural". The first also generated a positive response in terms of what respondents would like the ideal agency to be, compared with where mission movements generally are, but the level of support for it was less than a quarter, 22%. Could this suggest that while this is seen to be "a good thing" in practice it doesn't happen as much as ministers would like?

The fact that "Multicultural" was the one word which scored virtually the same on both lists suggests that the location of where the mission agency is operating (in the UK or abroad) and the type of work which is being done are being given the "right" amount of priority by agencies. In an ideal agency "multicultural" activity is eighth in order of importance, and well behind empowering people and fighting for justice, the top two items. Empowering, transforming people and fighting for justice are the key factors irrespective of where or how these are undertaken.

So what has this chapter shown?

This Chapter has looked briefly at the mission questions asked by some of those who sponsored the Census. While a fuller report breaking down the answers by denomination, churchmanship, etc. will be made available to them, the outline findings are:

- Two-fifths, 38%, of churches had used the Alpha course, on average 5.6 times, especially in January or September, starting especially in the latter half of the 1990s, with an average of 20 people per year.

- The most popular alternative courses mentioned were Emmaus (7%) and Christianity Explored (3%).

- A quarter, 27%, of churchgoers read the Bible at least once a week personally apart from when they are in church, a percentage highest in Avon (40%) and lowest in the Isle of Man (18%). Almost two-thirds of those attending New Churches (66%), Independent (64%) and Pentecostal (62%) churches read their Bible, as did half (48%) of those in Broad churches.

- Women read the Bible marginally more than men (28% to 26%), and non-white people more than white (40% to 25%). Those in their 20s read it most (34%), followed by those 85 or over (31%). Those in churches with between 11 and 25 people are most likely to read their Bible (47%) and those in churches 400 or over the least (13%).

- Ministers and their congregation felt that preaching/teaching should take priority in using their church's resources. They differed however on the second priority – evangelism for ministers and the church fabric for the congregation. Children and Youth Work came third for both, however.

• Giving to long-term projects was the favoured mechanism of giving to the Third World, but 4%, twice the 1989 percentage, did not reckon on giving at all to the Third World.

• The things which are most likely to cause a church to give are: The project fits with the vision of the church (44%), or where the church has a tradition of support for that agency (43%), or the church is in receipt of an impressive appeal (41%).

• Half, 46%, of the responding churches said they were involved in political action, either nationally or locally, and a third, 32%, of churches said they were involved with "popular or higher Arts".

• Transforming, Empowering people and Spirit-led were the three words or phrases where the difference was greatest between how mission movements are currently seen and what respondents would ideally like them to be. This is probably irrespective of where or how mission is undertaken.

Looking behind the detail

There are some positive elements in this list and some of concern.

A) Evangelism is highly important for ministers, but less so for the congregation. Alpha (and other) courses are one means to that end, but they involve the congregation; are they a mechanism of helping the congregation to see the importance of evangelism? Evangelism is seen as a key component of mission agency activity, but was deemed to be of less importance in the ideal agency than it currently is. There is a critical issue here of how to engage and encourage ordinary people in spreading the faith.

B) Previous chapters have shown the growing percentage of Evangelical churchgoers, and the implication that Evangelical churches are likely to be growing in the future. But the evidence of this chapter is that Evangelicals read their Bible less than non-Evangelicals, if Catholics (who read it least of all) are excluded. Is this why ministers put preaching and teaching top of their priorities? Is the Bible becoming a closed book among those who say they follow it most strongly?

C) The necessity for mission agencies to meet the needs of individual churches is evident from these findings, which implicitly support the importance of larger agencies (rather than smaller ones) since presumably they have the resources for maintaining a local presence. The work they are wanted to do, however, is transforming, empowering, Spirit-led which may well include (and indeed necessitate) evangelism, but the top phrases used by respondents did not include that word. Has it gone out of fashion in the desire to be involved politically and with the Arts, or is it just a cultural change?

12   God believes in the Church
[Where do we go from here?]

Is the church in England dead? Absolutely NOT! Is it in terminal decline? NO, though it may show symptoms of such. Could the churches in this country die, as those planted by Paul in Asia Minor did? Yes, that is possible. Is that likely? No, not if churches respond vigorously and far-sightedly to the challenges and opportunities ahead. Can the church pull out of the nosedive and start climbing again? Absolutely, YES! Reginald Bibby quotes Don Posterski and Andrew Grenville in his book on Canadian research as follows:

> "Clearly, many Canadians believe in God, God believes in the Church. To bring these two realities together is the challenge, and the opportunity, for the Canadian church in the new century."[1]

That is absolutely true for England also. The purpose of this Chapter is to draw together the many threads this book has revealed, not reporting the facts again *per se*, but to give the author's opinions and thoughts for the future. Unlike the 1998 study no one factor has emerged which dominates the scene. Instead we have a *pot pourri* of items, nearly 50 in total[2], and so it is important to seek to distil the key elements locked within them. This Chapter concerns itself with the implications arising from these individual findings. "You may have dozed off reading all the tables, but hopefully this Chapter tells you what I am trying to say[3]!"

It would seem to me that there are five broad themes that emerge from this analysis – four positive and one negative. Let us look at each of these in turn, the positive items not being given in any special order.

Positive: Release of energy

Energy may be seen in several different ways. Chapter 2 reported an explosion of ethnic diversity churches; that growth happened in part because people made worship joyful and meaningful and invited their friends to join in the ethnically appropriate expression of their faith.

Age and denomination are related. The Independents, New Churches and the Pentecostals attract the greatest proportions of churchgoers aged 20 to 44, the age-groups where energy is flourishing and is seen in the numerous church activities these people help to run. This ties in with two other findings – that this age-group, together with younger people and non-white people, are attracted to the growing, "successful", churches. Growth needs energy, but the energy feeds the growth. These growing churches are often the larger churches, especially if they are Anglican. This energy is also seen in the higher proportion of people between 20 and 44 (and their children) in Remoter Rural churches, where to belong is to make a difference, and to be an active part of the culture of village life.

The other related finding is the growth of midweek worship and midweek activities, even if they attract fewer people. This then becomes a strategic issue, perhaps seen in the fact that the larger churches tend to have *pro rata* fewer midweek activities. Other research has shown that successful churches have midweek activities *for a purpose*, and invariably an evangelistic purpose[4]. This suggests controlled energy, focussed on something in particular, rather than unquestioning adherence to already established patterns of church life.

There is also the 65 to 74 age-group, the largest decadal group. These people, in general terms, were born in the 1930s, grew up during the Second World War, and went to school in the 1940s or 1950s. As a cohort they have been loyal to the church, sticking at it with a commitment not seen in younger cohorts, which have included those who have dropped out of church for a while and then returned. This is the grandparent Third Age group whose time and energies will often be willingly given if asked and if able.

All this is underlined by the desire of church attenders that mission agencies should tend to be transforming, empowering and Spirit-led – all dynamic words. This perhaps is exemplified too in the popularity of Christmas church attendance, one person in 7 in the population, with two-fifths of such attendance being in an Anglican church.

Walter Brueggemann points out that Jesus released energy: His "imagination and action stood against all the discerned data and in the face of the doubt and resistance of those to whom He came. That ultimate energising gave people a future when they believed that the grim present was the end and only possible state of existence."[5] He also said that "the task of prophetic imagination and ministry is *to bring to public expression those very hopes and yearnings* that have been denied so long and suppressed so deeply that we no longer know they are there."[6]

Energy is required if we are to pull out of the nosedive!

Positive: Growth is happening

A third, 34%, of English churches grew between 1998 and 2005, considerably more than the 21% which grew between 1989 and 1998. Not only did more churches see their congregations grow, but those who attended them were, on balance, coming slightly more regularly (an extra four times a year). The midweek attendance added roughly 10% to the numbers of Sunday attendance, and that percentage is also higher than it was in the 1990s.

Growth is seen reversely in that the Evangelicals are declining less rapidly than the non-Evangelicals, and are thus becoming a larger proportion of the whole, 40% in 2005. The reasons for this might be worth ascertaining, especially as "the people of the Book" are reading it less than the non-Evangelicals! Within Evangelicalism, it may be asked why the Charismatic Evangelicals are declining least rapidly of all (and are therefore becoming a larger proportion within the evangelical movement)[7].

Perhaps growth is happening because many ministers see evangelism as a priority, albeit after preaching and teaching their existing congregation. This is in marked contrast to many in their congregations who put looking after the church fabric as the second highest priority for church resources rather than evangelism or growth.

This has two implications. The importance of the Suburban and Town church attendance strength cannot be overlooked. They are the main engine of church attendance in this country, and if the church is to pull out of its nosedive and take off again, some of that will have to be seen in these key environments.

The other implication is the way in which "growth" happens. As Reginald Bibby reminds us, "Jesus didn't just tell people to go into all the world. He told them when they got there, to say something."[8] In an increasingly multi-cultural society, more and more communication is cross-cultural. However, the principles of cross-cultural communication are also relevant in the 54% of "white-only" congregations; perhaps some of the growth is due to this being done in an increasingly effective manner.

Positive: Leadership vision

Growth and leadership are closely related. Much of the growth that has been seen has come through leaders with a vision. Part of the reason why the Anglican Diocese of London has repeatedly seen both its Electoral Roll and Sunday attendance figures increase through the last decade is that each incumbent is required to work to a five year vision programme.

Perhaps this emphasis in Dioceses like London (and Hereford) is one of the reasons why the Church of England's attendance has not declined as much as expected. While the lack of younger ministers brings problems of relating to similar age cohorts, one benefit of older leaders may be that they have learned more leadership skills perhaps before they were ordained, as well as subsequently. The training of leadership is also of crucial importance, and an essential part of this needs to be in the skills of developing teams[9].

So is the need to match the different leadership abilities with the varying size of churches. Smaller churches require different skills from those of larger churches; it is important this is recognised so that suitable training (and preparatory experience) can be provided. Furthermore, it is important that the particular skills of any one person are matched with the leadership needed for any particular church.

As it happens, all the leaders of churches with more than 300 in their Sunday congregation who replied to the Census are male, although one imagines this will change over the next decade. At the other end of the scale, when individuals are often responsible for multiple congregations, the stress factor in being asked to look after too many without adequate lay support needs also to be monitored. Two ministers who replied were each responsible for 16 congregations.

Positive: Greater London is booming

Greater London is different! It has 11% of the entire country's churches, but 20% of its churchgoers. Its churches are on average twice the size of those outside the capital. Mission activity and ethnic activity have helped to increase the number of churches by 6% in the 7 years ending 2005 to over 4,000. It is home to 23% of Evangelical churchgoers, an incredible 53% of Pentecostals in England, and 57% of churchgoers aged 20 to 29.

Most of the largest (non-Roman Catholic) churches in the country are located in Greater London, whether black majority (Kingsway International, Ruach or Jesus House), Pentecostal (Kensington Temple), Anglican (Holy Trinity, Brompton and All Souls, Langham Place), or Independent (Hillsong). These largest/mega churches are all evangelical, but other large churches in London follow other traditions (especially several all called St Mary's in west London). There are also the major cathedrals: St Paul's, Westminster Cathedral and Westminster Abbey. These City Centre churches have huge resources and expertise; can their knowledge and experience be shared elsewhere, perhaps especially outside the metropolis?

Likewise, the Inner City, both in Greater London but also elsewhere, is a kaleidoscope of cultural differences and varying traditions. How can these be shared, so that "iron sharpens iron" and the different strengths of each can mutually support and develop each other? Because so much growth is happening there, particularly in Inner London, it is important that the principles and values that are being expressed and worked through should be shared with other, especially white, congregations both inside and outside of the capital. It may well be that what happens in the capital can influence other parts of the country also.

There is a downside to this, however. If Greater London has so many positives, and so much relative strength, it means that the other 46 counties in England have fewer positives and less strength. It is easy for those based in Greater London to assume the rest of the country is similar, but the stresses and opportunities are actually quite different.

One way of pulling out of the nosedive could be through the use of the "Minster Model"[10]: essentially, the sharing of resources and the supervision of these shared opportunities. This approach might well help to focus enough energy and power to be able to level out from the downward spiral, and even to start soaring again.

Negative: Apathy is rife also

Although there are many positives flowing from this research, there also areas of grave concern. Half, 50%, of the churches declined during the period 1998–2005, and the collective strength of their losses far outweighed the gains of the churches which grew. Let us not assume all is well. It isn't! It is probably strictly unfair to totally correlate apathy and decline; there are many struggling church leaders passionate about change which somehow isn't happening.

There continues to be a very considerable absence of work with young people, who are continuing to leave the church, albeit in smaller proportions than were seen during the 1990s. Two-fifths of churches have *no work* among those under 11; half *no work* with those aged 11 to 14; three-fifths *no work* with those aged 15 to 19 (Chapter 10).

There is the suggestion that black youth may be falling away as well as white youth. Girls are leaving more than boys; indeed there are slightly more young men aged 15 to 19 in church than young women (51% to 49%). There is perhaps an awareness-of-own-identity issue here. There is also the issue of authority, seen in South Africa[11] but also in this country, whereby church teaching on lifestyle and behaviour is simply not being followed.

The 30 to 44 age-group especially are seeing greater annual losses than during 1989 to 1998, and so is the age-group 45 to 64. These losses began in the 1990s, but were drowned by the huge numbers of young people leaving. This "loss" in reality is folk coming to church less frequently – once a month perhaps rather than once a week. 72% of those no longer present so regularly aged 30 to 44 are women, as are 63% of those aged 45 to 64. During 1998 and 2005, 1,000 women per week ceased regular attendance. A key question emerging from this is whether such changed frequency of attendance will continue into the future as these cohorts grow older? If it does, then an additional vacuum will emerge in general church attendance.

Many of those aged 30 to 44 are married with a family. Lacking in the church in this age-group or younger are many who are co-habiting, with or without children, and lone parents, despite these groups becoming an increasingly large percentage of families in the UK.

Other issues are whether small churches, especially in rural areas, are truly viable, with perhaps the emphasis on Commuter Rural (rather than Remoter Rural) where the average age of attendance is higher than average. Are Commuter Rural churches less inclined to reach out in evangelism?

The difficulty of women ministers who appear to serve in declining, small, liberal, rural congregations needs to be faced. The key issue here is location – being in a Rural church is likely to bring with it the other factors. Equally it needs to be stated that many women cannot be held responsible for the decline; they were appointed to an already declining congregation. However, some women appointed to a declining congregation are now looking after a growing church, though the reverse is also true. But this is no different to male ministers; growth and decline are related to leadership and vision, not gender. The challenge is perhaps to encourage ministers to be change agents.

Are there ways in which these various factors can be used to make challenges to church leaders for the period ahead? I believe there are.

Challenge 1: Double the congregation!

The first challenge that might be made to church leaders is to *double the size of your congregation over the next five years*, say by 2012. Before reading the next paragraph, just ask if you were going to do this, what steps would you take.

This could be undertaken in a
variety of different ways,
perhaps in conjunction with
each other:

Do you
have a
friend?

CHALLENGE 1
DOUBLE THE
CONGREGATION

- Could a "Fresh Expression"
  congregation be started?

- Could a specific church
  plant be made outside your
  congregation?

- Could another, multiple,
  congregation be begun within the existing church, say for
  older people, or a Youth Service?

- Could a new service be held at a totally different time, say at
  4.00pm or after school mid-week?

- Could you refresh your church website or begin one?

- Could you appoint a Children's or Youth Worker? 20% of
  churches have one.

- Hold an Alpha (or other) course, perhaps again?

- Organise a follow-up course for those who have already
  attended a teaching course, perhaps more of a discipleship
  course?

- Talk with other successful churches that you feel you could
  learn from?

- Consider whether there are things you cannot do alone but
  could do in cooperation with another local church?

- Make the preaching more relevant? "Relevance is vital," says
  Jeff Lucas[12], one of the leaders of Spring Harvest.

- Work out a strategy of where you're going, or where you'd
  like to be in, say, 5 years' time?

Starting new services at quite different times has worked in some churches. A Leicestershire Baptist church took the brave decision to abolish its Sunday morning service, which had been held since the church started 70 years previously, and substituted a 4 o'clock service, with tea and cake at 3.30pm. Children could play football on the Sunday morning, or rehearse with their music band, and still come to church! Shopping could be fitted in, and the visit to relatives, all before church. Their congregation doubled from 100 to 200 in a month.

A church website is an extension of its public face to the community. It should be welcoming and informative to curious visitors and church members alike, demonstrating "church" to be a positive and friendly experience. Church websites outnumber other Christian sites by 5 to 1 and can often be a person's first point of contact with a church. They therefore have huge potential for outreach and to create a good "first impression". "Week in, week out, more visitors turn up at our church on a Sunday because of the website, than anything else", said a church leader in Kingston[13].

It may be that your church of 25 people has 20 people over 60 in it; can you accomplish what some others have done and encourage these older people to invite their friends, neighbours and relatives to come to church, and so increase the number of those over 60 in your congregation? There is no law which says a church must have so many young people, nor any against having a growing congregation of older people. A number of churches with elderly congregations have seen their numbers double, even triple, over a few years – could yours do the same?

If the numbers increase, the energy, enthusiasm, effort, excitement, excellence will abound (the abundance of 'E' factors that Charles Handy recognises in successful organisations[14]). "The talk is about 'we', not 'I', and there is a sense that the organization is on some sort of mission, not just to make money, but something grander, something worthy of one's commitment, skills and time."[15] Recent research shows that, if present in church, those in their 20s are often very highly committed[16]; perhaps some of their energy can be released into a church's leadership; you could aim for 35% of your leadership being under 35.

If growth is occurring, people are having to work together. The priorities of minister and congregation, rather than being different, have to begin to merge. So the impact is felt throughout the church, and, inevitably, in its neighbourhood also. Success leads to success and more people will come along just "to see what is happening". Church resources, both in financial and human terms, will also increase.

Confidence in the church, in each other, and in the Gospel itself returns when the church is growing. "A confident church is one which knows in whom it believes," according to Archbishop Rowan Williams at a Conference[17].

Why suggest the five year period? Because it is important to have a definite objective or target. In the Anglican Dioceses of both London and Hereford the emphasis is on leadership over a five year period, with specific objectives, and through a church team (although this is constituted differently in the two Dioceses). Both of these Dioceses are growing, and the example their senior leaders are setting, and giving, can be replicated elsewhere. Some people object to goals being set, but Jesus worked to goals, so why can't we? Jesus had Jerusalem as His target in a particular time-frame, and He achieved it[18].

Challenge 2: Have more midweek activity!

Nearly two-fifths, 38%, of churches have tried Alpha, and a further 24% of churches have used other courses, perhaps a total of say 60%, assuming some churches will have used more than one. Three-fifths of the churches in the country either have used or are using teaching-Christianity courses of one kind or another. In the main, they are doing so successfully if, as the Alpha usage recorded in Chapter 11 shows, they continue to hold the course for at least 3 years, and perhaps for six[19].

Midweek worship is increasing, and more people are coming to midweek events. Alpha and other like courses are nearly always held on a weekday. They require partnership between leadership and lay people, and demand much energy in the process. But the activity seems to work and more people are contacted, some of whom come to faith and start attending church, while others are enabled to re-start church again following a previous lapse.

That leaves two-fifths of the churches in the country who perhaps could try such a course, or other midweek activity. Research has shown that midweek activities held purposefully, that is, specifically related to the church's overall vision, are often successful in bringing people in. Effectively the midweek activities mostly help to grow the church "fringe" and there are a number of pieces of research which show that those joining the church are much more likely to be those who have been on the "fringe" in the first instance, sometimes for several years.

In one large London church, a couple started coming. The lady was a believer with an excellent voice (so joined the choir), but her husband was not. However, he felt he should accompany her to church, and sat during each service, sometimes singing a hymn or otherwise participating, but other times not. He also came with her to a friendly midweek luncheon club for older people organised by the church. After 10 years, when the minister was about to move to another position, the husband told him one day, "I've prayed the prayer". When someone said how glad they were he had been converted he said, "I'm just a baby in the faith, so please pray for me" – despite having listened to 2 sermons every Sunday for 10 years!

Four years later, their lodger, a widow in her late 60s, also made a commitment.

Could your church *consider extra weekday or other activities to reach out to those in your local community*? Nigel McCulloch, Bishop of Manchester, started a "Back to Church" Sunday in 2004 which resulted in some 1,200 people coming to a church on the Sunday in question (encouraged by a goody bag of Divine chocolate donated by the local Co-op). Of these, 600 were still coming to church 6 months later[20]. Other Dioceses have since taken up the idea.

Do you have "Third Agers" (those aged 65 to 74) in your church? Some of these may have a vision for change, and an energy to make it happen. Could they start an extra midweek activity – perhaps a course on "How to be an effective Grandparent"?

Challenge 3: Think strategically!

While vision is important, knowing how it may be fulfilled is even more crucial! Working out what to do is vital if the church is to move forward, and such *strategic thinking needs to take place at all levels*. It needs to take place[21]:

- At the most senior level – the strategic significance level – where lateral thinking, thinking outside the box, spanning past and present, wide-ranging thinking can happen. It is where the leader decides on the big picture he/she would like to see in 5 years' time, and tries to answer the question of how it may be accomplished.

- At the operational impact level – where it is translated into management areas, making it functional, being broad but specific, with delegated responsibility to others as appropriate. It is where the Youth Worker thinks through the syllabus to be followed, and which schools he or she should visit. He answers questions like: *What* to do? *Which* to do first? *When* to do it?

- At the tactical success level – where the rubber hits the road, where it is practical, detailed, day to day, at ground level. It is where the Sunday School teacher works out how to explain the Battle of Ai to his or her 13 year olds next Sunday.

Not everyone can think strategically. Some church leaders may need help. Bob Jackson, Archdeacon of Walsall and Church Growth Officer in the Diocese of Lichfield, spends some of his time discussing the local situation with clergy and then comes back after a few weeks to suggest a strategy he/she and their Parochial Church Council might consider following. Others may wish to visit ministers responsible for large churches whose very responsibility requires them to spend much time thinking strategically. Others may wish to approach a Mission Agency.

What is "strategy"? It has been defined as "a small number of big decisions which determine the future direction of a church over a period of 3 to 5 years"[22]. In other words, the church leadership in effect says, "We are going to do the following . . ." with the aim of completing the action in a given period of time.

Why is this critical? "The core of leadership is vision. Vision is seeing the potential purpose hidden in the chaos of the moment, but which could bring to birth new possibilities for a person, a company or a nation."[23] Strategic thinking has to take a church through the chaos of the moment, perhaps through the chaos of many moments, in order that a particular end may be achieved. Vision, integrity and judgement are the leadership qualities people seek, but only 30% see them in their leaders[24].

Vision is linked to values; and what better than the Christian values like freedom, family, gospel, community and nation[25]? Professor Yang Huilin of Renda University in Beijing was asked about Christianity in China. He replied, "China doesn't need a new religion. It needs a new value system and a new way of thinking."[26] So does the UK!

Clearly it is therefore important that leaders are trained to think strategically, and that where groups of key leaders meet together, some of their collective time is spent trying to answer where, as a body, they want to be in, say, 5 years' time. Not every gathering of senior leaders does this. I once asked a Diocesan Bishop if he had to explain what his Diocese was doing over the next 5 years at one of the regular meetings of the House of Bishops, whether that would give him greater determination to fulfil it; he said it would!

How do you begin to think strategically? Try answering questions such as:

- If you could change one thing about your present position (or your life), what would it be and why?

- What is the biggest hindrance you currently face with respect to evangelising your local community and how would you remove it?

- If resources were not a hindrance what feature would you innovate in the next 6 months?

- What would an effective, growing church look like in an era in which the church had pulled out of the nosedive?

Is strategic vision enough to make it happen? Actually no. As Sir Terry Leahy, Chairman of Tesco, said, "Strategy is only part of the battle. The difference between success and failure is the difference between implementing, say, 80% or only 50% of your plans."[27] In other words, perseverance, or cold-blooded determination or guts, is also required. But where leaders have this strength, growth invariably takes place. The winners of the Best Paper award at the 2004 Market Research Conference would agree – "the management of the process rather than the actual insight generation itself" is the key[28].

Challenge 4: Greater London as a model!

Greater London is different in its church life from almost any other part of England, in terms of the local environment, the number of larger churches, the growth in its congregations, the size and vibrancy of the ethnic majority churches, the size of its churches, the skills of its leaders, the age of its attenders, etc. How far can all these work together for mission?

London has a unique happening in a few years' time – the 2012 Olympic Games, which provide an immense opportunity for mission to the thousands of competitors and millions of visitors who will attend. Can the collective senior leadership, across all the denominations and ethnicities, work together with the leaders of, say, the largest churches in the capital, to generate an impressive momentum of mission for the Olympics which can spill over into other areas and further years? There are many meetings of church leaders and others on this very subject to discuss how this might be accomplished, and in the coming years a clear strategy needs to emerge and be implemented.

The importance for such a working together is not just vital for the Olympics and for the Greater London leaders involved in the process. Such collaboration could well be a model which other groups throughout the country could follow. *Greater London*'s uniqueness in church life could then perhaps become *a springboard by which its impact could be felt across the whole of England. That* is the real challenge!

Challenge 5: Pray!

Find another person (or more) in your church or local area burdened for the state of the country, the future of the church, particularly in your locality and those who have no living personal relationship with Jesus Christ. Pray together regularly and persistently for the growth of Christ's kingdom in your church.

Bob Jackson's conclusion is valid: "Within a declining . . . Church there is enough spiritual renewal going on to enable and empower significant church growth."[29] You *can* pull out of a nosedive!

So what does all this say?

Five challenges! Why not *go for it*? Conrad Hilton, who gave his name to the hotel chain, once said, "What I speak of is a brand of imaginative thinking backed by enthusiasm, vitality, expectation, to which all may aspire"[30]. Absolutely! You will never know whether or not you would have succeeded if you do not try.

> *"One does not discover new lands without consenting to lose sight of the shore."* (André Gide)

> *"Almost nothing that's possible is too improbable ever to happen."* (Andrew Brown)[31]

> *"Only he who sees the invincible can do the impossible."* (Michael Guido)[32]

> *"If you had faith as a mustard seed,"* said Jesus, *"you would say to this mulberry tree, 'Be pulled up by the roots and be planted in the sea, and it would have obeyed you.'"*[33]

Notes

Introduction

1 For those interested the actual formula behind these figures is $P = 196 \times \sqrt{[\{p(1-p)\}/N]}$, where p is the percentage in question, and N is the number on which it is based. When p = 6.3%, then (1 - p) is 93.7%. N = 18,720. Thus we have $P = 196 \times \sqrt{(0.063 \times 0.937/18720)} = 0.348$.

2 Advice given by Sir John Boreham prior to the 1989 English Church Census who acted as Statistical Adviser. At that time he was the Head of the Government Statistical Service (a post that today is now called the National Statistician), the highest statistical officer in the country.

3 A similar Table was published when the results of the 1998 English Church Attendance Survey were available. The Church of England figure was estimated at 975,900 and when published by Church House, the official figure was 976,800.

4 These figures are taken from the annual Catholic Directory and are 1.6% higher than those reported in *Pastoral and Population Statistics of the Catholic Community in England and Wales 1958-2002*, edited by A E C W Spencer, Pastoral Research Centre Report, Taunton, Somerset, 2004.

5 *The Future of the Church, Religious Trends* No 5, 2005/2006, edited by Peter Brierley, Christian Research, London, 2005, Table 12.14.1.

Chapter One The overall findings

1 *12 Trends in British Society*, Some statistical trends and what they imply for church leaders, Peter Brierley, Christian Research, London, 2005, Page 4.

2 *The Future of the Church, Religious Trends* No 5, 2005/2006, edited by Peter Brierley, Christian Research, London, 2005, Figure 4.9.6 assuming one-third of singles are single parent families.

3 *Turning the Tide: The Challenge Ahead,* Report of the 2002 Scottish Church Census, Peter Brierley, Christian Research, London, 2003.

4 Op cit (Item 1, *12 Trends*), Page 5.

5 Op cit (Item 1, *12 Trends*), Page 7.

6 Op cit (Item 2, *Trends* 5), Table 12.14.1.

7 The number of Christians attending church once a year has *fallen* by about 280,000 in the same period.

8 *Mission-shaped Church,* General Synod Committee, chaired by Rt Rev Graham Cray, Archbishops' Council, Church House Publishing, 2004.

9 Missionary shaped churches are: focussed on God the Trinity, incarnational, transformational, relational and making disciples (op cit Item 8, Page 81).

10 *International Alpha Courses in 2005*; private research report for Holy Trinity, Brompton, Christian Research, London, Peter Brierley, May 2006.

11 *The 2005 Alpha Invitation and Autumn Course*; private research report for Holy Trinity, Brompton, Christian Research, London, Peter Brierley, January 2006.

12 Quoted in *The Christian Challenge*, Vol XLIV, No 5, November/December 2005, Page 30.

13 *Secular Lives, Sacred Hearts,* Rev Alan Billings, SPCK, London, 2004, Page 37.

14 Article "Religious belief 'falling faster than church attendance'" by Matt Barnwell and Amy Igguiden in *The Daily Telegraph*, 17th August, 2005.

15 *The Death of Christian Britain*, Callum Brown, Routledge, London, 2001.

16 Such as *The Church Invisible*, Nick Page, Zondervan, Grand Rapids, Michigan, 2004; *A Churchless Faith*, Faith Journeys beyond the Churches, Alan Jamieson, SPCK, 2002; *Mission After Christendom*, David Smith, Darton, Longman and Todd, London, 2003; *Church After Christendom,* Stuart Murray, Paternoster, Carlisle, 2003; *The Church beyond the Congregation*, James Thwaites, Paternoster, Carlisle, 1999; *Post-Christendom,* Stuart Murray, Paternoster, Carlisle, 2004; *Invading Secular Space,* Martin Robinson and Dwight Smith, LionHudson, Oxford, 2003 and *The Next Christendom,* Philip Jenkins, Oxford University Press, Oxford, 2002.

17 Study undertaken for the Chartered Institute of Management in 1997 of 1,360 managers by Cary Cooper, Professor of Organisational Psychology, University of Manchester Institute of Science and Technology.

18 *Archdeacons in the early 21st Century,* Report for the National Archdeacons' Forum, Christian Research, London, May 2004, Page 9, with a further 22% working between 70 and 79 hours a week, and 43% between 60 and 69 hours a week.

19 Article in the *Church of England Newspaper*, 4th November 2005.

20 The intentionality behind some church plants is "to plant a church which in 5 years will plant another" (Martin Robinson, Director, Together in Mission).

21 Sermon by the Most Revd Rowan Williams at the Commissioning Service for the Fresh Expressions Team, 22nd September, 2005 at Lambeth Palace Chapel.

22 Where necessary they are included as part of the "Independent" group to reflect their autonomy.

23 Listed in *Religious Trends* No 1, 1998/1999, Page 2.18.

24 All Orthodox priests are non-stipendiary, except for two Greek Orthodox priests based in London. Bishops are however given a stipend.

25 Comment in personal letter from John Glass, General Superintendent, Elim Pentecostal Church.

26 Some earlier figures have been revised.

27 About 300 of these "closures" are simply transfers of Independent churches deciding to become linked to various New Church streams, which accounts for about two-thirds of "openings" of New Churches between 1989 and 1998.

28 Article "Time to close?" by Andy Peck in *Christianity*, December 2005, Page 14, which was followed by a further article "Finishing well" in the January, 2006 issue, Page 18.

29 For example in the article "Church closure and membership statistics: trends in four rural dioceses" by Carol Roberts and Leslie J Francis in *Rural Theology*, Volume 4, Number 1, Issue 66, 2006, Page 37.

30 Points made by Rev Dr Martin Robinson at European Church Growth Conference (now called Euronet), Kristiansand, Norway, April 2005.

31 Some arguments, for and against, are given in op cit (Item 2, *Trends* 5), Page 2.3.

32 *Restless Churches,* How Canada's Churches can contribute to the emerging religious renaissance, Reginald Bibby, Wood Lake Books, Novalis, Ontario, Canada, 2004, Page 33.

33 Grace Davie, Professor of Sociology at the University of Exeter, was speaking at the Conference in op cit (Item 30).

34 This is worked out in more detail in *Religion in Modern Europe, A Memory Mutates*, Grace Davie, Oxford University Press, Oxford, 2000, especially Chapters 3 and 4.

35 Article "Help! I'm lost in the crush at Ikea" by Iain Hollingshead, *Daily Telegraph Features*, 30th May, 2005, Page 13.

36 It is recognised that such chaplaincies are unable to undertake customary parochial activities, but as a Royal Navy Chaplain explained in a letter, "the Chaplaincy has extensive weekly input in the training programme" – in this case of HMS Raleigh, in Torpoint, Cornwall.

37 Like Surbiton Hill Methodist Church who took the Census on 15th May.

38 In terms of location, the Ashford Local Authority in Kent gave the highest response – 90% of its churches completed the Census form, followed by Dover (87%), Cotswold (84%), East Hertfordshire (80%), St Albans, Hertfordshire, Staffordshire Moorlands, Suffolk Coastal and Spelthorne, Surrey (all from 79%), Maidstone, Kent (77%), the town of Stroud, Gloucestershire (74%), the London Boroughs of Hillingdon (74%) and Richmond (73%), West Lindsey, Lincolnshire (73%) and the town of Chelmsford, Essex (70%).

39 Also called "Little-Easter" Sunday.

40 Courtesy of Noel Ford, *Church Times*, 13th May, 2005.

41 If all the churches not holding a service on Census Sunday were in Remoter Rural areas that would be 7% of the total. As the majority would be Anglican, however, the total number is 11.5% of all Anglican Remoter Rural churches, one church in 9.

42 These numbers can be put another way, by saying that between 1979 and 1989 numbers dropped at the average rate of 70,000 per year, between 1989 and 1998 numbers at 110,000 per year, between 1998 and 2005 numbers at 80,000 per year, and between 2005 and 2015 numbers they could drop at 70,000 per year. These figures indicate that the *rate* of decline is decreasing, as might be expected with smaller overall numbers. If the rate of decline reduces by 10,000 a year every 10 years, then it will be 2085 before it stops. Unfortunately by then there will be virtually no-one in the church to notice.

Chapter Two Going down Lewisham High Street

1 Peviously called "ethnic minority groups".

2 A helpful list of such is given in *Look what the Lord has done*, Mark Sturge, Scripture Union, Milton Keynes, 2005, Table 3, Pages 90f. which gives the location of the International Headquarters.

3 As with all the graphs in this chapter, it should be noticed that the years are not equally spaced apart, but the years in which the relevant Census took place.

4 The Anglican and Catholic figures are lower than those implicit in *Religious Trends* No 5, as the actual attendance levels in 2005 are lower than anticipated. Linear regression has used to estimate the 2015 figures here and elsewhere as there is insufficient data for more sophisticated forecasting methods.

5 The decline 2005 to 2015 is at a faster rate than between 1998 and 2005 partly because of the drop in numbers of young people.

6 See previous note; the total of all 4 Institutional Churches is 1,866,000 on these figures, just 7,000 above what is actually observed.

7 Using a dampened linear extrapolation of the three earlier figures would suggest a 2005 attendance of 973,000 for Catholics, 99,000 for the United Reformed and 36,000 for the Orthodox, but 758,000 for the Anglicans.

8 These changes are illustrated in *The 2005 English Church Census, Religious Trends No 6*, 2006/2007, edited Peter Brierley, Christian Research, London, Figure 2.13.3.

9 A graph illustrating the re-entries is given in *Church Statistics* 2003/2004, Research and Statistics Department, Archbishops' Council, Church House publishing, 2005, Page 43.

10 These counties (not Dioceses) were: Staffordshire (–1%), Gloucestershire (–2%), Leicestershire (–3%), Greater Manchester (–4%), Cleveland and the Isle of Man (–5% each), Buckinghamshire, Cambridgeshire, Cheshire and North Yorkshire (–6% each), Shropshire, Somerset and West Sussex (–7% each), Lancashire (–8%), Berkshire and Northumberland (–9% each). The changes are illustrated in op cit (Item 8, *Trends* 6), Figure 2.13.1.

11 Some of the thinking implicit in this situation may be found in the booklet *Challenges and Opportunities facing the Church of England over the next 15 years*, Christian Research, London, 2005.

12 See also John Hayward's article on the possibility of change in *Quadrant*, Christian Research, London, May 2006, Page 1.

13 Op cit (Item 8, *Trends* 6) at the bottom of Table 2 in Section 12 on left hand pages, that is, those with even numbers.

14 Many from the URC feel that as the only Uniting Church in the country they should be in a category by themselves; this argument would have more validity if they were larger!

15 Illustrated in op cit (Item 8, *Trends* 6), Figure 2.13.8.

16 An exception was made at the *Orthodoxy in the West Today and Tomorrow* Conference held in Swanwick in August 2004 when the policy of ordination was explained by the Bishop responsible for them.

17 Illustrated in op cit (Item 8, *Trends* 6), Figure 2.13.5.

18 Derbyshire, Greater Manchester, Lancashire and Merseyside.

19 West Sussex, Hampshire, Isle of Wight and Surrey.

20 Avon (Bristol), Essex, Greater London, Staffordshire, South Yorkshire, Warwickshire, West Midlands, West Yorkshire, but less so in Tyneside.

21 Lincolnshire and Shropshire.

22 See, for example, the front page article "Sharp drop in number of youngsters in churches" by Nick Lear, *Baptist Times*, 6th October, 2005.

23 The Baptist Union of Great Britain saw its membership increase from 141,000 in 2003 to 142,000 in 2004, and baptisms increase from 4,800 in 2003 to 5,000 in 2004. Much of this growth was in their Black Majority London churches.

24 East Sussex, Greater London, Greater Manchester, Lincolnshire, Shropshire and Somerset.

25 Sometimes the only way to classify them is through their name, or association with another body. Those with a Baptist association are put in the "Independent Baptist" category; those which are black are put as "Other Pentecostals"; those with a specific national identity are included with "Protestant Overseas Nationals" within the "Smaller denominations" group; those with a New Church or white charismatic background are usually located as "Other New Churches"; while the remainder are included in this group of "Other independent churches".

26 A detailed examination of the theology and culture of these churches both in the UK and USA at the turn of the century can be found in *Becoming Conversant with the Emerging Church*, Understanding a Movement and its Implications, Professor D A Carson, Zondervan, Grand Rapids, Michigan, 2005.

27 Article "Defining a fresh expression" by Rev Dr Steve Croft in *The Church of England Newspaper*, 12th May, 2006, Page 11.

28 Article "Why fresh expressions are needed in every parish" in *Church of England Newspaper*, 3rd March, 2006.

29 An assessment of the 2004 event may be found in *Quadrant*, Christian Research, London, March 2005, Page 1.

30 Rev Michael Moynagh reported at the Strategic Thinkers Forum held in February, 2005 that one church he knew had only 8 conversions out of 200 people who had newly joined their church.

31 An excellent list may be found in *The Road to Growth: towards a thriving Church*, Bob Jackson, Church House Publishing, London, 2005, Chapter 7.

32 For example, Rejesus.co.uk is one such site started in 2002, which on 8th May 2005 had 1,640 visits.

33 After the report *Mission-shaped Church*, Church House Publishing, London, presented to the Church of England Synod from a committee chaired by the Bishop of Maidstone, Graham Cray, in 2004.

34 *Breaking the Mould of Christendom: Kingdom Community, Diaconal Church and the Liberation of the Laity*, David Clark, Epworth Press, Peterborough, Cambs., November 2005.

35 As cited by the Archbishop of Canterbury, the Most Rev Rowan Williams speaking at the National Conference of Archdeacons, Swanwick, January 2005.

36 *The Emerging Church: Introductory Reading Guide* (50 titles), Darren Cronshaw, Zadok Paper Number S143, Summer 2005, Fitzroy, Australia, Page 9.

37 Article "Church coffers are half full, not half empty" by Rt Rev Richard Chartres in *The Times*, 18th June, 2005.

38 Talk given at the Strategic Thinkers Forum, Mulberry House, High Ongar, Essex, February 2005, organised by Christian Research, London.

39 *Rapid Increase in Alternative Forms of the Church*, Barna Update, barna@barna.org, accessed 24th October, 2005, Page 2.

40 Some do not follow all of the "shepherding", or "mentoring" discipleship programmes advocated by many New Churches.

41 *Religious Trends* No 5, 2005/2006, Christian Research, London, 2005, Table 9.10.5.

42 In 2004, Covenant Ministries International changed, with its member churches choosing to affiliate themselves with Lifelink International, Ministries without Borders or remaining with the re-formed Together. The largest of these is Ministries without Borders; the other two groups are included within "Smaller New Church Streams".

43 At least 10% increases in Avon, Cambridgeshire, the Channel Islands, Cleveland, Greater London, Greater Manchester, Hampshire, Herefordshire, Nottinghamshire and Oxfordshire, and smaller increases in Bedfordshire, Buckinghamshire, East Sussex, Merseyside, Northamptonshire and West Yorkshire.

44 Quakers encourage others to join what they call the "Quaker Quest: a spiritual path for our time", leaflet produced by the Manchester Quakers.

45 Cheshire, Derbyshire, Gloucestershire, Somerset and Worcestershire. These are illustrated in op cit (Item 8, *Trends* 6), Figure 2.13.9.

46 Story from Nick & Kerry Coke taken from *Urban Expression Newsletter*, February 2006, Page 3. www.urbanexpression.org.uk

47 For English Church Census purposes the congregations in these churches are split equally between those denominations which form the LEP; thus, for example, a congregation of 60 people in a Anglican/Baptist LEP would be taken as being 30 Anglican and 30 Baptist. In this way double counting is avoided. Likewise the church itself would be counted as $^1/_2$ Anglican and $^1/_2$ Baptist.

48 *Church Statistics,* 2003/4, Research and Statistics Department, Archbishops' Council, Church House Publishing, London, 2005, Page 1.

49 Berkshire (469 to 478), Dorset (685 to 688), Hampshire (1,005 to 1,010), Northamptonshire (574 to 579), Oxfordshire (681 to 683), Suffolk (871 to 874), West Midlands (1,231 to 1,281) and Wiltshire (604 to 614).

50 Details of the composition of their congregation during different years in the 1990s by ethnicity are given in op cit (Item 2, Sturge), Table 1, Page 45. For example, in 1997 their congregation was 47% African, 19% Caucasian, 12% Caribbean, 7% Asian, 4% Chinese and 11% others.

51 Article "Church: full on" by Gill Troop, *Christianity*, April 2005, Page 22.

52 Martin Robinson speaking at *Euronet* Conference, Kristiansand, Norway, April, 2005. Another Hillsong congregation was being started in Guildford, Surrey in 2006.

53 Article "Church thriving on a message of hope" by Chris Bond in *Yorkshire Post*, 24th May 2005, Page 9.

Chapter Three Halfway up the candle

1 Rev Thomas Moore, of St James' Church, Bushey, Hertfordshire.

2 Such as those carried out as Strategic Reviews of Anglican Deaneries in the Diocese of Rochester by Christian Research at the turn of the 21st century.

3 *Religious Trends* No 6, 2006/2007, edited by Peter Brierley, Christian Research, London, 2006, Page 5.13.

4 See, for example, *Painting by Numbers*, Peter Brierley, Christian Research, London, 2005, Chapter 6.

5 Op cit (Item 3, *Trends* 6), Page 5.12.

6 Probably using the word in its old meaning of "universal", and distinct from those Anglicans who are "Anglo-Catholic".

7 In previous studies a number ticked both the "Charismatic" and "Catholic" boxes, but the number doing so in 2005 was very small, only 21 churches, 13 of which are included within "Catholic" and 8, who also ticked "Evangelical", counted as "Charismatic Evangelical".

8 Churchmanship was not asked in the 1979 English Church Census.

9 The detailed figures are given in op cit (Item 3, *Trends* 6), Table 12.2.4.

10 *The Spiritual Revolution*, Paul Heelas and Linda Woodhead, et al., Blackwell Publishing, 2005. ISBN: 1 4051 1959 4.

11 Ibid., Page 75.

12 *Evangelicals Etcetera, Conflict and Conviction in the Church of England's Parties*, Rev Kevin Randall, Ashgate, Aldershot, Hampshire, 2005.

13 This needs to be set against the growing importance of church attendance in Greater London as a whole, which is increasing from 14% in 1979 to 17% in 1989, 20% in 2005 and a forecast of 23% by 2015. The Evangelical percentages of the total are consistently greater than these figures.

14 Nor should it be seen as attempting to count numbers associated with groups called "Mainstream Anglicans" or "Mainstream" in the United Reformed Church.

15 Op cit (Item 3, *Trends* 6), Page 5.15.

16 97 people in 2005 in Greater London compared with 84 per congregation in England as a whole.

17 *The Road to Growth towards a thriving church*, Ven Bob Jackson, Church House Publishing, London, 2005, Chapter 8.

18 Op cit (Item 3, *Trends* 6), Table 5.15.

19 Op cit (Item 3, *Trends* 6), Page 5.14.

20 The Table includes revised figures for 1998.

21 Op cit (Item 3, *Trends* 6), Table 5.14.2.

22 Op cit (Item 17, Jackson), Page 107.

Chapter Four Oh, to be in England!

1 Robert Browning, *Home-thoughts, from Abroad,* as in *The Concise Oxford Dictionary of Quotations*, Oxford University Press, Oxford, 1967, Page 44.

2 Up 8% between 1989 and 1998, *Religious Trends* No 3, 2002/2003, edited by Peter Brierley, Christian Research, London, 2001, Table 12.42.1. The figures for Inner London, given in that Table as increasing 9%, were subsequently revised by the government to be +7.2% against the +7.6% for Remoter Rural areas; these later figures being given in *The Future of the Church, Religious Trends* No 5, 2005/2006, Christian Research, London, Table 7.12.1.

3 Another 11% of churchgoers lived in Commuter Rural areas in 2005, compared with 15% of the population.

4 90% replied to the question on environment, out of a total response of 70%, meaning that 63% of churches on the Christian Research data base have an environmental classification given by their minister. The others have been estimated.

5 *Religious Trends* No 6, 2006/2007, edited by Peter Brierley, Christian Research, London, 2006, Table 1 on the odd-numbered pages in Section 12.

6 The actual wording on the 1989 form was "Rural: Commuter/Dormitory area".

7 The actual wording on the 1989 form was "Rural: Other areas".

8 Total of areas labelled E, F, $^1/_2$ of G, I, L, M, S and U in Table 12.42.1 in op cit (Item 2, *Trends* 3).

9 The actual numbers are given in Table 12.3.1 in op cit (Item 5, *Trends* 6).

10 Op cit (Item 5, *Trends* 6), Tables 5.16.3 and 5.17.3.

11 Taken as fewer than 3% of the total number of churches in that denomination.

12 *Seeds in Holy Ground,* A Workbook for Rural Churches, edited by Jill Hopkinson and Anne Richards, Archbishops' Council, Acora Publishing, GC Misc 803, 2005, Page 11.

13 *How do we keep our Parish Churches?*, Trevor Cooper, The Ecclesiological Society, 2004, Table F1, Page 67, for the Church of England figure, and *The Tide is Running Out*, Peter Brierley, Christian Research, London, 2000, Page 205 for the Methodist figure.

14 Article "Financial plea from Church to State over buildings" in the *Church of England Newspaper*, 20th January, 2006, Page 2.

15 Such as St Augustine's, Addlestone, Surrey in 2005, according to the report on Page 1 of *The Herald*, Diocese of Guildford, Number 209, October 2005, to the Surrey Islamic Trust.

16 Examples taken from op cit (Item 12, *Seeds*), Pages 36f.

17 Report "Why the nation needs to support country churches" on the February 2006 Synod meeting, in the *Church Times*, 10th February, 2006, Page 18.

18 *Changing Rural Life*, A Christian response to key rural issues, edited by Jeremy Martineau, Leslie Francis and Peter Francis, Canterbury Press, Norwich, 2004, Page 23.

19 This is an excellent example of a Community-led church, shaped by community engagement, as mentioned in Chapter 2.

20 Taken from *Inside Out*, the CWM magazine, June-August 2005, Number 45, Page 4.

21 The detailed figures are in op cit (Item 5, *Trends* 6), Table 5.18.3.

22 See, for example, *Leadership, Vision and Growing Churches*, Christian Research, London, 2003, Page 22.

23 Some may find useful *The Urban Church: A Practitioner's Resource Book*, edited by Michael Eastman and Steve Latham, SPCK, London, 2005.

24 Article "Use of Monte Carlo simulation for the public sector" by Roberto Foa and Melanie Howard in the *International Journal of Market Research*, Volume 48, Issue 1, 2006, Page 27.

25 The numbers on which these percentages are based are given in op cit (Item 5, *Trends* 6), Table 5.18.1.

26 Op cit., (Item 5, *Trends* 6), Table 12.75.4.

27 Report "Busy agenda set for February Synod" in the *Church of England Newspaper*, London, 20th January, 2006, Page 2.

28 Article "Utopia UK" by John Dyson in *Readers' Digest*, London, February 2006, Page 121.

29 If, say, 7% of these were churchgoers, that's 24,600 people or 9.5% of all the Remoter Rural churchgoers mentioned in 2005 in Table 4.3.

30 Op cit., (Item 28, Article).

31 Article "Psychological type preference of rural churchgoers" by Charlotte Craig in *Rural Theology*, Volume 3 Number 2, 2005, Page 128.

32 The numbers on which these percentages are based are given in op cit (Item 5, *Trends* 6), Table 5.18.4.

33 The other two environments where the proportion attending twice weekly is higher than average are Separate Towns and Other built-up areas. These are the two environments which also have the highest percentage of stable churches, and whose percentage of growing churches is least. Since older people are much more likely to attend church twice on a Sunday than younger people this accords with the previous finding of a high proportion in these environments who are 65 or over (although not the highest as it happens).

34 These percentages are derived from the figures analysed in Chapter 8.

35 Details of the Commission for Rural Communities are on: www.exchange.ruralcommunities.gov.uk

Chapter Five Beating the drums

1 Article in *The Yorkshire Post* 1st December 2005.

2 It was then called the Central Statistical Office.

3 It should be noted that the ONS category "Chinese" does not include Korean and Japanese which are included in their classification as "Other Asian".

4   Full details of the 2001 Population Census expansion of the categories are given in *The Future of the Church, Religious Trends* No 5, 2005/2006, edited by Peter Brierley, Christian Research, London, 2005, Table 9.20.4.

5   *Population Trends*, Office for National Statistics, Number 105, Autumn 2001, Page 9.

6   At the time of writing no later breakdown of the English population by ethnic minority groups had been published so the figures in Table 5.1 are an extrapolation from earlier years.

7   *Population Trends*, National Statistics, Palgrave Macmillan, Number 123, Spring 2006, Page 23.

8   214,300 in Table 2.1 out of 525,600 in Table 5.1.

9   *Look what the Lord has done!*, Mark Sturge, Scripture Union, Bletchley, Hertfordshire, 2005, Pages 91–93.

10 An example of such is in Chapter 5 on "Body and Soul" in George Alagiah's forthcoming book.

11 An example is Main Road Baptist Church in Sidcup, London Borough of Bexley where an almost entirely white congregation called a black minister as its Pastor. The same happens in other countries also: an article "African initiated Christianity in Eastern Europe" by J Kwabena Asamoah-Gyadu describes a church of 20,000 largely white Ukrainians led by a Nigerian-born Pastor Sunday Adelaja in *International Bulletin of Missionary Research*, OMSC, Connecticut, United States, Volume 30, Number 2, April 2006, Page 73.

12 Article "Americans reveal their top priority in life" by George Barna, *Barna Update*, The Barna Group, Ventura, California, United States, March 2006, Page 2.

13 Research project "Migration and social mobility: the life chances of Britain's minority ethnic communities", *Findings*, Joseph Rowntree Foundation, York, November 2005.

14 A map illustrating this spread is given in *Religious Trends* No 1, 1998/1999, edited by Peter Brierley, OM Publishing, Carlisle and Christian Research, London, 1997, Figure 4.5.4.

15 Op cit (Item 10).

16 Although generally I quote percentages in whole numbers, some of the proportions need to be given to a decimal place for clarity.

17 Article "Accounting for the Uncounted" by Roger Finke and Christopher Scheitle, in *Review of Religious Research*, Illinois, USA, Volume 47, Number 1, September 2005, Page 14.

18 Only two counts of black churchgoers were undertaken prior to 1998. The Methodists had 16,000 in 1985, and the Anglicans had 27,200 in 1992.

19 *Religious Trends* No 6, 2006/2007, edited by Dr Peter Brierley, Christian Research, London, 2006, Table 5.19.1.

20 Ibid., Table 5.19.3.

21 The black proportion of Evangelicals is 17%, half as much again as the 11.7% of adherents in the United States, op cit (Item 17, *Review*).

22 Based on the actual African and Caribbean percentage when measured in 1997 but not since, unfortunately. Given in Table 1, Page 45 of op cit (Item 9, Sturge).

23 Article "Church coffers are half full, not half empty", by Rt Rev Richard Chartres, *The Times*, 18th June, 2005.

24 Tomorrow Project, citing *Mapping Guide*, Leicester Statistics, 2005.

25 Avon, Berkshire, Cambridgeshire, East Sussex, Essex, Greater Manchester, Hertfordshire, Northamptonshire, South Yorkshire, Staffordshire, Surrey, West Yorkshire and Worcestershire.

26 Op cit., (Item 19, *Trends* 6), Page 2.19.2.

27 From David Beales, leader of DNA Networks, 10th September, 2005.

28 Interview between Geoffrey Smith, Christian Friends of Israel, and Messianic Rabbi Moshe Laurie, 15th March 2005, issued by CFI Communications.

29 *The Church of England Newspaper*, 3rd March, 2006, Page 15.

30 Article "Family building intentions in England and Wales", Steve Smallwood and Julie Jefferies, in *Population Trends*, Number 112, Summer 2003, Office for National Statistics, London, Page 24.

31 Article "Barna Reviews Top Religious Trends of 2005" in *Barna Update*, 20th December 2005, www.barna.org, Page 2.

32 Op cit. (Item 9, Sturge), Page 31.

33 Article "Black majority" by Jonathan Oloyede in *Christianity*, October 2005, Page 26.

34 *Respect*, Understanding Caribbean British Christianity, Bishop Joe D Aldred, Epworth, Peterborough, Cambridgeshire, 2005.

35 St Mary, Our Lady of Reparation, Roman Catholic Church, Croydon, Surrey.

36 McGavran's "Homogeneous Unit Principle" of church growth – people are attracted to churches where those of similar culture, background, education, etc. are present – is seen to be working here, even though the church is multi-racial.

37 Op cit. (Item 33, Oloyede).

38 Personal conversation, May 2006.

39 Article "Terrorism should not end our rights" by Ram Gidoomal, *The Church of England Newspaper*, 2nd September, 2005, Page 15.

40 Proverbs Chapter 29, Verse 18.

Chapter Six "Hallowed be Thy Game!"

1 Session "The allure of celebrity and its relation to Implicit Religion" by Claudia May, at the Network for Implicit Religion Conference, Denton, North Yorkshire, May 2005.

2 Revd Paul Simmonds, Mission Adviser, Coventry Diocese, 1999.

3 For example, the article "The Celtic canary in the UK's coal mine" by Mark Steyn in *The Daily Telegraph*, 24th January, 2006.

4 The total numbers are graphed in Figure 1.3.

5 Such as Above Bar Church, Southampton, which has been undertaking regular surveys of its congregation every June since 1996. Details from Clive Osmond.

6 *Restless Churches*, Reginald Bibby, Wood Lake Books, Novalis, Toronto, Canada, 2004, Page 43.

7 Ring Lardner, quoted in *Father's Wit*, edited by Rosemarie Jarski, Prion, 2005, Page 88.

8 *Winning Them Back*, Eddie Gibbs, MARC, Tunbridge Wells, Kent, 1993, and *Finding Faith in 1994*, a survey undertaken for Churches Together in England, a summary of which was published in *Quadrant*, Christian Research, London, March 1998.

9 Article "Parishes asked to aid clergy pensions" on BBC News website, 3rd May, 2001, read 24th May, 2006, www.news.bbc.co.uk/1/hi/uk/1309961.stm

10 But does not prove it; detailed mortality calculations would be needed to do that.

11 Op cit., (Item 6, *Restless Churches*), Page 99.

12 *Youth Matters Green Paper*, Department for Education and Skills, www.dfes.gov.uk/ publications/ youth, accessed 24th August 2005.

13 In *Reaching and Keeping Tweenagers*, Peter Brierley, Christian Research, London, 2002, Page 9, they are taken as those born between 1984 and 2002, and also called "Mosaics", while Generation Z, "Kaleidoscopes", are those born after 2002.

14 Article "Today's teens: happy but with no need for God in their lives" by Sylvia Collins-Mayo in *The Church of England Newspaper*, 12th May 2006, Page 7, quoting from *Making Sense of Generation Y*, Sara Savage, Sylvia Collins-Mayo, Bob Mayo with Graham Cray, Church House Publishing, London, 2006.

15 Ibid.

16 These figures may be expressed in a different way, as some churches may have had some aged, say, under 11, but none aged 11 to 14: one third, 33%, of churches had no-one under 11, or 11 to 14, or 15 to 19, that is, no-one at all under 20. Almost the same proportion, 35%, had no-one under 15, indicating that in 2% of churches the youngest attending is someone aged 15 to 19. Over two-fifths, 43%, of churches had no-one aged between 11 and 19, implying that 10% of churches had children under 11, but no-one aged 11 to 19.

17 See, for example, "Exciting times in Religious Studies!" by Dick Powell, Culham Institute, Abingdon, in *Audenshaw Papers*, AP213, Hinksey Network, 2005.

18 *Being Single*, The Challenge to the Church, Philip Watson, Darton, Longman and Todd, 2005, Table 5.

19 *The Future of the Church, Religious Trends* No 5, 2005/2006, edited by Dr Peter Brierley, Christian Research, London, 2005, Figure 4.9.2.

20 Private survey, *Attitudes to Morality and Religion among Secondary School Age Young People*, by Christian Research for Josh McDowell Inc., 2005, put the percentage at 1%.

21 Article "Granny, will you have the kids?" by Catherine Butcher in *Christianity*, July, 2005, Page 34.

22 Op cit., (Item 13, *Tweenagers*), Page 117.

23 Op cit., (Item 13, *Tweenagers*), Table 2.12.

24 Op cit., (Item 19, *Trends* 5), Figure 4.9.6.

25 *Turning the Tide, The Challenge Ahead*, Report of the 2002 Scottish Church Census, Dr Peter Brierley, Christian Research, London and Church of Scotland, Edinburgh, 2003, Page 55.

26 This is partly why, for example, Mark Greene, Director of the London Institute for Contemporary Christianity, emphasises the importance of work in church life.

27 *The Future of the Church: The Impact of Weekend Working*, Patrick Carroll, Papri Research, email of 24th November, 2005, papriresearch@btconnect.com

28 *Focus on Gender*, Office for National Statistics, London, 2004.

29 Survey of 1,360 managers for the Institute of Management (now the Chartered Institute) in 1997.

30 In the article "Till death (or divorce) us do part" by Clem Jackson, in *Christian Marketplace*, January 2006, Page 16, it was suggested that the divorce rate "among Christian couples is over 30%", but the author could not source this percentage when asked.

31 Op cit., (Item 20, *McDowell*).

32 For example, *Church Survey*, Rev Jon Willans, Ecumenical Research Committee, 2005, based on 14,000 replies to advertisements and requests for people to write about their church experience.

33 Article "Larger Church of England Churches", Dr Peter Brierley, *Church of England Newspaper*, 16th February 2005, based on private research.

34 Op cit., (Item 7, *Wit*), Page 237.

35 See respectively Table 4.7 and Figure 5.8.

36 The Anglican figure equates to 143,100 under the age of 15, of which 142,600 would be Church of England, a figure which is close to the official 2003 figure of 145,000.

37 The underlying figures for the Table and percentages for earlier years are given in *Religious Trends* No 6, 2006/2007, edited by Dr Peter Brierley, Christian Research, London, 2006, Tables 5.6.1 and 2.

38 The correlation co-efficient, r, is obtained from the closeness of a straight-line fit between, in this case, the percentage rate of decline 1998–2005 and the average age in 2005. It is a statistical measure which must fall between +1 and –1, so to be as close to –1 as –0.84 is very high.

39 Baptist Union of Great Britain Annual Returns Report for 2003.

40 Op cit., (Item 19, *Trends* 5), Figure 5.8.3.

41 Op cit., (Item 19, *Trends* 5), Figure 5.8.2.

42 Op cit., (Item 19, *Trends* 5), Table 5.8.1.

43 Op cit., (Item 19, *Trends* 5), Table 5.8.2.

44 Op cit., (Item 19, *Trends* 5), Figure 5.8.1.

45 *Older People and the Church*, Christian Research survey for the Sir Halley Stewart Project, February 2000.

46 Op cit., (Item 37, *Trends* 6), Table 5.7.2.

47 Op cit., (Item 19, *Trends* 5), Figure 4.9.6, based on *Marital Status projections for England and Wales*, News release by Government Actuary's Department, www.gad.gov.uk/news/marital_ status_projections; Christian figures compiled from 6,594 people including 1,910 Anglican churchgoers in the 2003 Cost of Conscience survey, published in *The Mind of Anglicans*, Christian Research; 939 churchgoers in a private 2003 survey about Methodist care services undertaken by Christian Research; 2,656 churchgoers across three Deanery Strategic Reviews undertaken for the Diocese of Rochester by Christian Research between 1999 and 2002; and 1,089 churchgoers across all denominations in a private survey about Bible Reading undertaken by Christian Research in 2003.

48 Op cit., (Item 20, *McDowell*).

49 Op cit., (Item 18, *Being Single*), Page 198.

50 Op cit., (Item 26, *Turning*).

51 Article "So what happened to the men?" by Kenwyn Pierce, editor, *CWM Inside Out*, June-August 2005, Number 45, Page 18.

52 Article "In spiritual matters, kids take their cues from Dad" by David Murrow, in Rick Warren's Ministry Toolbox, www.pastors.com/RWMT, downloaded 9th June 2005, Page 1.

53 For detailed figures of the percentage for each age-group by denomination see op cit. (Item 37, *Trends* 6), Table 5.8.1.

54 Ibid., Table 5.8.2.

55 Ibid., Table 5.8.3.

56 Op cit., (Item 20, *McDowell*), Table 3.3.

57 And as against 41% and 23% respectively for those who only rarely or never go to church.

58 *Sex, Alcohol and Other Drugs*, Exploring the links in young people's lives, Jeanie Lynch and Simon Blake, National Childrens' Bureau, London, 2004. The support and education we offer children often treats these issues in isolation.

Chapter Seven Prayerful sunbathing

1 Article "How the nation loves its church buildings" by Rev Lynda Barley, in *Church Times*, 3rd February, 2006, Page 10.

2 *The Prophetic Imagination*, Walter Brueggemann, Fortress Press, Minneapolis, United States, 2001, Page 27.

3 The church of St Helen's, Wheathampstead, St Albans, quoted with permission.

4 This is based on assuming that "every week" in practice means 44 times a year (allowing for sickness, etc.), twice on Sundays, 88 times a year, fortnightly 26 times a year and monthly 12 times a year. In 1998 the average was then 44 and in 2005 it was 48.

5 A t-test gave the value t = 4.98; with $v = 4$, $P > 0.001$.

6 Article in *Review of Religious Research*, Volume 46, Number 3, March 2005, Page 250.

7 *Barna Update* of 24th October 2005 which stated two-thirds of adults in a house church attend in any given week, www.barna.org accessed 31st October.

8 Article in *Religion Watch*, North Bellmore, New York, United States, January 2006, Page 6.

9 Fewer slips were returned from young people (as might otherwise be expected), so the age proportions have been amended to reflect the overall age-groups percentages.

10 Chapter 4 has already looked at the variations of frequency of church attendance by environment (Figure 4.8), showing that those living in Rural areas attended least frequently, Remoter Rural less often than Commuter Rural (11% and 14% twice, respectively), but this almost certainly reflects the lesser frequency with which services are actually held. Chapter 5 showed the variations of ethnicity by age of churchgoer (Figure 5.8).

11 Article in *Christianity* magazine, March 2006, Page 10.

12 Article "Selection Effects in Studies of Religious Influence" by Mark Regnerus and Christian Smith, in *Review of Religious Research*, Volume 47, Number 1, September 2005, ISSN 0034–673X.

13 84% for black people and 82% for all other non-white.

14 9% black and 11% other non-white.

15 Mark Chapter 2 Verse 27.

16 *Notes on the Miracles of Our Lord*, Richard C Trench, Pickering & Inglis Ltd., London, 1953, Page 343.

17 Church of St Mary, Our Lady of Reparation, Croydon, Surrey, quoted with permission.

18 *Church Statistics*, 2003/4, Research and Statistics Department, Archbishops' Council, Church House Publishing, London, 2005.

19 Usually only 27% of churchgoers attend Anglican services, so this is 10% more.

20 *Steps to the Future*, Dr Peter Brierley, Scripture Union, Milton Keynes, Bucks and Christian Research, London, 2000, Page 68.

21 Barna Research Group, taken from *Jaffarian's Missions Research Ezine*, January 2006, michaeldawna@earthlink.net

22 The non-Roman Catholic congregations include: Kingsway International Christian Centre, Hackney (10,000), Kensington Temple (Elim), West London (5,500), Hillsong in central London (5,000), Ruach Ministries, Brixton (4,000), House of Praise,

Woolwich (2,500), St Thomas Crookes, Sheffield (2,500), Holy Trinity, Brompton, West London (2,490), Jesus House for All Nations, Brent (2,200), All Souls in central London (2,000), Holy Trinity, Cheltenham (1,680), Basingstoke Community Church (1,450), Community Church, Southampton (1,400), St Andrew's, Chorleywood (1,400), Renewal Christian Centre, Solihull (1,400), Tonbridge Baptist Church (1,250), Kingdom Faith Church, Horsham (1,200), Woodlands Church, Bristol (1,100), St Ebbe's, Oxford (1,080), Jesmond Parish Church, Tyneside (1,030), Christian Centre, Nottingham (1,000) and Gold Hill Baptist Church, Chalfont St Peter (1,000).

23 *A Vision for Growth*, Prof Robin Gill, SPCK, London, 1994.

24 The average figures for each size category have been kept the same as were used in both the 1989 English Church Census, and the 1998 English Church Attendance Survey being, respectively for the different size groups, 5, 12, 30, 55, 110, 165, 220, 330, 440 and 550.

25 *Restless Churches*, How Canada's churches can contribute to the emerging religious renaissance, Reginald Bibby, Wood Lake Books, Novalis, Ontario, Canada, 2004, Page 132.

26 Private research report for USPG, *The Image of USPG*, Christian Research, London, May 2003.

27 These percentages vary somewhat from those given in *The Body Book 2005*, 10th Edition, published by Pioneer, Leatherhead and Christian Research, London, 2004, Page 5, partly because these were 2004 figures rather than 2005, and also because some of the smaller New Churches are not listed in that book.

28 Strictly the separate research has focussed on Anglican churches, not cathedrals, which are 350 or more in their regular Sunday congregation.

29 Paper "The increasing significance of the larger Church of England churches", Peter Brierley, Christian Research, presented at the National Larger Anglican Churches Conference, Swanwick, June, 2005.

30 Article "Is bigger always better in public services?" in *Public*, February 2006, Page 33.

31 Giving Evangelicals an overall average of 82, roughly double that of all non-Evangelicals, if Catholics are excluded, of 46.

32 *Religious Trends* No 6, 2006/2007, edited by Dr Peter Brierley, Christian Research, London, 2006, Pages 5.14 and 5.15, from which the average size of a church may be ascertained in any denomination and churchmanship combination for 1989, 1998 and 2005.

33 These are the same as the bottom line in Table 4.5.

34 *Whatever happened to the Brethren?*, Graham Brown, Partnership, Tiverton, Devon and Paternoster Press, Carlisle, Cumbria, 2003.

35 Fellowship of Independent Evangelical Churches; *Report of FIEC Churches Consultation*, Andrew Phelps, FIEC, London, May 2004.

Chapter Eight In the Country, Ma'am!

1 *Religious Trends* No 4, 2003/2004, edited by Dr Peter Brierley, published by Christian Research, London, 2003, Table 2.21.1.

2 *Church Statistics*, 2003/4, Research and Statistics Department, Archbishops' Council, Church House Publishing, London, 2005, Page 27. The percentage relates to Diocesan clergy

3 This number is used as the base for the calculations in this chapter.

4 *Religious Trends* No 3, 2001/2002, edited by Dr Peter Brierley, Christian Research, London, 2001, Table 2.21.1.

5 *Leadership, Vision and Growing Churches* survey on behalf of the Salvation Army but across all denominations in England in 2003. Results of ministerial age published in op cit (Item 1, *Trends* 4), Table 5.2.2.

6 Taking "Under 30" as 25 and "70 and over" as 75.

7 $t = 2.63, v = 5, P = 0.023$, not significant at 1% level.

8 For example, see *Hope for the Church*, Bob Jackson, Church House Publishing, London, 2002, Page 160 or *Church Growth in the 1990s*, research commissioned by Springboard, Abingdon, Oxon and Christian Research, London, June 2000.

9 *The Road to Growth*, Bob Jackson, Church House Publishing, London, 2005, Page 43.

10 Op cit (Item 2, *Statistics*), Page 33.

11 *Believe it or not!* by Revs Robbie Low and Francis Gardom, and *The Mind of Anglicans*, by Dr Peter Brierley, both co-published by Cost of Conscience and Christian Research, London, 2003.

12 Variations about the mean of 12% for all environments gave $t = 6.07, v = 7, P < 0.001$.

13 At least one Church of England Diocese, the Diocese of Chelmsford, undertakes a risk assessment of safety issues when placing women clergy.

14 Op cit., (Item 8, *Growth*).

15 Joel Chapter 2 Verse 28.

16 *The Road to Growth*, a survey of UK businesses, Financial Times and The Royal Bank of Scotland, 2005, based on a MORI survey in last quarter of 2004, Page 23.

17 *Seeds in Holy Ground*, A Workbook for Rural Churches, edited by Jill Hopkinson and Anne Richards, Archbishops' Council, Acora Publishing, GC Misc 803, 2005, Page 19.

18 *More than one Church*, private research for the then Bishop of Norwich, Rt Rev Peter Nott, by MARC Europe, 1989.

19 Article "Burnout and the practice of ministry among rural clergy: looking for the hidden signs", by Christopher Rutledge, in *Rural Theology*, Volume 4, Part 1, Issue 66, 2006, Page 57.

20 This is because not every minister looking after more than one church completed a form for each of their churches in this Census.

21 The average number of churches per minister was 3.0 for Methodists, 2.3 for Anglicans, 2.1 for the United Reformed Church, 2.0 for the Orthodox, 1.3 for Smaller Denominations, 1.2 for Roman Catholics and Pentecostals, 1.1 for Independent and New Churches, and 1.0 for Baptists.

22 Professor Leslie Francis has undertaken much research on stress levels of clergy; he can be contacted at l.j.francis@bangor.ac.uk

23 See, for example, op cit (Item 4, *Trends* 3), Table 2.21.1.

24 Published by Church Pastoral Aid Society, Warwick; phone 01926 458 458; www.cpas.org.uk

25 Available through MasterSun, New Malden, Surrey; phone 020 8942 9442; www.mastersun.co.uk

Chapter Nine Building Churches without Buildings

1 Article in *Christianity* magazine, March 2006, Page 10.

2 Taken from an advertisement in *Leadership* magazine, Summer 2005.

3   *The Mind of Anglicans*, private survey for Cost of Conscience, April 2002. Some results were printed in two booklets jointly published between Cost of Conscience and Christian Research, London: *Believe it or not!* and *The Mind of Anglicans*.

4   10,227 churches in only the 1989 English Church Census; 1,234 churches in only the 1998 English Church Attendance Survey, and 4,158 churches in only the 2005 English Church Census (which of course will have included some churches which did not exist in earlier years).

5   4,030 churches completed forms in both 1989 and 1998; 7,523 churches completed forms in both 1989 and 2005, and 2,025 churches completed forms in only 1998 and 2005.

6   When looking at 1989–1998 and 1998–2005 individually a further 4,030 and 2,025 churches may be added respectively; the samples are assumed to be unbiassed.

7   They were, respectively, 7.7% to 18.9%, 19.0% to 29.8%, 29.9% to 44.0% and 44.1% and over. Negatively they were –7.9% to –20.9%, –21.0% to –32.8%, –32.9% to –51.0% and –51.1% and over.

8   For 1989 to 1998, or between –7.8% and + 7.6% for the period 1998–2005.

9   For subsequent analysis, this 14% is assumed split 3% for 40%–59% and 11% for 10%–39%.

10 As given in *Church Growth in the 1990s*, private report for Springboard by Christian Research, London, June 2000.

11 Based on 5,038 churches (=100%).

12 See *Religious Trends* No 6, 2006/2007, edited by Dr Peter Brierley, Christian Research, London, 2006, Figure 5.3.1.

13 Article "Catholic laity to preside at services and run parishes" by Jonathan Petre, *The Daily Telegraph*, 26th May 2005.

14 Op cit., (Item 12, *Trends* 6), Table 5.3.1.

15 Ibid., Figure 5.3.2.

16 This one churchmanship contributes over half, 57%, of the total variation.

17 Op cit., (Item 12, *Trends* 6), Table 5.3.2.

18 *Leadership, Vision and Growing Churches*, research undertaken across all denominations for the Salvation Army by Christian Research, London, and published in 2003, Page 22.

19 Op cit., (Item 12, *Trends* 6), Table 5.3.3.

20 "In Brief" news note in *The Church of England Newspaper*, 26th May, 2006, Page 2.

21 Ibid.

22 *The Shape of the Church to Come*, Revd Canon Graham Hedger, March 2005, Page 25; my italics.

23 *Restless Churches*, Reginald Bibby, Wood Lake Books, Novalis, Ontario, Canada, 2004, Page 171.

24 Op cit., (Item 13, *Trends* 6), Figure 5.3.3.

25 *Being Single*, Philip Wilson, Darton, Longman and Todd, 2005, Page 195.

26 See *12 Trends in British Society*, Dr Peter Brierley, Christian Research, London, 2005, Page 9.

27 Table 2.2. The actual difference in numbers attending between 1998 and 2005 is 548,000.

28 Private research for the Diocese of Rochester, *Electoral Roll*, December 2003, Page 7.

29 Op cit., (Item 23, *Restless*), Page 40.

30 Article "Protestant Churches Inflow and Outflow" quoting the 2001 National Church Life Survey results, in *Pointers*, Christian Research Association Bulletin, Melbourne, Volume 16, Number 1, Page 16.

31 Fertility rates by age of mother as given in *Population Trends*, National Statistics, Palgrave Macmillan, Basingstoke, Hants., Volume 123, Spring 2006, Page 56.

32 The proportion of the population of child-bearing years who are married is 40% (ibid., Table 1.5, Page 50), but this is taken as 51% to allow for the fact that more church people are married than in the general population (proportion from Figure 6.9). In addition there will be some church children born to unmarried parents.

33 *The 2005 Alpha Invitation and Autumn Course*, private research report by Christian Research, London, January 2006.

34 Op cit., (Item 18, *Leadership*), Page 18.

35 Detailed in Chapter 11.

36 *Winning Them Back*, Rev Prof Eddie Gibbs, MARC, Tunbridge Wells, Kent, 1993.

37 That this number is 31% not 35% is still consistent with the Anglican figure, since Anglicans have the third highest average age of churchgoers; in other denominations the percentage who die will be lower as there are fewer churchgoers over 65.

38 Conversation with Mark Elsdon-Dew, Publicity Officer at HTB.

39 *Grow Your Church from the Outside*, George Barna, Regal, Ventura, California, 2002.

40 *Church Survey*, Rev Jon Willans, Ecumenical Research Committee, 2005.

41 *Being Strategic About Leadership: the principles that work in God's world*, Jill Garrett, Christian Research Lecture 2006, Christian Research, London, 2006.

42 Ibid.

43 These are taken from op cit., (Item 18, *Leadership*), Page 22.

44 One facet of such church planting is not just starting churches in the immediate neighbourhood of a church, but starting a church overseas, for example. One such is documented in *Great Commission*, Jim Montgomery (who began the DAWN organisation), January 2006, Page 3.

45 A point made strongly in *The Road to Growth*, Ven Bob Jackson, Church House Publishing, London, 2005, Part 3.

46 *Back from the Brink*, Heather Wraight, Christian Research, London, 2007.

47 www.thegoodnews.co.uk website accessed 11th August 2005, when Tony Campolo was speaking at the 2005 Faithworks Conference.

Chapter Ten Open seven days a week?

1 *Leadership, Vision and Growing Churches*, results of a private survey for the Salvation Army, undertaken by Christian Research, London, and published in 2003, Pages 14 and 15.

2 Article on Rick Warren in *The New Yorker*, 12th September, 2005, quoted in *Jaffarian's Mission Research Ezine*, January 2006, michaeldawna@earthlink.net

3 National Evangelical Anglican Church Conference, held in Blackpool, this information being presented by the vicar, Canon Mark Bailey.

4 *Reaching and Keeping Tweenagers*, Dr Peter Brierley, Christian Research, London, 2002.

5 *Ministry among Young People*, private research project for the Church of Scotland, Church of Scotland Parish Education Department, Edinburgh, Autumn 2000.

6   *Electoral Roll*, private research for the Diocese of Rochester by Christian Research, London, December 2003.

7   *Turning the Tide: The Challenge Ahead*, Dr Peter Brierley, Christian Research, London and the Church of Scotland, Edinburgh, 2003, Page 95.

8   189,000 compared with 176,000 in 2004. The 189,000 is one year later and includes some Anglican but non-Church of England churches.

9   Op cit., (Item 7, *Turning*), Page 98.

10 *Resourcing Mission within the Church of England*, Interim Report of the Group established by the Archbishops, Church House Publishing, London, GS 1580B, 2005, Page 3.

11 Op cit., (Item 7, *Turning*), Page 98.

12 *Annual Returns* Report 2003, Mission and Research Department, Baptist Union of Great Britain, Page 2. 199 churches out of 1,780 reported employing a Youth Worker.

13 *Background to the Task*, Evangelical Alliance and Scripture Union, London, 1968.

14 *Attitudes to Morality and Religion among Secondary School age Young People*, private research report for Josh McDowell Inc. by Christian Research, London, May 2005.

15 In order to give comparability those over 20 have been ignored, assuming that these are all adult helpers, and those on the form aged 12 to 14 increased by one-third to cover those aged 11.

16 Op cit., (Item 4, *Tweenagers*).

17 Op cit., (Item 7, *Turning*), Page 99.

18 The proportion of churches answering the question by denomination was: Anglican 18%, Baptist 28%, Roman Catholic 4%, Independent 29%, Methodist 26%, New Churches 25%, Orthodox 3%, Pentecostal 18%, United Reformed 42% and Smaller denominations 20%.

19 Op cit., (Item 1, *Leadership*), Page 14.

20 Ibid.

21 Those who attend "fringe" activities midweek are not included in this 10%.

Chapter Eleven Beyond the Numbers

1   The computer field for this question was not large enough to take HTB's answer! No other church has had attendance in five figures.

2   *The 2005 Alpha Invitation and Autumn Course*, private research report by Christian Research for Holy Trinity, Brompton, January 2006.

3   *Church Growth in the 1990s*, research commissioned by Springboard undertaken by Christian Research, May 2000.

4   Op cit., (Item 2, *Alpha 2005*).

5   Ibid. Alpha courses held other than in the autumn each year and at times other than the evenings generally attract fewer people. Also the number of people coming to each Alpha course has been consistently increasing for the last 7 years.

6   Ibid.

7   This is more than the Census figures gross up to, probably because numbers attending Alpha courses held prior to the arrival of the current minister, or at churches where Alpha is no longer regularly held, were omitted.

8   Other courses mentioned by more than one church were: Credo (0.34%), Disciples (0.27%), York courses (0.20%), Essence (0.16%), Beta (0.13%), Journey in Faith (0.12%), Hearts and Minds (Quaker course) (0.11%), Circuit Discipleship (0.08%),

Discovering Christianity (0.06%), Simply Christianity (0.05%), Come as You Are, Confirmation course, Purpose Driven Life, SEAN and Share the Light (0.03% each), and Catch the Vision, Diocesan course, Faith comes by Hearing, Firm Foundations, Freedom in Christ, Good News Course, Just Looking, Life Bible Course (CPO), Living Faith (Tom Wright), New Directions, Omega, Presence, RUN, Saints Alive, Start Rite (Ichthus) and This is our Faith (Jeffery John) (0.02% each).

9   *The Barna Update*, George Barna, The Barna Group, Ventura, California, email of 11th April, 2005, www.barna.org

10 *Church in Change*, The Evangelical Lutheran Church of Finland from 2000 to 2003, Dr Kimmo Kääriäinen, Dr Maarit Hytönen, Dr Katio Niemelä and Kari Salonen, translated by Virginia Mattila, Publication 55, Church Research Institute, Tampere, 2005, Page 23.

11 The others, non-evangelical, collectively were 25%, made up of 14% for Anglo-Catholics/ Catholics, and 38% for those of Broad/ Liberal/ Low Church/ Other persuasions.

12 It should also be remembered that a number of these larger churches are either Mainstream or Charismatic Evangelical, whose Bible reading is less than the overall average, from Table 11.2.

13 This may be because of legal requirements for disabled access etc.

14 *'Christian' England*, Peter Brierley, MARC Europe, London, 1991, Table 75, Page 193.

15 The overall percentage from congregational surveys in Anglican churches in the Diocese of Rochester as part of Strategic Deanery Reviews undertaken by Christian Research 1999–2002.

16 *Religious Trends* No 5, 2005/2006, edited by Dr Peter Brierley, Christian Research, London, 2005, Table 5.3.1.

17 One respondent commented on this question: "How can you include WEC, CAFOD and CWM etc in one set of answers? The only sensible thing to do was leave it blank or tick every box. We chose to leave it blank."

Chapter Twelve God believes in the Church

1   *Restless Churches*, Reginald Bibby, Wood Lake Books, Novalis, Toronto, Canada, 2004, Page 51, taken from the article "The Complicated and Irrepressible Canadian Church" in *Envision*, Spring 2004, Page 6.

2   Counting the items picked out in the "Looking behind the detail" at the end of each chapter.

3   Wording suggested by op cit., (Item 1, *Restless*), Page 142.

4   *Leadership, Vision and Growing Churches*, booklet summarising a Salvation Army survey across all denominations, Christian Research, London, 2003.

5   *The Prophetic Imagination*, Second edition, Walter Brueggemann, Fortress Press, Minneapolis, United States, 2001, Page 102.

6   Ibid., Page 65, his italics.

7   There could be, however, a tension looming with the increasing numbers of non-Evangelical female ministers.

8   Op cit., (Item 1, *Restless*), Page 124.

9   Emphasised for instance in *An Ecology for Sustainable Church Leadership*, Malcolm Grundy, Foundation for Church Leadership, April 2006, Page 3 and article "A dog's view of leadership" by Peter Hunter in *Professional Manager*, January 2006, Page 26.

10 For example, Nick Spencer in *Parochial Vision*, The Future of the English parish, Paternoster Press, Carlisle, 2004.

11 Article "Confirmation and condoms" by Claire Shelley in *The Church Times*, 28th April, 2006, which contained this paragraph: "As for religious teaching, 72% of respondents indicated that the Church had taught them something about sexuality, through sermons, Sunday schools, confirmation classes, or other programmes. But of those who had received teaching, 31% had had sex, compared with 32% of those who had not received any teaching."

12 Article "Thirteen things I wish I'd known about preaching" in *The Church of England Newspaper*, 26th May, 2006, Page 12.

13 Article "Church Sites – Another missed Opportunity" in *Lausanneworldpulse.com*, April 2006, Page 19. Church website resources can be found at www.ied.gospelcom.net/church.php.

14 *The Hungry Spirit*, Charles Handy, Hutchinson, London, 1997, Page 158.

15 Ibid, where "mission" has been inserted in place of "crusade" in the original.

16 Private research for OMF International by Christian Research, London, March 2006.

17 Speaking at the National Archdeacons' Conference, The Hayes, Swanwick, January 2005.

18 The New International Version actually uses the word "goal" in its translation of Luke 13:32.

19 On the assumption they hold one course per year.

20 Article "Back to Church Sunday" in *Quadrant*, Christian Research, London, March 2005, Page 1.

21 This is explained in more detail in *Coming Up Trumps!*, Dr Peter Brierley, Christian Research, London, 2004.

22 Dr Bill Lattimer, Business Development Manager, Christian Research.

23 William van Dusen Wishard, but actual source unknown.

24 Vice-Admiral Sir James Burnell-Nugent speaking on "Positive Reduction: Managing Strategic Change" at the National Archdeacons' Conference, The Hayes, Swanwick, January 2005.

25 Leader "The Tories' fight for life" in *The Daily Telegraph*, 21st July 2005.

26 *Jesus in Beijing*, David Aikman, Monarch, Oxford, 2003, Page 253.

27 Patience Wheatcroft, City Editor of *The Times* in *Management Today*, December 2004, Page 27.

28 Article "Insight as a strategic asset – the opportunity and the stark reality" by Steve Wills and Pauline Williams, *International Journal of Market Research*, Volume 46, Quarter 4, 2004, Page 404.

29 *The Road to Growth, towards a thriving Church*, Ven Bob Jackson, Church House Publishing, London, 2005, Page 217.

30 Conrad Hilton, *Be My Guest*, Simon & Schuster, 1994.

31 Comment by Andrew Brown in *The Church Times*, 24th March, 2006, on the story of Professor Ronald Mann who had a fatal heart attack while driving along a twisty road. Dying, his car crashed into a tree, and the impact flung him on to the steering wheel with such force that his heart restarted.

32 *Seek First*, the magazine of St Philip and St Jacob Church, Bristol, Spring 2006, Page 24.

33 Luke Chapter 17 Verse 6.

Index

If a page number is followed by "n" it means the Note of that number. Thus "65n4" means Note 4 on Page 65. Titles of books, booklets and reports are in italics.

Over the last 9 years *Religious Trends* has become a highly respected reference volume for anyone wishing to know the facts about the Church, Christianity and other religions in the UK. It is widely quoted, and is seen as an essential tool for church leaders, media, schools, reference libraries, politicians, researchers, the business community and others.

This volume is a companion to *Pulling out of the Nosedive*. It gives the detailed statistical data emerging from the Census, including:

- A colour section of maps showing the strength and changing nature of Churchgoing in England, by both county and Local/Unitary Authority

- Extensive analyses by denomination, churchmanship, environment, and age and ethnicity of churchgoer

- Analyses of how churchgoing has changed in the four Church Censuses, since 1979

- Charts showing church attendance as a percentage of the population, and numbers giving this broken down for every local authority in England

- Analyses by size of church, by growth/decline of church congregations, by frequency of attendance, midweek meetings, and the ethnicity of churchgoers

- Information on the age and gender of ministers

- Data on Bible reading, and how this varies by denomination and geographically across England

- A comprehensive index.

UK CHRISTIAN HANDBOOK
RELIGIOUS
TRENDS 6

PULLING OUT OF THE NOSEDIVE

A contemporary picture of churchgoing: what the 2005 English Church Census reveals

Statistics • Maps • Charts • Trends • Analysis

CHRISTIAN RESEARCH   EDITED BY PETER BRIERLEY   2006/2007

'Everyone who was anyone in the town of Midwich showed up at the Jolly Lion sooner or later. Matt and Bill had been going for years, and had debated politics, sport and women over many a pint.

Then one night a stranger came in. He ordered a pint and looked around in a friendly manner. Matt and Bill nodded as he caught their eye.

"Hello," said the stranger, "I'm Mike – the new vicar at St John's. May I join you?"'

(from the Preamble by Anne Coomes)

So began an acquaintance during which Mike described to Matt and Bill how to 'paint the church by numbers'.'"Statistics", said Mike. "They are the numbers which the specialists can use to paint a picture of what our churches are like."'

Dr Peter Brierley is recognised as a specialist on 'painting the church by numbers'. *Painting by Numbers* is a user-friendly look at those numbers and other aspects of church life. It is designed to help church leaders and lay people understand what is happening in the church in the UK in the present decade.

PAINTING BY NUMBERS

Peter Brierley

An Introduction to CHURCH STATISTICS

CHRISTIAN RESEARCH

"What do you want to become?"

We all need to answer this question but too often we can come up with the dreams but not know how to achieve them. To help us do so, Peter Brierley tackles the following issues:

- The place of vision • Forward planning • Setting targets
- Identifying goals • Formulating a life plan
- Learning God's vision for your life • Thinking objectively

"Applicable to individuals, churches or Christian organisations, *Coming up Trumps!* Makes frequent use of case studies, tables and diagrams, providing a clear understanding of strategic thinking."
Foreword by Pete Broadbent, Bishop of Willesden

"... describes a crucial dimension for the health and growth of the church - strategic thinking. He provides a helpful overview of four models of strategizing, integrated with practical examples and wise insights, showing its relevance to the church."
Dr Rick Love, International Director, Frontiers

COMING UP TRUMPS!

Four Ways into the Future

Dr Peter Brierley

Who is
Christian Research?

■ We are a registered charity which began in 1983, but changed to its present name in 199

■ We publish the *UK Christian Handbook* and its companion volume *Religious Trends*

■ We are a membership organisation giving our members the results of the latest researc whether undertaken by ourselves or others as well as discounts on publications and seminars

■ Members receive our bimonthly bulletin *Quadrant*. For a sample please copy and send back the slip below

■ We are happy to help in any way we can in the field of church research

■ We run Briefings and Forums to discuss the implications of current trends. If you would like details, please contact us

We hope you have found this book stimulating, and look forward to hearing from you!

Please send me

☐ details of membership to keep information coming my way

☐ a sample copy of your *QUADRANT* bulletin on latest statistics

☐ your monthly email

☐ Religious Trends No 6 £34 (inc p&p)

☐ Painting by Numbers £8 (inc p&p)

☐ Coming up Trumps! £10 (inc p&p)

I enclose a cheque to 'Christian Research' for £ _____
or order online at www.christian-research.org.uk

Title: _____ Name: _____

Address: _____

_____ Postcode: _____

Email: _____

Christian Research
Vision Building, 4 Footscray Road, Eltham, London SE9 2TZ
Phone: 020 8294 1989   Fax: 020 8294 0014   Email: admin@christian-research.org.uk
Web: www.christian-research.org.uk and www.ukchristianhandbook.org.uk